TRIBUTE TO A HERO

Dedicated to every recipient of the Elizabeth Cross

For the mothers, fathers, brothers, sisters, children & comrades of our fallen. Your story is written, and the world knows of your courage and sacrifice, the depth of your pain. But above all, at what price, their freedom.

TRIBUTE TO A HERO

The Life and Loss of Major Paul Harding MiD at Basra

GARRY McCARTHY & PAULA HARDING

Pen & Sword
MILITARY

AN IMPRINT OF PEN & SWORD BOOKS LTD.
YORKSHIRE – PHILADELPHIA

First published in Great Britain in 2022 by
PEN AND SWORD MILITARY
An imprint of
Pen & Sword Books Limited
Yorkshire – Philadelphia

Copyright © Garry McCarthy & Paula Harding, 2022

ISBN 978 1 39908 970 8

The right of Garry McCarthy & Paula Harding to be identified as Authors of this work has been asserted by them in accordance with the Copyright, Designs and Patents Act 1988.

A CIP catalogue record for this book is available from the British Library.

All rights reserved. No part of this book may be reproduced or transmitted in any form or by any means, electronic or mechanical including photocopying, recording or by any information storage and retrieval system, without permission from the Publisher in writing.

Typeset in Times New Roman 11.5/14.5 by
SJmagic DESIGN SERVICES, India.
Printed and bound in the UK by CPI Group (UK) Ltd.

Pen & Sword Books Limited incorporates the imprints of Atlas, Archaeology, Aviation, Discovery, Family History, Fiction, History, Maritime, Military, Military Classics, Politics, Select, Transport, True Crime, Air World, Frontline Publishing, Leo Cooper, Remember When, Seaforth Publishing, The Praetorian Press, Wharncliffe Local History, Wharncliffe Transport, Wharncliffe True Crime and White Owl.

For a complete list of Pen & Sword titles please contact
PEN & SWORD BOOKS LIMITED
47 Church Street, Barnsley, South Yorkshire S70 2AS, United Kingdom
E-mail: enquiries@pen-and-sword.co.uk
Website: www.pen-and-sword.co.uk

Or

PEN AND SWORD BOOKS
1950 Lawrence Rd, Havertown, PA 19083, USA
E-mail: Uspen-and-sword@casematepublishers.com
Website: www.penandswordbooks.com

Contents

Introduction		vii
Chapter One	Hobson's Choice: Master Garry McCarthy	1
Chapter Two	Summer of 85: Miss Paula Bendall	12
Chapter Three	Conflicts: Corporal Garry McCarthy	32
Chapter Four	Wedded Bliss 87: Miss Paula Bendall	39
Chapter Five	Winchester to Iraq: Mrs Paula Harding	66
Chapter Six	Africa to Iraq: WO1 Garry McCarthy	72
Chapter Seven	Iraq (Again): Mrs Paula Harding	88
Chapter Eight	Notification: Captain Garry McCarthy	104
Chapter Nine	Home Coming: Mrs Paula Harding	114
Chapter Ten	Operation PABBAY: Captain Garry McCarthy	128
Chapter Eleven	Death of A Hero	146
Chapter Twelve	In the footsteps of Kings: Mrs Paula Harding	148
Chapter Thirteen	The Regimental Family Gathers: Capt Garry McCarthy	162
Chapter Fourteen	The Epiphany: Mrs Paula Harding	166
Chapter Fifteen	It Feels Like Yesterday: Major Garry McCarthy	193
Chapter Sixteen	Bright as A Rainbow: Mrs Paula Harding	207
Chapter Seventeen	Once More unto the Breach: Major Garry McCarthy	224

Chapter Eighteen	John 15-13: Lieutenant Colonel Garry McCarthy	239
Chapter Nineteen	Life's Greatest Lesson: Mrs Paul Harding	243
Acknowledgements		246

Introduction

Freedom is not free. It is mortgaged to a nation and paid for by a few remarkable people. Remuneration is taken in blood, emotional grief and a lifetime of incomprehensible pain. There is no end to these repayments and for the rest of their lives, the families of the few will forever pay daily installments to the bank of ever diminishing patriotism and Christian values.

Rousingly powerful, inspiring and emotionally highly charged, this story recounts the most remarkable journey of a family anonymously bankrolling a nation's freedom. Yet this is no tale of woe, nor is it a plea to perpetuate the memory of a military hero. The words herewith in, exemplify the love and resilience of two young men and a widow paying off our mortgage of freedom. But to be clear. Freedom is not free.

Chapter One

Hobson's Choice
Master Garry McCarthy

3rd January 1982. Psychedelic electric blue lights and blinding white halogen beams bounced around the inside of the cockpit. The intensity of the light was amplified by winter skies and dreary urban streetlights. A swift glance in the rear-view mirror confirmed the situation had just worsened. The unmistakable wedge shape Rover Vitesse 3.5 litre Police pursuit car was so close to my bumper, the turbo could be heard whining to capacity. Double-tone sirens trapped in the inner-city suburb masked the high-pitched screams bleeding from the hugely inferior 1.6 litre Mk1 Ford Escort car it chased. Darting through the busy streets of Wavertree, the brake lights illuminated a plethora of pursuing Police cars. Leading the chase, PC Robbie Kilshaw. Old school and uncompromising, Kilshaw was a notorious traffic cop with a fearsome reputation for busting persistent car thieves, and repeat juvenile offenders.

The caustic stench of burning clutch flooded into the car with increasing intensity. Engine power ebbed away as oil constantly spewed onto the red-hot manifold. Swirls of grey smoke poured through the heating vents and the floor wells reducing visibility inside the car. Frantically flapping at the handle, the driver's side window was opened so the smoke could dissipate. Speeding through the narrow Victorian streets on the outskirts of Liverpool City Centre, escape looked highly unlikely. My limited driving skills and fading Ford were no match for Kilshaw's twenty years of experience. This chase would come down to who was prepared to take the greatest risks. Flying through red lights, mounting pavements to circumvent static traffic, the stakes had escalated in the extreme. Such reckless manoeuvres were creating gaps between Kilshaw's Vitesse and my Escort, but if escape was to be realised, levels of recklessness needed to overmatch Police tolerance.

TRIBUTE TO A HERO

It had taken less than ten minutes for the pursuit to reach its peak. The fear of lengthy incarceration morphed into desperation, fuelling repeated flirtations with death. Police cars appeared from every side street. Cutting off escape routes and clearing traffic, their tactics were obvious, and there was little choice but to conform. A well-rehearsed drill funnelled the chase into the open expanse of Sefton Park. The water drenched emerald grass viciously reflected the stream of blue flashing lights. Shadows cast by trees and hedgerows as cars jockeyed for blocking positions and headlights swirled in endless circles searching for possible escape routes. Travelling at breakneck speeds, ploughing up the fields and bouncing over footpath after footpath, the pantomime was nearing its end. A line of Police cars followed in one straight line, lights ablaze, sirens wailing, turning and twisting in my wake. The Police had settled for containment, biding their time ahead of the inevitable decant.

Sefton Park is a massive expanse of well-kept grass with sporadic treelines and mature hedgerows running neatly around the edges. Narrow footpaths cut directly through the centre of the park linking a sequence of sports pitches with Smithdown Road. On three flanks, multi-storey Victorian townhouses stood proudly in leafy avenues. The final boundary, an ever-expanding cemetery hemmed in by the Liverpool main rail line, set the scene for textbook handling of a dangerous joyrider. On every track, at every exit, a Police vehicle. Cornered in a place where the threat to life and property was minimal, this high-octane game of chess prepared for checkmate. Seemingly, with no escape plausible, it was all over, less an arrest. After several laps of the park, the full gravity of the situation could be understood. Black vans carrying beat cops massed on the tracks waiting for the foot pursuit to begin. The only unguarded boundary was the railway line, but the formidable fence at the base of the embankment presented a significant obstacle.

Kilshaw's Vitesse was still leading the chase, yawing and spinning every time we changed direction. With its long chassis and powerful rear-wheel drive, the beastly Police car couldn't make quick turns on the wet grass of a local park. But what it lacked in cornering, it made up for on the straight. It would take less than five seconds before the Rover made up the ground and closed the gap to nothing. In my mind, an opportunity could be seen. If it worked, there was a slim chance of escape! If a few quick turns generated a five-second gap between the cars, time could be traded for space, and if the fence guarding the railway line could be breached, an escape was plausible. Conceivably the car's roof could provide the elevated platform required to clear the high fence before the foot race got underway. The Police would not expect this, with any luck, there would be no one on the far side, and a getaway would be likely.

One final look at the size of the fence, which had to be over eight feet high, a few deep breaths to calm the nerves, it was now or never. A couple of fake turns to keep Kilshaw guessing, and a game of 'chicken' with a smaller Police car, the gap was created. Eyes closed, body braced, the passenger side of the Daytona Yellow Escort was smashed hard up against the railings. The deafening screech of the passenger doors concertinaing backwards was terrifying. Glass rained down from all angles as the car shuddered to a halt. The manoeuvre worked perfectly. In a flash, I was on the roof of the car and jumping clear over the railings. A quick rearward glance whilst crossing the railway tracks, a cheeky wave to the Police who had not yet come to a stop, and the decant was complete. As the pursuing cops scrambled up the embankment, the gods smiled on me as two trains denied Police access, and the escape was almost assured.

In less than five minutes I had disappeared into the alleyways of urban Wavertree and boarded the first bus, arriving on Smithdown Road. Comically, it was en route to the city centre via Sefton Park. The euphoria of my escape was irrepressible. As I slumped on the bench chair at the rear of the bus, the Police could be seen flying in every direction. Pursuit cars and beat cops were in meltdown clearing the trail of destruction left by the chase. My heart pumped fiercely as a peal of nervous laughter seeped from my mouth. Fifteen minutes later and the bus pulled into the depot at the Pier Head, escape confirmed. Resting on a cast iron bench overlooking the River Mersey, watching ferries go to and fro, the events of the chase ran through my head. The trains were a blessing, a huge slice of luck. Unquestionably the additional 30 seconds allowed me to select an escape route without being seen by the Police. Slowly the euphoria subsided as the enormity of my irresponsible behaviour emerged from the chaos of the last two hours. Driving on the pavement at speeds in excess of 50 mph dodging pedestrians, jumping red lights on the wrong side of the road, wrecking parked cars, and destroying a family's pride and joy, it was fortuitous that no one had died. More alarmingly, it wasn't the first time! Somehow, this was rapidly becoming a common theme and a way of life. Fighting the conflict of emotions, a change was needed. On the long bus ride home, guilt had gripped my every thought. Recalling the terror etched on the faces of the pedestrians, this was not who I wanted to be.

Twenty-four hours later and life returned to normal. A small crowd of friends from dysfunctional families, just like mine, gathered to learn the fundamentals of vehicle mechanics. Tinkering with motorcycle and car engines, and teaching others how it all worked, was a pleasant distraction from the tedium of unemployment. Occasionally we would enjoy the thrill of riding bikes or driving cars on council waste ground when fuel could be purchased. Mid-flow of teaching the kids how to set the timing on an old Robin Reliant engine, PC Kilshaw pulled up outside the front of our house. Six-foot six, nearly seven-foot tall wearing his headdress, he prised himself out of the low-profile pursuit car. The pristine white forage cap framed his blotchy red face and did little to disarm his menacing look, despite an attempted smile. Like a Venus flytrap, his white Rover Vitesse with the broad orange stripe, still covered in grass and mud from last night's chase, attracted attention from everyone within sight. Kilshaw had patrolled our neighbourhood for as long as anyone could recall, and still had warrants out for a few of the neighbours. Much of his time was invested in understanding 'who was who' in the motor theft trade. Regularly, Kilshaw would visit car thieves in prison, urging them to convince their children not to follow the family path. Although it wasn't understood in the late 70s, we now recognise this as 'early intervention'.

PC Kilshaw was no stranger to me. This mountain of a man had previously felt my collar for riding motorbikes without MOT, tax or insurance, as well as driving a car without a licence. Singlehandedly, he had put many from the neighbourhood in prison for car-related crimes. But notwithstanding this, he was widely respected, no easy feat for a Policeman patrolling such a deprived borough like Huyton. Never violent or patronising, not judgmental or arrogant, just brutally truthful and ruthlessly efficient, the respect afforded to Kilshaw was a testimony to his professionalism. Nosing around the shed, he picked up a few tools and inspected them, before breaking his silence.

'Scram kids, me and McCarthy need a chat.'

There was no confrontation from the group, as they were only too happy to get away from this legendary copper. Kilshaw remained silent a little longer, writing down the engine number of the block we had been working on.

'What were you up to last night McCarthy?'

'Nothing. Why?'

'There was someone recklessly driving a stolen Escort around Wavertree. Nearly killed himself. Nearly killed a few pedestrians and risked the lives of a few good coppers.'

'Yes well, that wasn't me. I was here tinkering with this engine block, which incidentally was given to me by Yew Tree school to help kids develop their mechanical skills. So, feel free to check the engine number out when you get back to the bizzy station.

'McCarthy. You are a good lad. We all see how much you are doing to keep kids off the streets, and away from drugs. But at sixteen you are little more than a kid yourself.'

The sage old copper continued to nose around the shed giving us both time to think. It never dawned on me that the little motor club had become a semi-quasi social programme.

'Look, McCarthy! Apart from doing more harm than good, you are a danger to yourself. I am here to tell you CID has lifted a clean set of prints off the car. If I was a gambling man, I'd bet they will match yours.'

'You're crazy mate! Ask my Mum. Why don't you do something more useful and catch the blokes who beat her up, as she walked back from the Labour Club and robbed her of her last two cigarettes on Friday night?'

Kilshaw's body posture and tone changed. Gone were the soft tones he opened with as he took off his peaked cap and poked me square in the chest with it.

'McCarthy, I am not stupid. I was behind you for fifteen minutes yesterday. It was you so don't dick around with me and pin your ears back. You can't inspire these kids from inside the Scrubs, or a coffin. Do yourself a favour, take a trip to the Army Careers Office. Enlist before you go to court. Maybe, just maybe, the judge will spare you a sentence. It will take the CID a week or two before they lift you. Your third offence McCarthy. It's a guaranteed custodial sentence. It's Hobson's choice, McCarthy. Jail, or the Army ?'

TRIBUTE TO A HERO

Kilshaw had called it right. In a heartbeat, CID had lifted me, and a court date was set. Had it not been for the fact that my start date to join the Army had already been set, life would have looked so very different. Whether intentionally or by accident, Kilshaw's intervention introduced me to a family that would reshape the values and standards that had been corrupted during my formative years on the streets of Liverpool.

The transformation was not without its bumps. At the start of the 80s, the British Army was nearly 200,000 strong, and not an awful lot going on. Veterans of Borneo, Brunei and Aden mixed with those now fixed by the troubles in Northern Ireland. Stories of 'do and dare' had grown beyond all recognition as the service hankered for a war that would break the doldrums. Alternatively, anyone seeking a change in routine served at one of the many recruit training depots around the United Kingdom. Some of those selected for this most important of duties were nothing short of bullies, desperate to find someone vulnerable to berate and belittle.

The first words ever redundant spoken to me by a recruit instructor still ring loudly in my ears. Having just stepped off the mail train at Winchester Station, life was looking up. Clutching my Co-op carrier bag containing an iron that cost me a week's wage, a change of underwear, and one or two other items, it felt like manhood had arrived. Bristling with pride, standing on Platform 2, I waited until the hordes of commuters disappeared before deciding where to go next. As the station cleared, a soldier was standing by a minibus. A few nervous people sat patiently in it. The soldier was facing the other way. Thinking he would welcome me with open arms, I smiled and tapped him on the shoulder.

'Is this minibus going to the Recruit Training Depot mate?'

'Mate! Mate! You're either very stupid, or very brave! So, where the fuck are your medals ?'

'Ain't got none mate!'

'So that makes you stupid.'

It had been a pleasant day up to this stage. At such a young age, travelling the length of the country, eventually arriving in Winchester on time was a huge achievement. The soldier dressed in his ceremonial uniform and a chest full of medals didn't agree. Stinking of cigarettes and booze, he pushed his forehead hard up against mine and whispered:

'I ain't your fucking mate, don't want to be your mate, never will be your fucking mate. The Training Depot is half a mile in that direction, up the hill. Start running and make sure you get there before the bus, fuck-face.'

Slightly overweight, but an imposing figure of a man, he pointed his pace stick towards a large hill and flicked his head in that direction. I was too stunned to move. Surely, he wasn't serious. Weren't all soldiers battle buddies, in it together and all that? At least that's what the Sergeant at the Recruiting Office had told me. A new family, one that understood me. The soldier screamed some more obscenities; a combination of the speed and thick Somerset accent made it impossible to understand. One poke in the chest with his pace stick and the message was clear. To this day, the smell of cigarette breath still makes me nauseous. It reminds me of his stinking saliva raining down on my face as he issued his instructions. By the time the front gates of Peninsula Barracks came into view, sweat was pouring down my back. The thought came that maybe jail would have been an easier option, and a damn sight less stressful.

Standing at the entrance to Peninsula Barracks, Winchester, the journey from leech on society to an honourable soldier was afoot. Digesting the grandeur of the breath-taking architecture of the historic barracks caused a mild panic. Bright red brick and sandstone lintels, arched windows all gracefully guarding a huge grey drill square. Captivating and intimidating in equal measure, this was once the home of royalty, politicians and military legends such as Sir John Moore and Lord Wellington.

Twenty-two weeks of basic training and early morning fitness smashed all of the ill-discipline out of my system. With unbelievable clarity, I could now look back on my life in Liverpool and reflect on how lucky I had been to get a second chance. Even though I had replaced a life of comfort with one of hardship, I had discovered a sense of belonging never experienced before. Streetwise boys from London, bear-like characters from Bristol, and bizarrely behaved anaemic short men from the Northeast. We shared everything, and bonded against the common enemy of the staff. The intensities of our relationships were intoxicating. I was desperate for more.

Having made the grade, my new family were enjoying a rich vein of success. Conflict in the South Atlantic and an upturn in the UK economy came with a pay rise, and the rise of the Iron Lady who loved the Army. Then, as if all the gods had decided that they wanted to give me more, the news broke that my parent battalion, 2RGJ, was going back to Belfast for another operational tour of duty. Preparations would get underway immediately. Training programmes were drafted, cascade training and specialised courses filled our days. In all too short a period, summer leave was a week away, but first, we needed to enjoy our pre-deployment parties.

For a man of a lowly rank like me, these parties meant extra duty. Normally it would consist of approximately twenty soldiers playing the role of waiter or barman. For the pitiful sum of £5, those selected single soldiers would be directed to 'wait' on the Warrant Officer's and Serjeants Mess during their annual Summer Ball. Allocated tables and rehearsed to death, it was customary that soldiers waited for the Serjeants, and officer guests, of the rifle company to which they belonged. Typically, on one table, there would be three serjeants, one colour serjeant, and one serjeant major, all with their wives and girlfriends.

The Serjeant's Mess of any military organisation is the most exclusive club in existence. It's exclusive because you can not buy your way into it. Unlike the Officer's Mess, which affords a rite of passage after one year of basic officer core training at Sandhurst, the Serjeant's Mess only admits entry after approximately eight years. Not that it's a waiting list; you need to prove you are capable of leading soldiers under fire, you need to qualify and pass the fiercest of assessments. Only the very best soldiers gain entry to the Serjeant's Mess. It is a place steeped in tradition and protocol, but none weirder than the unique spelling of Serjeant with a J as apposed to the normal spelling with a G. Sergeant is a French word, derived from Latin *serviens* = serving, or implied servant. The Royal Green Jackets typically rebelled against the notion of serving anyone and bastardised the word by replacing the letter G with a J. The unique spelling differentiates the mindset of a Serjeant in The Royal Green Jackets from any other member of the military who attained this rank. The nuance represents more than tradition, it epitomises the fundamental belief in fighting for our great country as a volunteer and not a paid servant.

In traditional fashion, I waited on my platoon serjeant, his wife, my Company Serjeant Major (CSM) and the remaining Senior Non-Commissioned Officers (SNCOs) from D Company. In between the endless food dishes, and the racket of a ten-piece orchestra, there was the misery of drunken wives wearing their husbands' rank. Fetch this, fetch that, 'pour me more wine, waiter.' I was clueless and devoid of the tolerance that those in the trade possess. It was hugely degrading. There had been plenty of warning that junior riflemen would suffer at the hands of the odd drunken wife or tyrannical serjeant. Low on enthusiasm and guarding myself against accidentally irking the protagonists, I avoided eye contact with the diehard party-goers who were refusing to leave the venue. Predictably, a drunken wife decided I was going to be her show pony and demanded I dance with her. The more I declined, the more she insisted. It was clear to me that this was going to get ugly. Burley and uneasy on her feet, cigarette hanging from her mouth, she gripped my arms with all the strength of a seasoned scaffolder. To compensate for my refusal to dance, she ragged me left-to-right attempting to force my participation.

In slow motion and comedic fashion, the woman slipped several times before eventually succumbing to a combination of the laws of gravity and biology. Spread-eagled on the floor, drunk, disorientated, embarrassed and now angry, she accused me of pushing her. Frozen in fear and riddled with anxiety I waited for her husband to arrive and give me a beating for just being in the wrong place. I was stuck between a rock and a hard place. Run, and I would look guilty. Stay, and she would convince people I am guilty. Her fall had not been graceful. Drinks had fallen from the table she collided with. Broken glass littered the scene and her voice shrieked like a macaw searching for a mate. Voices of dissent became louder, and the passing crowd became more interested, I braced for impact as a hand grabbed my shoulder from behind. A tight grip on my collar bone purged the blood from my arm and with little more than a disappointing glance from the assembled crowd, I was escorted to the rear of the kitchen. I braced myself for a kicking.

'McCarthy, you fancy yourself as a squash player?'

Fearing this was a euphemism for who do you think you are? (normally a prelude to a beating) I denied the claim.

'No Serjeant. No. I am not.'

Serjeant Paul Harding was the newest platoon serjeant to join D Company where I had now been for nearly two years. If I was to be given a kicking for my perceived indiscretion, it would be down to the new serjeant to deliver it. He'd been promoted and drafted into 15 Platoon ahead of the upcoming Belfast tour. We had encountered each other on numerous occasions over the previous few months, and frequently passed each other whilst running the routes of the stunning parks surrounding our German camp in Minden. Before his promotion to Serjeant and subsequent move to Delta Company, he had been a corporal with A Company and lived in a different camp. Ironically, only days before, we had been kicking lumps out of each other during the Annual Inter-Company Football Competition, part of the Bramall Trophy (a highly sought-after accolade, many reputations were won and lost whilst competing for this prestigious trophy). On this occasion, honours finished even, and I had hoped to have impressed some of the Regimental legends like Jimmy Mitchell, Ginge Starkey, Bernie Smith and Richie (Mark) Richmond. If nothing else, we had the foundations of one of those professional respects for each other that men never discuss.

Paul was one of a number of Regimental legends Riflemen often discussed during their idle moments in the bar, or during NAAFI break. Riflemen love to embellish stories about those who inspire them. Although I never served in the same fighting company as Andy McNab, I would often recount stories of his courage whilst fighting Irish Republican terrorists. Andy's history was one every Rifleman was proud of. In a similar fashion, Paul had a history that immediately endeared him to the Rifleman. He had originally applied to join as an officer, but during the placement process and suitability assessments, Paul had changed his mind and decided to join the ranks instead. He would forever be remembered as the man who had more integrity than the people who invented it.

'Bollocks McCarthy' he said.

'I know you play, I have seen you at the court with Paul Dunne and Jonny Mabb. What are you doing tomorrow morning?'

'It is Sunday morning! By the time this is over, I am probably doing my ironing ready for guard duty.'

'Good, so you are up early then? See you at the squash court at 0900 hrs for a knockabout. Now go, get on home to bed. Best you leave before you get dragged back into the bar by another drunken wife.'

With a wry smile and a nod of his head, I was set free, relieved to escape the wrath of drunken serjeants. It was surreal. I climbed into my bed at 0200 hrs unsure if that had just happened. The dream was still playing through my head when the bottom of my bed shook violently.

'Oy! It's 10 past nine. Get your racket and meet me at Court Two in five minutes.'

Bleary-eyed and dog tired, I opened the door to a frozen squash court. Still struggling to gain my senses, two voices were bouncing off the cavernous space, one of which was female.

'Sorry I am late Sarge, I didn't think you were serious. Sunday morning squash after a Summer Ball, and all that.'

For an hour, we smashed the double yellow dot squash ball around the court. Paul insisted on playing with a 'double yellow dot' squash ball because it makes the players play faster and harder. Despite my high level of fitness and enthusiasm, I was no match for Serjeant Harding. Game after game, he ran me ragged until eventually he was done. At no stage did he let up, not even at eight-nil. With the briefest of handshakes, we headed out the door. He was accompanied by a beautiful young lady. Porcelain skin, shining brunette hair and a smile that oozed warmth. As clear as day, I could see the beginnings of a loving relationship. The chemistry between the serjeant and his mystery woman was tangible.

Back in my room, dripping wet with sweat, I contemplated what life must be like for a man who had everything. Serjeant Harding was popular, brilliant at sport, phenomenally fit, and blessed with a dry wit and mischievous sense of humour. He listened more than he spoke and found time for everyone irrespective of rank or seniority. Like Andy McNab once said, 'everyone wanted to be in Paul's patrol when you had to do a tour of Belfast'. From my very junior position, it was hard not to be envious. With his young drop-dead gorgeous girlfriend, a trophy cabinet full of winner's medals, and a social circle littered with fast motorbikes and elite soldiers, he was the epitome of a successful soldier.

Chapter Two

Summer of 85
Miss Paula Bendall

Friday, 2nd August 1985. Hanover was much warmer than London, maybe this trip wouldn't be as unbearable as I had imagined. So far, the summer of 1985 had been full of days on Bournemouth beach and nights in the town's clubs and wine bars. I was just 19, Paul Hardcastle's anti-war single '19' had reached number one and, on 13th July, we had been transported through Live Aid into a whole new world where, through the lingua franca of rock and pop music, Bob Geldof had empowered us to address the issue of starvation in, what we called then, 'Third World Countries'. But, most importantly, at last, I was finally finished with school and exams.

For the past year, I had been retaking my A-levels at a not so salubrious sixth form college in the London Borough of Hounslow. A hugely diverse community, there were always running battles between the Hindu and Sikh boys, security guards and local authorities. Such a dramatic change in my domestic and educational situation had been a total culture shock. Previously from the ages of 7 to 18, I had been educated in a charming private single-sex school in Twickenham. Positioned on the Thames, surrounded by large imposing Victorian mansions, and taught by the Catholic Sisters of Mercy, I couldn't have wished for more pleasant school years. However, at the end of my Lower Sixth year, my Biology class of just 4 girls was sent on a field trip to Kew Gardens, and there I met Dominic, a handsome fellow sixth former from a nearby single-sex boarding school.

At 6'4" with Viking-like chiselled features, Dominic was the ideal distraction for a 17-year-old convent school girl. In no time at all, we were dating over his exeat weekends and holidays. Not surprisingly my studies suffered, I was partying harder than revising, and inevitably the following year I achieved dismal A-level grades. However, all was not lost, the situation was retrieved by enrolling with Hounslow College to retake the exams, whilst Dominic deferred his place at Plymouth University. The second time around I was determined not to repeat the same mistakes; I studied hard and that Summer my predicted grades were on target and my place at Plymouth Hospital's School of Nursing was closely becoming a reality. Dominic and I plotted our escape, hatching a plan to spend the first semester in our respective student accommodation, before moving on to rent a flat together.

There was a fly in our ointment of bliss though. My father and mother had earned their T-shirt of life, and were deeply concerned about Dominic and my relationship developing further, for although he had come from a privileged background, his immediate family were disjointed and somewhat dysfunctional; this was reflected in his emotional behaviour. His mother had her struggles and was using alcohol to cope with the loss of her marriage; his father had remarried but did not want Dominic to live with him. Inevitably, Dominic experienced rejection and had been sent to a boarding school, where he excelled at rugby and had found some stability. However, demons still chased him; in my teenage naivety I imagined I could 'fix' his issues, believing that he just needed the love that I had been blessed with. This was not the case, as two years into our relationship his insecurities had manifested into controlling behaviour, and my family and friends' reaction was to surreptitiously cast a doubt in my mind about the health of our relationship.

My mother had suggested that I spend the month of August in Germany with my eldest sister and her husband, to help with their two small children. My brother-in-law was serving with the 2nd Battalion, The Royal Green Jackets (2RGJ). He was a serjeant major, otherwise known as a Warrant Officer Class 2 (WO2). Quite a formidable man at 6' 5', known by everyone as Lofty, he had several 4-month intense counter-terrorism tours of Northern Ireland under his belt. He had always been a gentle giant with me. I was as much his kid sister as could be. My sister had married Lofty when I was 13, and for the past 4 years they'd been stationed in a German garrison town called Minden, 50 miles west of Hanover. The town is positioned on the River Weser, north of the Porta Westfalica Gap, between the ridges of the Weser and Wien Hills. The Summers there are scorching hot and the long winters are wonderfully cold and snowy. I had happily spent several Summer and Christmas holidays with them but, after working so hard at my studies, I had just wanted to spend the whole of the Summer of 1985 with Dominic in his mother's flat on the Dorset coast.

Dominic had begged me not to go to Germany, professing a concern that I would meet a soldier and proverbially 'dump' him. I laughed out loud at this. I had witnessed first-hand the life of a soldier's girlfriend, and then wife, and I had no intention whatsoever to follow in my sister's footsteps. Shortly after Lofty had proposed to my sister, he was selected to serve with 14 Intelligence Company, referred to as 14 INT or the DET. This unit was part of the British Army Special Forces established during the troubles in Northern Ireland. Primarily, they were responsible for undercover surveillance operations in specific parts of the six counties of Ulster. From its inception through until the *'Troubles'* played out, 14 INT carried out numerous undercover operations, mostly following and observing suspected terrorists. These painstaking intelligence-gathering efforts often led to the arrest of terrorists by the RUC, as well as discoveries of weapons caches.

His work meant that Lofty's leave was rare and sporadic, but he managed to get some time off for their wedding. Lofty was unable to get married in uniform for fear his photo might appear in the local press and blow his cover on the job he was working on in Belfast. He had long hair and a moustache that would have given Clint Eastwood a run for his money in *The Good, The Bad and The Ugly!* Fourteen months after their marriage, my nephew was born, followed eighteen months later by the birth of my niece. Lofty was away for 80% of the time and my sister frequently returned to our parents' home and stayed. It was a constant worry for our whole family that Lofty might get injured, or worse. During my holidays with them, I had become acquainted with other wives living on my sister's 'patch' (the term used to describe married quarter estates). I witnessed these stoic wives and mothers spending several months a year alone, whilst the men were on exercise or on tour, living with the constant worry of an IRA bomb or bullet about to snatch their man from them, and perpetually coming second to the 'green machine'. During these visits, I determined that there was absolutely no way I was going to be an Army wife! So, I assured Dominic I would be landing back in London in just under a month, and together we would prepare ourselves for our move to Plymouth in the first week of October.

Yes, it was definitely warmer than London, and now I was in Germany, I'd just have to make the most of it. Lofty was flying down the autobahn in his brand new Volvo 740 Turbo. I was beginning to relax as we talked about taking the children to the lakes and Potts Park, the local amusement park. I'd been told to pack a long dress for the Serjeants' Mess annual summer party. Known to everyone as *'The Rifle Ball'*, it was being held the following evening in a huge marquee on the lawn of the Warrant Officer's & Serjeants' Mess and, being of age, Lofty had bought me a ticket. I was conscious that such events were governed by strict protocol, and 'punishments' for breaching rigid dress regulations were a regular occurrence. However, the only full-length dress that I owned was the apricot-gold bridesmaid dress I had worn to my sister and Lofty's wedding five years previously. Fortunately, it still fitted me, and my talented other sister had altered the neckline and transformed it into an *'off the shoulder'* ball gown. My sister added a black satin ribbon sash and handmade drawstring black velvet evening bag; this along with my mother's pearls and stud earrings had transformed my bridesmaid dress into the perfect evening attire.

We passed the autobahn exit for Rinteln, the home of one of the Army's military hospitals, I had been taken there with a broken wrist by Lofty three years previously. Lofty then broached the subject of the Ball the following evening. He tentatively started with the opening gambit of how he wasn't "matchmaking or anything", but the tables were set for 12, and with myself added to his party I made it an odd number of eleven. To round up our numbers up to the requisite amount he had asked one of the single serjeants to join our table. I knew that Lofty did not favour Dominic, but I also knew that he didn't want to distress me, and so I just replied that it was fine and joked that he should not expect me to dance with this mystery guest.

On arriving at the married quarter all thoughts of this mystery guest were forgotten: elated to see my sister, nephew and niece I threw myself into my unpacking and catching up on their newly acquired skills of walking and building Lego structures. That night I lay in bed thinking about what Dominic might be doing, and how I was to fill the next four weeks until my return to the UK.

The following evening, I readied myself for the Rifle Ball. I was not at all excited, and even contemplated feigning some malady. However, guilt got the better of me and so I found myself, struggling in my kitten heels, with evening bag in one hand and ball gown gathered up in the other, pulling myself up and into the back of an Army minibus to be trundled through the married quarters, past the Guard Room, into Clifton Barracks. It was a warm, airless summer evening and I was relieved to be in a cool dress, and not the woollen uniform of tight trousers and bolero jacket worn by Lofty and his fellow mess members. The Serjeant's Mess was festooned with garlands of balloons, flower displays and swags of silk. Candles flickered on the dozens of circular tables which were adorned with silverware dating back to the Napoleonic wars, circa early 1800s. The atmosphere was full of anticipation, greetings being shouted out back and forth as guests arrived, above the orchestra playing light jazz. Lofty was greeted by a mess waiter, who then carved a way for us through the mingling party-goers to our table. I walked around it, in an anti-clockwise direction, searching out the chair that would be my island of sanctuary for the evening. A place card caught my attention, in neat italics the name 'Sjt. P Harding' had been scribed to the right of a glossy black embossed Green Jacket cap badge. I held my breath as I read the next place name 'Miss P Bendall'. Exhaling, and taking my seat, I remembered Lofty explaining to me before that the spelling of Serjeant with a 'j' and not a 'g' was not a mistake, and this peculiar tradition had given me a telling insight into the kind of people attending the night's revelries. The history of this Regiment, and its antecedents, forged through time before and during the reign of Queen Victoria, when Britain really ruled the waves, were still firmly entrenched in the contemporary lives of its soldiers. There was certainly a difference about them that suggested adventure, bravery, innovation and just a hint of trouble. I took my seat and began to read the programme and menu. That year the Ball was honouring the Riflemen who had sailed on HMS Warren Hastings, a ship that had been launched in April 1894. As in similar reference to HMS Titanic, reports at the time of its launch had claimed her to be 'practically unsinkable' because of her 33 watertight compartments. On 6th January 1897, Warren Hastings departed from Cape Town, bound for Mauritius. Onboard were 526 members of the King's Royal Rifle Corps (a forerunner to the Royal Green Jackets), 20 wives (known in those days as 'camp followers'), 10 children, and 253 crew members. On 13th January at 0400 hrs, in thick fog and with a 'magnetic disturbance', which caused the compass to malfunction, she struck a rock 30 metres from the shore of Reunion Island, and began to sink.

When the captain ordered an evacuation, Rifleman N. McNamara, strung a line between the ship and the shore, and heavier ropes were subsequently set up. The ship was completely evacuated by 0530 hrs. Two people died during the evacuation. So impressed was Queen Victoria at the miraculous rescue that she personally wrote to the ship's Captain to congratulate his Riflemen for their discipline and calmness during the disaster. As confusing as my emotions were on the night, standing amidst such tangible history was very special. The very green jackets worn by this unique collection of men represented much more than just pomp and ceremony. It somehow brought the 1800s to life, and inspired an esprit-de-corps that was potent.

In the centre of our table were the most intricate pieces of sugar paste artwork. The chefs had created edible life rings the size of a small side plate, with the names of the ladies of the table piped on each one, along with the ship's name. The life rings were crammed with delectable looking handmade chocolates and truffles. I noticed that the last 'a' of my name had chipped off so that it now read 'Paul', but I didn't mind and looked forward to tucking into the chocolates at the end of the meal.

I felt Lofty nudge my arm and heard him say:

'Serjeant Harding is over there at the bar.'

I turned to look at two men at the bar in mess uniform, facing each other in a close tete a tete. They suddenly flung their heads back accompanied by loud belly laughs and they clinked their pints of beer. As they replaced their glasses on the counter, the taller of the two turned and looked me straight in the eyes as guests and waiters mingled through our view. My stomach lurched and I felt a mixture of intense excitement and dread. Something was about to change my whole world.

The Mess Manager announced it was time for everyone to prepare themselves for dinner, guests began checking the seating plan and searching out their respective tables. I held my breath to see which serjeant was going to be seated beside me. Both were good looking and obviously very fit, but when the taller of the two, with broad shoulders and extremely short dark hair, turned and walked towards our table I began to enjoy the evening, despite myself. A Bugler played the call for silence and, following mess etiquette, we stood behind our chairs, bowed our heads and a deep voice behind me said grace. When I opened my eyes and looked up Sjt. P Harding had his face turned towards me, taking in every one of my features. He then, in one swift movement, pulled back my chair and offered to help me to take my place at the table. Feeling a blush bloom across my face, I turned to look at Lofty, who gave me a surreptitious wink before assisting my sister into her chair to his right. We introduced ourselves and mused over having the same name in its respective forms. To my horror I was lost for words, and trying to find anything to talk about turned to the menu card in front of me. Scrutinising it intently I noticed that there were sections labelled 'Indian Bar' and 'Chinese Bar', and with my nerves getting the better of me I blurted out:

'It's terrible that the Army is so racist!'

Paul looked at me incredulously; without breaking eye contact he asked:

'What do you mean?'

'Well, that the Indian soldiers and Chinese soldiers have to eat separately in their own bars!' I replied. To my horror, I saw his face turn into an enormous grin and heard that same laugh that I'd heard before.

'You Wombat', he said, 'That's the Indian and Chinese food bars.'

From that moment I was to collect a whole plethora of 'Wombatisms', and although I felt pretty stupid at that point, he had such a way that it just didn't seem to matter that I had just made a ridiculous faux pas. And the faux pas did not end there, that night.

Playing the role of host personified, Serjeant Harding invited me to join him at the buffet, a spectacular array of the finest cuisine imaginable. Sparkling ice sculptures adorned the centre table, bouncing light erratically across the exotic colours of the continental collection of food. I was completely overwhelmed by the magnitude of the display and the variety of dishes offered. The artistry that the chefs employed in creating their displays was breath-taking. Then I saw the fish bar; the vibrant red lobsters lying prostrate on crushed ice with their velvet-covered antennae were simply irresistible. So, using the silver pincers provided, I chose a beautiful, glossy and extremely large specimen of a claw. Placing it upon my plate I proceeded along the line, adding spoonfuls of salads and rice. It wasn't until I approached the end of the buffet table that it occurred to me that my chosen piece of lobster, complete with its claw shell, was totally inaccessible. I had no way of cracking said shell to release the juicy lump of pink lobster meat within. I took a sidelong glance at Paul, who was following me with his already laden plate of cold meats and salads, he seemed to be busy chatting to one of the chefs serving, so I swiftly took hold of the lobster claw and secreted it under the stack of napkins perched at the end of the table. Returning to our places we proceeded to devour our delicious assortments. Feeling a sense of relief at how I had deposited the rather large lobster claw undetected, I quietly commented to Paul what an achievement it was, on the chef's part, to produce such a delicious spread, and how full I was. He replied:

'But you haven't finished yet.'

Then, in an instant, from his sleeve appeared a paper napkin parcel. The lobster claw dropped out and clattered onto my plate. I was aghast at being caught, but he gave me that direct look again, staring straight into my eyes, followed by that broad grin. Again, that same feeling swept over me, my world had subtly shifted.

Once everyone had finished eating a lady called Lynne reached forward and picked up one of the sugar paste 'life rings'. Smiling at her husband who was called 'Doc', even though he wasn't a doctor, Lynne offered the chocolates to him. Paul then reached forward and picked up the iced ring and its chocolates with the missing 'a' at the end and offered me one. A little cheeky of him I thought, but I smiled and thanked him for the offer, but explained that I was full. Without blinking, Paul, like a child let loose in a sweetshop, demolished the majority of the truffles and petit fours. His cheerful countenance vanished though when Lofty fixed a cold stare on his actions.

'Serjeant Harding! What do you think you are doing?' chided Lofty.

'Erm, just eating my sweets Sir', replied Paul.

'I think you'll find you've just polished off Paula's after-dinner chocolates actually.'

Paul looked around more closely at the iced rings, and I inwardly smiled as I saw the comprehension that only the ladies had these special gifts made by the chefs. Now it was my turn to smile and look him in the eyes, and there it was, that huge laugh and sparkling brown eyes. I hadn't drunk any alcohol but felt intoxicated, and when he asked my forgiveness I gladly gave it, with a gentle kiss on his cheek.

We chatted all evening, learning everything we could about each other during precious moments between speeches and ceremonies. The meal and ceremonies concluded, he took my hand and led the way onto the dancefloor where we moved to the syncopated baselines and synthesisers typical of an 80's disco. The evening was passing far too quickly. I savoured every moment in this man's company, feeling frustrated when he briefly disappeared around 1:30 am to settle some disturbance caused by guests who had consumed copious amounts of alcohol and were becoming leery. Upon his return to our table, Sjt Harding crouched down beside me on his haunches and with a whisper in my ear, suggested we might go for a walk around the grounds. Escaping the miasma of nicotine, chatter and bass, breathing freely in the crisp, cool fresh air and being able to hear his voice clearly, was a relief. We wandered aimlessly around the camp, occasionally crossing paths with patrolling Riflemen on guard duty, who would nod and acknowledge his rank. We talked about our life plans, I learnt that he would turn 28 in two weeks, and I realised quite quickly that he was a career soldier, he loved his work. He was passionate about his platoon and their training to ready them for deployment to Belfast in the coming November. I explained my prospective place in Plymouth, adding how I would be starting my Student Nurse training in the Autumn. However, with cold culpability running through my veins I omitted the part about Dominic. Becoming closer with every step we took, I felt Serjeant Harding slip a tentative hand into mine, and as goosebumps covered the skin of my arms we came to a stop behind the stables. Standing perfectly still as Earth's star began to explore a new day above Germany, we watched our first sunrise together. He slipped off his woollen mess jacket and wrapped it around my shoulders, whispering that I looked cold. Despite the warm material now covering my exposed shoulders, the hairs on my arms did not comply and relax, the goosebumps refused to dissipate, this was a whole new sensation that I was feeling, that had nothing to do with the temperature of the air around us. Paul placed a hand on each of my shoulders, and slowly turned me to face him; I could hear the birds heralding a new day, as I closed my eyes and felt his lips on mine.

We returned to the mess and enjoyed a full fry up, complete with bratwurst sausages, for breakfast, washed down by the obligatory glass of Champagne. Then Lofty found us and declared it was time to get the transport home, and I was to meet him at the front of the mess in 2 minutes. I didn't want to go, I wanted this night to continue its spell over me. Conscious now of the other guests finding coats and their transport rendezvous points, I began to mumble how lovely it had been to meet him when he put an index finger to my lips.

'I'm playing squash at 9 am, would you like to watch the game, and then go for cake and coffee at my favourite place, Café Lenz'?

Without hesitation, I agreed.

I lay awake until my niece toddled into me at 7 am, and crawled under the duvet to sing nursery rhymes, but I was buzzing with anticipation and unable to stay in bed long. After a quick shower, I readied myself for what was feeling increasingly like a date; I felt pangs of guilt over Dominic, but couldn't stop myself from feeling intense excitement. When we had parted earlier, Paul had asked if I had a leather jacket. Bemused, I had replied I did, he then said 'wear it, with jeans and trainers', and he followed this instruction with a huge grin. When I asked, 'Why?', he declared:

'It's a surprise.'

So dutifully I walked through the married quarters, in jeans and leather jacket, to the camp gates, arriving at 8.50 am. Paul was waiting for me, wearing a tight polo shirt with the Green Jacket badge embroidered on his chest. Even tighter than his shirt were the white shorts he wore, I couldn't take my eyes off his legs, and as he caught me looking that cheeky grin slipped across his face, and I felt myself blush. He had a face that was not traditionally handsome, but with a retrousse nose, large dark hazel eyes and a broad mouth. I was becoming increasingly fond of his warmth, his half-smile, half inquisitive look that was comforting and endearing without being patronising. We walked to the squash courts, but I gathered Paul's opponent hadn't arrived when Paul asked me to 'wait one' whilst he went to give him a gentle nudge.

Paul returned a few minutes later and took me up to the viewing gallery. It was freezing in there, and I was glad for my jacket. Perhaps this was the reason for Paul's clothing request. Ten minutes went by and then a much younger, but familiar chap appeared in the court below us. Paul left me in the gallery and joined his opponent, their voices echoing in the cold, cavernous arena. I could differentiate between Paul's soft London accent and a strong Liverpudlian one. The two adversaries thrashed out several games, both were extremely fit, but Paul had the upper hand and was clearly an excellent squash player. Finally, they shook hands, and as I exited, I realised that the young chap had been one of the waiters at the ball and he must be exhausted.

We walked across the parade square to the Serjeants Mess, where Paul had a room, and I waited in the lounge area whilst he went to get showered and changed. Then he reappeared carrying two crash helmets and my jaw dropped.

'Come on' he said. 'Café Lenz is waiting.'

He took my hand and walked me to the car park where a huge silver BMW K100 was parked on its centre stand. Now I knew why he had stipulated the dress code of a leather jacket and jeans. Paul handed me a helmet and proceeded to rock the bike effortlessly off its stand. He got on the bike, put on his silver 'Alien' full-face helmet and nodded for me to do the same with the spare. I climbed on as pillion, put my arms around his waist, and felt the thrill of my first time on a motorbike.

By the time we had gone for our cake and coffee, then biked up to the Prussian Emperor Wilhelm's monument (affectionately known by the Riflemen as 'Kaiser Bill') and surrounding beautiful countryside, I was a converted biker. Most of all, I adored riding pillion to Paul and having an excuse to be so close to him. When he dropped me back at my sister's married quarter, he walked me to the door and kissed me again. I knew then I had to make a call, and after the sound of the K100 faded away I walked down the road to a payphone. I dialled Dominic's number. I needed to explain we wouldn't be going to Plymouth together.

The following day the battalion went on a training exercise, about an hour's drive away in Sennelager. I felt bereft for the next 7 days, and without any contact with Paul time dragged by. I kept as busy as I could, helping my sister, playing with my nephew and niece, or taking them swimming and for walks. Several times Dominic called my sister's house phone, he had managed to purloin the number from a girlfriend of mine, who had no idea that I had ended our relationship. I had tried to show compassion, I felt truly dreadful for hurting him so badly, but I knew my mind, and our conversations would go around in circles. Then on the evening of the 11th the house phone rang, I heard Lofty answer it and then he called out to me. I dreaded that it was going to be Dominic again, but could see a twinkle in Lofty's eye as I entered the hallway. I held my breath hoping to hear Paul's voice, and I wasn't disappointed.

The next few days were a whirlwind. He tried to teach me to play squash, but unsuccessfully. He spoiled me with gifts of every nature. We frequented the local cafés and enjoyed hot chocolates and cakes. A unique selling point for Paul was the banana pizzas he introduced me to in his favourite Italian restaurant, 'San Marco'. Our flourishing union was reinforced by the solitude we enjoyed on his motorbike. The peacefulness you feel as the pillion passenger is known only to those who have ridden with someone they trust and love. One evening he picked me up and we drove out to Kaiser Bill's monument. Paul parked up the bike, we took our crash hats and jackets off and sat on the steps leading up to the monument. The silence was only broken by the songbirds, calling to each other at the end of another summer's day. Enjoying the silence between us I watched as Paul unzipped a pocket in his leathers and took out a small jewellery box. I fell silent, and Paul said:

'It's OK, it's not a ring!'

For the first time in my life, the feeling of surrendering my heart consumed me. It was a feeling I had never experienced before. Everything about this man was wonderful. Previously I had thought I knew what love felt like, but in truth, it paled into insignificance compared to the feelings I was experiencing at that precise moment. I was in love, so much so that there was just a hint of disappointment when I heard his words. Perhaps it showed on my face? Maybe I had lost the plot? It's crazy to think we had only met twelve nights before. I opened the box to find a pair of gold, heart-shaped earrings, they were just beautiful. I was made up with them, but I think Paul was reading my mind because he then asked:

'What would you have said if it had been a ring?'

My true feelings were compromised, so I chose to say nothing, and replied with a simple kiss on his lips.

The following day was a Saturday, I made a cake for my 2-year-old niece and we held a little birthday celebration. I had discovered in one of the long conversations with Paul that his birthday was the following day, Sunday 17th. So whilst making my niece her cake, I made a cake for Paul. Although we were not going to see each other for a while because he was taking part in a training exercise with his platoon. In my head I thought, 'what better way to surprise him than with a 3D tank!?' sponge cake in green and brown icing with a chocolate flake as the gun! When

Lofty returned from his duties later that day, I asked him to take me into the Serjeants Mess so I could leave the cake for Paul, and surprise him when he returned to camp.

'Are you sure about this? Do you think Paul is going to like coming back to the Mess, with a tank birthday cake waiting for him in the hallway?' Lofty asked.

'Of course. He's going to love it!'

So off to the camp we went. Lofty parked up and said he'd wait in the car. On entering the Mess hallway, I saw a large, highly polished, wooden wall frame of pigeonholes. I found the pigeonhole with Paul's rank and name on the card in the brass nameplate and placed the cake on the shelf below. I had prepared a note saying, 'Happy Birthday, hope you like your cake, love Paula'. A few other mess members walked past me, and one of them stopped and asked where my Dad was? I was confused at this and asked him why, and he went on to say that kids shouldn't be in the mess alone. I was just coming up with an answer when Lofty appeared and asked me what was taking so long. The mess member who had spoken to me apologised to Lofty, calling him Sir; by now I was scarlet with embarrassment, and swiftly left with Lofty.

Paul called that evening to say the cake was magnificent, but there's now a rumour going around the mess that he is dating a pupil of Prince Rupert's, the local service children's school. I was aghast, I was 19 for goodness sake, but Paul just laughed, and said it was no one else's business. The following week Paul only managed to get a couple of hours off here and there as the training for the upcoming Belfast tour was becoming more intense. One of his Riflemen had commented that 'since the Sarge had started dating the daily fitness sessions were getting easier', so Paul had intensified the runs. The weekend was to be taken as leave, and Paul decided he was going to take me to Hanover for the day; he was craving a McDonald's of all things. So on the 24th August, 3 weeks after we had met, with only a week left of my stay in Germany, he picked me up early and we headed off up the autobahn to Hanover. I had to hunker down against Paul's back, with my arms tightly wrapped around his waist. It was freezing cold but the ride only took about 40 minutes, a lot faster than when Lofty had picked me up from the airport.

We parked up, and I soon started to thaw out as we walked and talked. I was happily taking in the sights when Paul said he sensed something was not quite right. He pointed out that the crowds had suddenly thinned out. I looked around, and saw that he was right; many of the shops had begun to close their doors. Paul quickly led me to the nearby McDonald's, we queued and chose our meals, and I followed him up to the first floor where we seated ourselves in a window with a view of the main street below. Within minutes a crowd of hundreds came surging down the main thoroughfare, only to be headed off by armed Federal Police, with water cannons. It felt surreal. I even wondered if this was an action movie being filmed. But, as we watched the water cannons being fired into the crowd, literally lifting people off the pavement and throwing them back like rag dolls, there was soon no doubt in my mind that this was not some film set, and these people were not actors. Those at the back of the crowd turned and tried their best to retreat, but the cannons were so powerful they forced even these rioters down. Suddenly the water jets stopped, and a large Police officer stood in the middle of the pedestrian thoroughfare. He began to address the now dispersing crowd. I didn't need my O-Level German to enable me to get the gist of what he was saying, and by the time we'd finished our apple pies, and Paul had drunk his fourth coffee, the streets were clear.

Paul announced it was time to go, and that he hoped I was enjoying the date, with his gruff laugh he said:

'I know how to show a girl a good time!'

He dropped me back at the house in the late afternoon. We arranged that he would pick me back up at 7.30, as he had heard of a lovely little restaurant near Petershagen, a town just north of Minden. So I quickly showered, and did my hair. I thought about how it was a waste of time, given that that the crash helmet would ruin it, but that I wanted to look my best when I greeted him at the door. Sure enough, it was a super little restaurant, in typical Germanic lodge style, wooden carvings everywhere and red and white gingham tablecloths. For a Thursday night, it was relatively quiet with only a few other tables occupied and Paul asked for us to be seated in the corner where we would be completely private. I was becoming addicted to the traditional Bratwursts with fries and mayonnaise and Paul ordered the same. He followed his with a large slice of black forest Gateau We were relaxed and giggling when the opening bars of Billy Paul's 'Me & Mrs Jones' cascaded over us. Simultaneously we began to hum along before breaking into song at the same time. We both laughed and declared our love for the track in unison. The love song epitomised the moment, and as we sang the words 'it's time for us to be leaving, it hurts so much inside', I could feel tears begin to sting my eyes. I was dreading my flight in 7 days, back to London, 500 miles from this man I had fallen in love with.

Paul was my everything now. I was only 19, but I knew what I felt was real. It wasn't just physical. Yes he was handsome, tall and athletic, but he was witty without being a comedian, gentle without being vulnerable, strong without being bullish. Sincerity flowed easily regardless of the topic and the overwhelming feeling of security in his presence was warrior-like. If there was a Hollywood moment in my life, this was it. I had found that one in a million.

As the song played its last bars, Paul glanced at the black dial of his diver's watch. He took a long, slow inhale of air and then looked me in the eye. Reaching across the table, he grasped my hands tightly. His giant fingers wrapped around my wrist and hands with space to spare. I was head over heels in love with this man and loved his boundless affection. He leant over the table to kiss me. Full of love and contentment, I leaned in too. But his lips brushed past my mouth, and he whispered into my ear:

'Will you marry me?'

My reply was instant. Yes.

The following day I requested a family meeting after breakfast. Lofty and my sister sat on the sofa, and as the children played with their playmobile on the floor between us, I explained that Paul and I were now engaged. Lofty was impassive, his face inscrutable. I had no idea whether he was about to blow a gasket or congratulate me. My sister was standing, with a collection of toys she had just picked up in her hands, and a look of deep concern etched across her face. I asked her if she was OK, but she just remained silent. They were clearly thinking of a response. Finally, my sister spoke, expressing her concern that I'd only met Paul three weeks ago, and was I sure that my relationship was over with Dominic? Then Lofty spoke:

'Paula, the battalion is about to go on a 6-month tour of Belfast. You need to understand that Paul will need no distractions. He's going to be working extremely long and arduous hours with the constant risk of an attack by terrorists. It is crucial he can focus on his job without any hindrance.'

'I know,' I replied.

And that seemed to be it. My sister got up, gave me a hug, and then said:

'You'd better call Mum and Dad then.'

So that afternoon I called home. My parents immediately booked themselves tickets for the British Airways flight to Hanover, on the following Thursday. They changed my flight home too, I was now going to stay until the 26th September! Giving Paul and I a further 5 weeks together.

I was concerned for both my parents. I didn't want to cause them any distress. In 1979, just before his 60th birthday, my father suffered a devastating blow. For thirty years he had been an aircraft engineer at Heathrow for British Airways, but he started to experience some strange symptoms, memory loss, sideways walking, and finally he had collapsed on his way to work. He had been admitted into The National Hospital for Neurology and Neurosurgery in Holborn. Dad was hospitalised for two years there, under the superb care of his surgeon, Sir Roger Gilbert Bannister CH CBE FRCP, and his diligent team of nurses and medics. Sir Roger carried out 6 operations to remove a benign brain tumour the size of an orange and designed shunts to transport the fluid that would build up in the cavity made by the tumour, draining it via the heart and venous system. Dad had suffered numerous complications, including septicaemia. My mother and I travelled most evenings after work and school to visit him at The National. This would mean driving to Hounslow West underground station, and then getting the Piccadilly Line to Russell Square, a 50-minute tube journey. I would complete my homework on the tube every evening and sit with Dad for a couple of hours before travelling back home and getting to bed around 10 pm. It had been an exhausting time for our family, and terribly hard for my two sisters, and their growing young families.

My parents had me later in life, my mother was 41, and my father 47. When people would ask if I had been 'an accident' he would always reply 'Paula is our bonus.' Dad was totally unselfish, loved his work at the airport, and loved his family unconditionally. Unlike my mother who had grown up in North Shields, in one of the poorest areas, and raised by her Grandmother, my Dad had been fortunate to have the most loving parents. Despite being born into post-war Britain in 1919, he had enjoyed a comfortable childhood with 5 siblings in Sunbury-on-Thames. My Grandfather had fought for three years during WW1. He was discharged with gunshot wounds to both legs and one arm. Dad joined the Royal Marines at 18 in 1937 and served with them until 1946. He was on active service throughout WW2. He spent his 21st birthday in Colombo, Sri Lanka (it was Ceylon in 1940), but was then selected to join the Mobile Naval Base Defence Organisation (MNBDO) which was essentially a Royal Marine base component of the larger Royal Naval part of beach landings. He had been part of the task force that built a military base for the Royal Navy in 1941 on Gan Island, the southernmost island of Addu Atoll, which is part of the larger groups of islands which form the Maldives.

As a child, I loved looking at the photos of him beside the pyramids of Giza, and of him sitting with little Dutch children after the liberation of Holland, but he never spoke of his times during the war, apart from to tell a humorous, self-effacing story. When I would ask him questions about the photos, like the one with the words written on the back 'Rouen, December 1944', he would brush my questions aside. I sometimes got more from my Mother. She told me how Dad had been part of the D-Day landings, and how he obtained the large scar across his shin bone by walking into buried metal whilst wading through the water to the beach. As a girl guide, I had marched at numerous Armistice Day parades, and asked why he didn't join us, and why didn't he have any medals? He would just smile and say he 'remembered everyone here' and point to his chest and head. It would not be until he was 80, and sadly moving to a nursing home, that whilst clearing my parents' attic, I found his medals hidden in several brown boxes. Still wrapped in their white wax paper, ribbons loose having never been threaded on, the enormity of his contribution was set in this array of valedictory medals, for all to see.

My father had been discharged from The National in 1980, but he was unable to ever work again. My mother and I cared for him between ourselves. It had been a long 6 years for our family, and I didn't want to be the reason for any further strain. I went with Lofty to pick them up from Hanover. Dad seemed really well, but Mum was a little frosty. Thankfully, once we arrived back in Minden, where my sister was waiting with excited children, the mood had lightened. During the drive, Lofty had told them a lot about Paul, his character, his loyalty, honesty, professionalism, he was an Infantry sportsman, and his career was going very well. I told them how he was handsome, funny, generous, kind and all-round gorgeous. As we helped them unpack, I explained that Paul would be coming to pick me up that evening, we were going to see a film at a charity run centre for soldiers, known as Red Fred's, but she and my father would get to meet him on Saturday at a house party Lofty had organised for their friends.

That evening I heard Paul pull up on his bike, but I was out the door and heading him off before he got halfway up the path. I knew my Mum and Dad were watching from behind the net curtains, and as he turned to walk back down the path to his bike, he ruffled my hair and big floppy 80's style fringe. We had another great evening and when I let myself in around 10 pm, my sister, parents and Lofty were all watching a video. I popped my head around the door to say goodnight, everyone replied the same, apart from my Dad when it fell quiet; Dad simply said:

'Don't you mess that boy around, I saw how he looked at you and touched your hair, don't you go breaking his heart. He's about to go on tour.'

I went and sat down next to my father, holding his hand tightly.

'Dad, I know what I am doing. I love him, and would never let Paul down.'

During the next four weeks, we were both very busy. Paul was back and forth to Sennelager, training with his platoon, and my parents and I visited Berlin. Whenever we could, Paul and I would pack a picnic and take a ride into the countryside on his BMW K100, however, time was moving too fast, and there was nothing I could do to stop the 26th September hurtling towards us. The flight was an early one. Paul came with Lofty and me to the airport; it felt as if my heart was breaking when we said goodbye. It was my first taste of what it was going to be like to be an Army wife.

On 10th October, I packed my belongings into an old Austin Mini and drove to Plymouth. With a mixture of excitement and trepidation, I moved into the nurses' home in Freedom Fields Hospital and began my studies. Although I was a four-hour drive from my parents, I was only half an hour away from my other sister Pamela and her family, who lived on Dartmoor. On my days off I would drive my very tired old Mini to stay with them. Their home was my haven to escape to. Spending time with my young nephew and niece enabled me to connect with the goodness in life, away from the pain and suffering I was coming across in my job. My sister taught me baking skills, and we would complete craft projects together. Practically, and to my great pleasure, I could guarantee a phone call with Paul. My room in the nurses' home was the furthest from the stairwell, and on the third floor, with one payphone on the ground floor. With Paul never knowing when he would get the chance to call, we relied on someone hearing the payphone ring and being kind enough to run up to my room, in the hope that I was in. It was often hit and miss, and I hated the fear of missing the opportunity of hearing his voice. Whilst nothing could replace hearing his voice, we had the consolation prize of the 'Bluey'. A Bluey was the term given to the military aerogrammes provided to troops on active service and to their families at home. There was no limit to how many could be sent, free of charge, via the Royal Mail and RAF, so I would write one in the form of a diary to Paul every day. Returning to the nurses' home after each shift I would hastily park up my old Mini and race to the entrance hall of the home, desperately hoping that there would be a 'bluey' tucked into the polished wooden pigeon holes. The emotional charge held in these aerogrammes was intense, they were my direct link to Paul, and enabled us to stay connected despite the lack of phone calls.

Then one afternoon, just before Christmas, a third-year student nurse called me from my room saying there was a chap looking for me in the common room. I hadn't heard from Paul in three days and my brain, racing ahead of me, rushed to the conclusion that he may have somehow been given leave and flown over from Belfast to surprise me. With blood pounding in my ears, I ran down the corridors and stairs and burst into the room, ready to leap into his arms. But, to my dismay, stood squarely in the centre of the room was Dominic. My disappointment was quickly taken over by guilt as he explained that he had been searching for me and had already been to the other two city hospitals attempting to track me down. He went to take my hand and saw my engagement ring:

'So I was right then?'

With as much sincerity as possible, I confirmed he was; without a word he stepped past me and left.

During January 1986, Paul was given his allotted leave, one day for every month spent in theatre. This precious rest and recuperation period, or R&R as it was called, provided the only days off that serving soldiers were given during a gruelling 6 months in the centre of the troubles. It was an exceptionally cold January, but we spent a glorious 4 days staying in a holiday cottage in Slapton Sands. Long walks on the beach, pub lunches, and then hunkering down in front of an open fire, it felt like paradise to me. Then the time came to 'meet the parents' and we drove up to where Paul had grown up: Walton on the Hill, a quintessential English village nestled in the Surrey Hills. The crowning glory of the village, apart from the Chequers Pub, was St Peter's church, where Paul and his father were choir members, and where Paul had been an altar boy. We stood silently basking in its simple splendour when Paul asked if I would be willing to get married here. It had been a very special part of his life, and I thought it was a perfect place to exchange our vows. Back at his parents' house, before he left for Belfast again, we sat down with our diaries and identified the first date we would both be available. This was not an easy task with the plans the battalion had, and my training schedule, but eventually we reached 11th April 1987, and there it was, inked into the appropriate page, and we began planning our wedding.

Chapter Three

Conflicts
Corporal Garry McCarthy

Our return to West Belfast was tough. As a Regiment the Royal Green Jackets had battled with the IRA on more occasions than many other organisations. There had been dramatic wins and painful losses. On the previous tour, the battalion had several skirmishes with the Irish dissidents over a four-month period and we had come out on top. But just a few short days before the tour finished, the IRA ambushed a mobile patrol exiting the rear of Springfield Road RUC Station, killing three Riflemen. Despite the heroic efforts of the patrol commander who pursued the killers through the back alleyways of Falls Road, the terrorists made their escape.

The pain of that loss weighed heavy on everyone's mind. There was a desperate desire to catch those responsible for the Crocus Street murders. It was not a sense of revenge but one of justice that drove the intensity of our efforts. Occasionally the terrorists would chance their arm in an audacious attempt to kill a Rifleman, but on most occasions we were coming out on top. With a combination of excellent planning and inventive tactics, we foiled several shooting attempts and identified a series of improvised explosive devices, long before there was an opportunity to detonate them. In this real-life game of cat and mouse, the IRA were left frustrated. On one occasion we executed a 'Mechanised Infantry' attack on the Divis Flats, the most notorious of Republican strongholds in the city. Three armoured Humber 'Pig' patrol vehicles raced into the high-rise flat complex to deliver thirty soldiers pumped up on adrenaline and hell-bent on catching terrorists unaware. The innovative operations had been the brainchild of our young platoon commander, Lieutenant Ed Butler.

Lieutenant Butler was calmness personified. Like Paul, he was assured and calculated in the delivery of his commands. If there was ever a man to match Paul's levels of fitness and professionalism, it was him. The audacious assault on the Divis Flats caught the IRA by surprise. In the blink of an eye, the estate was awash with Riflemen hot on the tail of suspected terrorists and dickers (the phrase *dickers* is army slang for somebody watching the activities of soldiers with a view to launch an attack, or warn the terrorists of military presence). For the remaining three months of the tour, the terrorists lived in fear of being caught out by the speed, surprise, and innovation of our tactics. Meanwhile, Paul and his platoon were conducting searches in the Beachmount area, uncovering weapons and ammunition used by terrorists to carry out punishment shootings and kneecapping.

No sooner had we returned to Minden, we were straight back on the roster for another tour of Northern Ireland. In fact, out of the next six years, a total of three and a half were spent protecting the innocent people of Northern Ireland from senseless acts of violence and murder. Occasionally there was a pleasant interlude or training course, but for the next ten years, Paul watched me develop from Rifleman to Colour Serjeant Instructor at Sandhurst, just as the next conflict had come along, Kosovo. It was fortuitous for the British Army that there was significant experience in dealing with religiously motivated conflict. No matter what excuse people wished to use to describe the violence that had caused the region to implode, the root cause was religious ethnicity. Although the British Army was unaware of it at the time, the unpredicted collapse of the Berlin Wall and the subsequent demise of the Warsaw Pact ushered in a new era of conflict, most of it underpinned by ethnic tension. As the former buffer states of the USSR split and fractured at an epidemic rate, ethnic cleansing forced NATO forces into global policing duties, as one dictator after another oppressed the innocent and vulnerable.

By the time our operational tour of Kosovo had concluded, my relationship with Paul had flourished into one of mutual respect. We had won football competitions together, fought the terrorists in Northern Ireland, and freed the oppressed in Kosovo. During domestic duties, he had demonstrated his professional standards and I had proved my desire and aspirations, or so I hoped. It was difficult to know if you had impressed Paul. Frequently he would raise a wry smile that said everything from: 'that was brilliant' to 'you are a complete fuck-wit'; you just had to make up your own mind as to what he meant.

A few years earlier, Paul had been dragged out of a comfortable appointment to rescue a failing group of elite soldiers training for the prestigious Cambrian Patrol Competition. For a variety of reasons, the group had become disinterested, fatigued and disillusioned. There was no one to blame for their mardy behaviour, but this was an international event that attracted participants from all around the world. If a team underperformed, it would tarnish the reputation of a regiment. It was not a risk that Lieutenant Colonel de Vere Hayes, Commanding Officer at the time, was prepared to take.

The two-day patrolling mission is a mind-melting, muscle-sapping forced march over 37 miles of the hilliest terrain in the Black Mountains. Competitors carry Complete Equipment Fighting Order (CEFO) weighing well over 50lbs. Sleep deprivation, hunger, blisters, bruises and random injuries are guaranteed. But just for good measure, the worst of the Welsh weather equalled the playing field for the other 1000 competitors, all of whom were trying to beat you.

The team Paul inherited consisted of the top 10 soldiers within the Regiment. There was no disputing their quality or ability, but they had lost their focus and motivation. His task was to arrest their falling morale, sharpen their skills and lead them to a winning position in the competition. Although I had not made the grade as a participant, Paul had called me into his team to deliver specialist combat engineering training. It was a timely rescue from the misery of a 'trials and development' task that had gone horribly wrong: what initially appeared to be great fun, with photo shoots for advertising campaigns and VIP visits, turned sour after Rifleman Geordie Staples destroyed the one and only prototype of the Trial's brand-new Warrior Fighting Vehicle. The first of its kind, it was deemed indestructible and Geordie reduced it to scrap metal after he reversed it into another armoured vehicle. For the eight men assigned to trial the vehicle's performance, life immediately became miserable as the Late Entry officer in charge of the trials, from another regiment, then took his frustrations out on everyone involved.

Late Entry (LE) officers are soldiers commissioned after completing their colour service of 24 years. Until the late 90's LE officers were commissioned into the rank of Second Lieutenant which would make them much older than the Sandhurst trained officer of the same rank. Only 3% of enlisted army personnel achieve the standard required to win a Late Entry commission. They are a highly regarded cohort that bring invaluable experience to a predominantly young officers mess of a typical combat unit. It would be fair to suggest that the old-style LE officers were short of quality leadership training. Until the start of the millennium when it was realised that the LE officer had much more to offer, their duties were confined to the tedium of functional roles. Consequently, they were short on patience, frequently grumpy and mostly suspicious or cynical. To vex a Late Entry officer of the early 90's was akin to poking a sleeping bear with a sharp stick.

Pleased to be removed from the vehicle trials, Paul had tasked me to teach the group basic combat engineering and demolitions, minefield breaching and how to avoid booby traps. There had been rumours that this year, the competition would include improvised bridge construction and basic mine clearance operations. Despite my eagerness to impress and incentivise, the group was gripped by tangible lethargy. The dynamics of the group left much to be desired. Knowing that Paul would not tolerate such a dysfunctional grouping, I fully expected him to lash out and thrash everyone to within an inch of their lives, and bring about a change of attitude.

The conditions were therefore set for Paul to dip into the perhaps traditional formula for eradicating lethargy, by 'beasting' his new team into obedience. Ten old school soldiers, maverick and rebellious, the outcome looked easy to predict.

Gathering the group at the rear of a four-ton truck, dressed in full kit, pensively flicking through his notebook, everyone feared Paul would explode into a tirade of abuse.

'Right fellas. Take your kit off. Sit on top of it, get your stoves out and knock up a brew'.

The bemused team followed the instructions. Sitting in silence, only the sound of water boiling and metal mugs clashing with steel cookers could be heard.

'I have been told by the Commanding Officer to pull this team together. He feels you have lost your direction and team ethos. In his words, 'you have become a bunch of individuals' or something like that. Do you agree?'

'Bollocks' Tami snapped. 'What the fuck does he know? All he does is sit in his ivory tower picking faults.'

A mountain of a man, Tami was of Fijian descent. His reputation as a hardened soldier was fearsome. He enjoyed a celebrity status within the Regiment after rumours circled that he had beaten up eight Military Policemen after they tried to arrest him on a night out in Minden. When eventually he and his battle partner, Rory McCaffery, were apprehended, the arrest file was over one hundred pages long. Tami did not suffer fools gladly, nor would he hold back his opinion. He viewed military life as a full-on democratic organisation where everyone had a right to their opinion, moreover, it should be heard. There was no rank or standing in his world; decisions were made by experience. Knowledge was the currency he traded in, and for those who didn't speak his language, he had little time. His response to Paul's statement had an undertone of resentment. It was a challenge to Paul's authority, a surreptitious test of his resolve. The blue touch paper was lit. Everyone watched in anticipation of an angry rebuke. Paul said nothing, he let the disgruntled gathering rumble on until their point became confused.

Paul seemed to be making it worse for himself. From my very junior position, it appeared as if he had invited criticism. For all the tea in China, there appeared to be no way back.

'Take a good look around you' said Paul, calm as a sleeping tiger.

'You believe you are a team, but I see ten stoves burning, ten mugs boiling, ten soldiers working as individuals. Even new recruits know to make a brew in pairs. So, I am sorry you feel that we have got this wrong, but the evidence before your very eyes confirms you have lost trust in each other. Collectively you have lost focus.'

The group fell silent. One sideways glance from Tami and the team knew Paul was right. It pained them all to agree, but they had become disconnected. You would have put your mortgage on the next step being a ten-mile forced march home as a punishment.

'Good. No one disagrees. So, we are going to start afresh. Scouse is here to do some demolitions and improvised bridging, 'fun training' I am calling it! We will start with a few simple command tasks to get us into the swing of it. Pompey. You are the youngest team member. You are in charge.'

It was genius. Paul had convinced Tami without embarrassing him, then totally disarmed him by placing a junior member in charge. With humility and parity, he had galvanised the group inside ten minutes.

It was my first real exposure to pragmatic leadership, something I would later identify as 'The Light Touch.'

Leadership in The Light Division is all about inspiring people through mutual respect and understanding. Although it would take me thirty years to understand the difference between The Royal Green Jackets (now The Rifles) and the rest of the Armed Forces, the fact is that a high proportion of combat 2-Star officers running the Army since the start of the millennium, and before, started life as a member of The Royal Green Jackets says it all. It is their unique style of leadership that makes them successful, and through osmosis, Paul had inherited this style.

It was indicative of Light Division Officer leadership that still endures today. In the mid-80s, I recall my first encounter of what is known as the Light Touch. My Company Commander, Major John Pentreath, displayed amazing composure after I made the most monumental navigation blunder. Somehow, I had navigated my section to the wrong FUP (Form Up Point) ten minutes before H Hour during a Battle Group Exercise on Salisbury Plain, with one hundred Riflemen poised to launch a surprise attack on a fictional enemy, and I was in the wrong place. Consequently, the enemy slipped out of their defensive position through a gap that I should have been plugging at Imber Clump and made good their escape. John had every right to go bananas at me. Not only had I ruined many hours of planning and tactical manoeuvring, I had let him and the rest of the company down. But instead of a public reprimand, he simply said: 'You're off my Christmas card list McCarthy. Move to the next location'. He never made reference to the massive blunder until we discussed it 30 years later.

Shortly after the Cambrian Patrol finished, life became increasingly chaotic as the Army reduced in size whilst simultaneously increasing its commitments. Back-to-back tours of Northern Ireland at the end of the '80's had drained me of enthusiasm. Specifically, my third tour of duty, because it fell at a time of major changes in the MoD. For the Army there would be job cuts and base closures; consequently, the planned eighteen-month tour of Omagh in County Tyrone turned into a massive two years and ten-month deployment. Notwithstanding the need for the British Army to rebalance its basing plan, the extension to an operational tour of duty was always going to present the chain of command with significant challenges. In an effort to keep me motivated and retain my services, the Commanding Officer, Lieutenant Colonel Nicholas Cottam, loaned my expertise to the Mozambique Advisory & Training Team who were located in Zimbabwe. It was sold to me as a busman's holiday, a chance to recharge my batteries, and ready myself for the next stage of my career.

The Rome Peace Accords (Portuguese: Acordo Geral de Paz), was a peace treaty signed between the government of Mozambique and RENAMO, ending the Mozambican Civil War in 1992. Nothing had happened for over two years and more importantly, nothing looked like happening for another two. Bernie Smith had just returned from the country and recounted stories of adventure, excitement, travel, and lots of extra pay. Above all, because RENAMO refused to take part in any training, there was no work.

Leaving Omagh was bittersweet in the autumn of 1991. The promise of an African adventure was irrepressible, but the guilt of leaving my close friends to continue to fight the terrorists was overwhelming. The fear of missing out on capturing bad guys and the fun of the brotherhood forged in the fire of adversity is intoxicating. For so many reasons, the tour of Omagh left its mark on me. It may have been the senseless loss of life, the near misses or the close camaraderie, but it cemented my love for the people of Northern Ireland and their brave unflinching resistance to terrorism.

Chapter Four

Wedded Bliss 87
Miss Paula Bendall

1986 - at the end of April the battalion vacated North Howard Street Mill, Belfast. Paul and I had made it. We had survived our first separation, our first six-month tour. There were times during those days, weeks, and months when I doubted my resilience. Times when at work, I would be washing a patient who had the BBC news playing on their bedside radio, when I would hear a news clip retelling how a British soldier had been wounded during contact with the IRA, and I would be praying inside my head that it was not Paul.

But, throughout these times I kept telling myself, 'if we get through this one, we will get through any tours they give us'. I'd hoped that we were going to see more of each other, but I was to learn the next lesson of the induction to life as a military wife. No sooner had Paul returned to Minden from Op Banner, than he was sent on one of the most demanding courses the Infantry had invented: The Platoon Sergeant's Battle Course (PSBC), known as 'Senior Brecon'. Although he had already been promoted, this was essentially the military confirming he was on course for success later in his career. He was fully committed to his career path, and by now I was accustomed to biting my tongue and supporting him wholeheartedly.

While Paul was giving his all on gruelling tabs (moving quickly across terrain, walking and running), with a full bergen and kit back and forth across the Brecon Beacons in South Wales, the Regiment had moved from Germany to Warminster in Wiltshire. After an outstanding performance during Senior Brecon, Paul was selected to sample life doing something other than operations, and found himself posted to the newly constructed Light Division Depot, Sir John Moore Barracks, Winchester. Ironically, he had been appointed Platoon Serjeant to 'Minden' Platoon, part of the Junior Leaders Course where the average age of the recruits was 16, and they were known as 'boy soldiers'. I quickly applied for a transfer of my nurses' training. Thankfully my reports so far had been good, so, after an interview, Winchester Hospital's School of Nursing accepted me. My move was swift, and my accommodation in the nurses' home within the hospital grounds was only a 15-minute drive from Paul's room in the Warrant Officer's & Serjeant's Mess. Life was good. Our plan was coming together.

The Light Division Depot had only just been built and would be officially opened in November later that year by Her Majesty Queen Elizabeth II. The first function I would accompany my fiancé to was a Ladies Dinner Night. I was rather nervous about the evening as it was my first event outside the security blanket of the battalion, and I literally knew no one. I was also missing my fellow student nurse and partner in crime from Plymouth, a dear friend, Kate, who would later become a Godmother to one of our sons. Typically, sensing my apprehension, and attuned to my emotions, Paul suggested we invite Kate too. It had been a lovely evening, but I noticed two of the wives were drinking heavily and getting rather belligerent with the Riflemen waiting on them. At Regimental events like this, no one should leave the table until the meal is finished, the port passed around the table, and toasts concluded. An announcement is then made that the 'ladies' are given permission to leave the table. Kate and I were pretty keen to adjourn, and making our way to the ladies toilets we joined the back of the queue. Free to talk openly at last, we chatted until we both noticed that the two wives that had caused the disturbances at the table had turned, and were staring at us. They were clearly in a pugnacious mood, probably fuelled by the copious amounts of alcohol on offer at the table. The atmosphere was becoming distinctly unpleasant when the louder of the two demanded:

'Who do you think you are? Walking around our mess, looking at our husbands.'

We ignored this outburst and quietly waited in the queue. Eventually it was our turn, and to my relief the cantankerous pair appeared to have simmered down and vacated the toilets. There were only two cubicles, but that was fine and we were grateful to have made it so far unscathed. However, stepping out of my cubicle, my relief was snatched away from me in an instant, as like a snarling wolf pouncing on its prey, the woman who had challenged us in the queue launched herself at me. Her long fake nails were like talons clawing at my throat, tearing my string of freshwater pearls from my neck, her acrid breath spitting expletives at me through the crimson lips of a 20 a day smoker. Stunned, I watched my pearls scatter in every direction, I heard the crunching noise of them being stepped on and looked down to see their creamy iridescence disappear down the central drain. Kate, upon hearing the commotion, burst out of her cubicle and tried to placate my assailant when, thankfully, the other half of the dreadful pair dragged her friend away. Kate gathered me into her arms, and we stood for a few moments catching our breath, before then washing our hands and heading back towards the dining room. Pushing open the swing doors into the foyer we stopped in our tracks, for Paul stood, arms folded with his back to the cabinets of silver cups and trophies. Concern etched into every line of his face, his eyes widening when he saw the scratches on my neck, my eyes red and puffy. Just as he stepped towards me, readying to question me as to what had happened, the heavy wooden door from the bar was flung open and again the same crimson lips were spitting:

'She's lying! I didn't break her necklace or touch her!'

Paul calmly turned to her, and rising to his full height explained that I hadn't said anything yet, so clearly she was the liar. At that moment her husband, a Warrant Officer Class 1 (WO1), and the Regimental Serjeant Major (RSM), both from another regiment, came into the lobby. Kate and I were asked to return to the dining room, and a few minutes later Paul joined us. I felt exhausted by the experience and we decided to call it a night. In the taxi back to the nurses' home I asked Paul what was the outcome, but he just gave a curt reply stating *'it's been sorted'*.

Over the coming weeks, I discovered just how unfair military life could be, for it was Paul who had been punished. The RSM had given Paul five extra 24 hour duties, on top of his regular ones. I was incensed at the injustice but Paul just shrugged it off, saying one shouldn't join up if one can't take a joke.

The beauty of moving to Winchester was the bonus of an extra two weeks leave together. Plans were well underway for our wedding in the following spring, and even though our leave dates were now changed we couldn't bring the wedding forward. Therefore, we made the most of the time off touring France on Paul's K100, driving south and enjoying the coast and then wending our way back up through the Alps. It was heaven to be away from the hospital, and the Army, and be totally alone for a full two weeks. We were camping and I had started to grumble about sleeping on a roll mat, and the toilet paper being the old Izal type we had back at school. One morning I woke to find Paul and the bike were gone, I hadn't even woken to the sound of the engine starting up. I was getting my wash kit together to go for a shower when I heard the unmistakable rumble of the bike slowly creeping through the campsite. I stood up and watched Paul riding tanned and handsome in the sunshine, wearing nothing more than flip flops, vest top, and union jack running shorts. As he drew closer, I saw a bag of twelve toilet rolls (the smallest pack Carrefour sold) and an air bed bungeed to the back rack. 'Yes,' I thought. 'He is a keeper.' This thought compounded when I learnt that when he had left to go shopping he had wheeled the bike out of the campsite before starting it up, so as not to wake me.

'Snake Bite Black' was my chosen poison as a student nurse, and the week before I became Mrs Harding I sampled the majority of that vile concoction that was on offer in Winchester. Surrounded by my fellow students we began our nurses' bevvy at the County Arms on Romsey Road, and then worked our way via The Westgate, a canter on Elisabeth Frink's bronze equestrian sculpture Horse and Rider, with a late-night burger in the Wimpy burger bar on the corner of the High Street, and Middle Brook Street. The problem was that by then Snake Bite Black had begun to take effect, and the bigger problem was that Minden Platoon was on a Friday night out, and had decided to have a late-night burger too. The following morning, as I lay in my bunk with a pounding head, I smiled as I remembered that Paul was taking his boys out on the range that day. I would have loved to hear their stories of the Sarge's Mrs in the Wimpy after several pints of Snake Bite Black.

It was a sunny, but extremely windy Saturday in April 1987 when I arrived with my father at St Peter's church, where our families and friends had gathered. Both my sisters and their husbands, nephews and nieces were all able to attend. Paul looked every inch a hero dressed in the dark green uniform and flanked by fellow Riflemen, Lofty, Phil Ashby, Jock Fleming, my cousin Bob Maddocks, Norman Gregson and Ted Deal (Physical Training Instructor for the Light Division Depot).

I arrived in a Rolls Royce Silver Shadow with my father. It had been a long drive of around 45 minutes. After extricating myself and my cathedral length veil out of the car, Dad and I began to walk along the gravel path, and under the lychgate. The doors into the church were open and Handel's 'Arrival of the Queen of Sheba' began to play. My heart was thumping, but just as we reached the entrance a gust of wind lifted my tiara and veil up, off my head, and into the yew tree. The ushers, seeing what had happened, quickly closed the doors, and Lofty climbed up the tree to rescue my headdress. My bridesmaids were my two small nieces, my closest friend from school, Maria, my friend Kate and Paul's sister Jonquil. Within seconds they had me back to looking like a bride. The doors were opened a second time and the music from the organ filtered out. As I drew close to Paul with his best man Phil Ashby, and his groomsman Jock Fleming at his side, he gave me that huge grin of his and a sidelong glance. He whispered, 'having second thoughts?' We both laughed, and I instantly relaxed.

It was the most perfect day, but one of the most magical moments for me was that my Dad, despite all his medical trials and tribulations, was able to walk me down the aisle, and give me to Paul. I had been talking about having a dog as Paul was away so much and it would be company for me, but Paul kept saying it would be too much of a tie. But after the wedding breakfast and speeches, he went out to his parents' car, and brought in a box with an 8-week-old Jack Russell puppy.

After our honeymoon, accompanied by our puppy, in a log cabin deep in the Scottish countryside, we moved into our first married quarter at Worthy Down camp near Winchester, home of the Royal Army Pay Corps (RAPC). That May, Paul bought me my first motorbike, an AE80 Kawasaki for my 21st, and bought me lessons with ROSPA in preparation to take my licence. We would often take rides out to the coast on our bikes. Having a swim in the sea, and a picnic in Stokes Bay was Paul's favourite way to spend some downtime. Then everything changed when at the end of June, on the same day Paul was promoted to Colour Serjeant, I found out I was six weeks pregnant. In less than two years we had met, married, and were now expecting a baby. I felt a little overwhelmed, still with a year left to finish my training and these huge changes in my life, but Paul took it in his stride and assured me that everything would work out.

TRIBUTE TO A HERO

That season of 1987/88, Paul was playing for RAPC Worthy Down regimental football team when he was spotted by a Hampshire County scout who asked if he would captain the Hampshire team. Paul was chuffed at this and enthusiastically began training with the county side. Their first game was on a Wednesday evening at Romsey Football Club. I was keen to watch and managed to swap my day off so that I could go with him. At five months pregnant, it was time to stop riding the bike and take to the newly acquired VW Golf. I offered to pick Paul up from Sir John Moore's Barracks, but I had forgotten to put petrol in the car. We were less than a mile away from the camp when to my horror the car stalled, and Paul pulled over into a lay-by. He exclaimed the petrol gauge indicated the fuel tank was empty. I was mortified and my profuse apology was met with a hard look before Paul realised that he had time to run back to camp and get a Jerry can of fuel. Off he went running back to the barracks. I sat there listening to the radio, but there wasn't anything on that I liked, so without a second thought I pushed my 'Eurythmics' cassette tape into the player and happily sang along with Annie Lennox. Paul arrived back half an hour later and emptied the full Jerry can that he had run back with, into the car's tank. By now it was dark and had started to rain. He jumped back in and announced we still had plenty of time to get to Romsey, and I was not to worry. Assured we were now ready to go, he turned the ignition key, and nothing happened. He tried again, and then looked at the radio and asked, 'have you been listening to a tape?'

It was then the horror of my actions sunk in; I had run the battery flat. Without so much as a cross word, Paul went running back to camp a second time, leaving me now cold, and feeling very guilty. Half an hour later he arrived back at the car in an Army Land Rover. We locked the car, I scrambled with my bump into the seat beside him, and off we headed, in silence, to Romsey. We arrived with 15 minutes to spare, and I watched Paul as he played one of the best games I was to ever see him play.

On 15th October, Michael Fish infamously announced during his weather report that a lady had rung into the BBC saying there was a hurricane on its way to Great Britain, but the lady was wrong and there would be wind and rain along the Southeast coast only. Paul's young recruits were conducting night exercises on Barton Stacey Training Area, about twenty minutes from the camp. I was on early shifts and exhausted, so went to bed early and slept through the night missing the winds gusting at up to 100 mph, and torrential rain. Meanwhile, Paul had one Land Rover, and spent the early hours ferrying the boys in groups back to camp until they, and all the staff, were safe in the barracks. The following morning at 6 am I could not drive down the road past the camp because six trees had been blown down. I was horrified to learn later that Paul had driven back and forth along that road several times during the night. There was massive devastation across the country that night, eighteen people were sadly killed, and about 15 million trees were blown down.

March 1988 was a busy one. Heavily pregnant, I took my nursing exams, only just being able to squeeze onto the chair behind the desk. A week later our son Christopher was born. He was 3 days overdue and knowing that my husband was about to be deployed on a training exercise, my obstetrician agreed to induce me. Christopher was born at 2.31 p.m. on a Saturday. However, the Hampshire Chronicle sportswriter reported on how 'Paul Harding, Captain of the RAPC football team, was not up to his normal prowess, and the mistakes he made that game allowed for several shots on goal by the opposition'. Clearly, no one had told him that Paul had been substituted. The following morning Paul visited me, and said his goodbyes, then went away to Brecon for a three-week training exercise with his platoon. I quickly learnt the reality of being alone and having to get on with things. It was left to my mother to come to the hospital to collect Christopher and me and to take us home to Worthy Down. Between caring for my poorly father and working for the MoD, every few days she would drive down from Twickenham to Winchester with bags of shopping and issue words of encouragement, but I missed Paul desperately.

By July we had bought our first property, a flat near Stokes Bay. The day that we 'marched out' of our quarter, I followed the removal van, and Paul was going to follow on his motorbike later that day. Christopher was three months old, so I wanted to get to our flat and unpack his cot and set up his nursery immediately. We arrived and I wondered what was keeping Paul. Then, as I was directing the removal men, a friend came bursting through the door saying Paul was in hospital in Winchester. When I got to the A&E department Paul was in a bad way. He had been on a roundabout crossing over the M3 when a lady in a Honda Accord had joined the roundabout, and had not seen him. She had hit him side on and thrown him into the air landing just inside the barrier. Another metre further and he would have been thrown over the barrier, and down onto the motorway beneath. Paul's arm and wrist were badly broken in several places, but what he was really upset about was that he knew this would jeopardise his application for Special Air Service selection. Paul received months of care at the Queen Alexandra's Hospital in Portsmouth, trying to fix and plate the bones of his forearm, but in the end, he had to accept that the radioulnar joint would never be fixed and would remain detached. As heartbreaking as it was, this along with us just having had a baby, Paul decided not to pursue his ambition of going to Hereford, and joining the Special Air Service.

Paul received a posting order to return to his parent unit, 2 RGJ, who were now in Connaught Barracks, Dover. I remained in our flat until the summer of 1989 but was finding the separation very hard. Then, when Christopher was fifteen months he was misdiagnosed by our GP who thought he was teething. Thankfully the mother instinct in me knew something was seriously wrong. The Royal Naval Hospital Haslar was nearby, so one morning, having been turned away by our GP again, I went straight to Haslar and walked onto the paediatric ward with Christopher like a rag doll in my arms. I explained our military connection, and we were ushered into a side room for a nurse to carry out observations on Christopher. Right on cue, he went totally limp in my arms as he went into peripheral shutdown. I had done plenty of paediatric nursing, but when it is your own baby it is absolutely terrifying. I had to step aside as he was taken into a high dependency room in front of the nurses' station. The Commander (Naval Consultant) was summoned, a crash trolley was brought out, and a paediatricians and nurses worked on Christopher, giving him oxygen, trying to get lines into him. Eventually, things calmed down and they stabilised him. A giant of a male nurse called Wilf was assigned to special care Chris; he was literally an angel. He asked about my connection to the Armed Forces, and I explained that my husband was stationed in Dover, giving him Paul's name, rank and number. He lifted the telephone receiver above Christopher's cot and dialled the operator, asked for Connaught Barracks, and within seconds he had got through to Paul. Wilf told Paul what had happened and replaced the receiver. He then said to me that Paul was going to try and get away, and pop down.

By now it was midday, Dover was 150 miles away, around a three-hour drive if the M25 was kind, I imagined Paul would get his work finished and head over late afternoon. The paediatrician had managed to extract just enough blood from Christopher to test for a variety of conditions. The Commander examined Christopher, then ordered Wilf to take Chris and me down to X-ray. He wanted to check Chris's lungs before giving him a lumbar puncture. We arrived back on the ward just as the lunches were being cleared away. It was now 1.30 pm and to my astonishment, as Wilf was hooking Christopher up to the monitors, Paul almost crashed through the double doors, still in camouflage clothing, holding his crash helmet in his hand. He had literally gone AWOL. The moment he finished the call from Wilf, he had taken his motorbike and covered 150 miles in an hour and a half. Relief flooded over me. I didn't care that he must have been speeding or that he was AWOL, he was there with me. We were in Haslar for two weeks whilst Christopher was treated for pneumonia. Paul secured some annual leave and we tag-teamed staying overnight with Christopher in his little room. Gradually we saw the colour appear in his limbs and face, his life could now begin. It was a turning point for me, as the following week I found out I was pregnant again, and I no longer wanted to be living apart from Paul. The reality of separation was too much to withstand, and we marketed the flat immediately.

I was 16 weeks pregnant when I experienced intense abdominal pain and a large loss of blood. Paul had deployed that same day for an exercise in Germany. I refused to see my GP after his treatment of Christopher and so went to the nearest A&E. I was examined and told by a most unsympathetic doctor that I had lost the baby. Trying not to be distressed in front of my toddler, I returned to our flat and called my sister in Devon. She immediately drove from Dartmoor to Gosport, collected Christopher and me, and took us home with her. As soon as we arrived, I fell into bed and slept for ten hours. The following day she called her own GP and requested a home visit for me. He examined me and announced he thought I was still pregnant and that possibly I had lost one of twins. The subsequent scan showed he was correct. So I had to stay on bed rest for the duration of Paul's deployment in Germany, and Christopher and I stayed with my family.

Thankfully the flat sold quickly, and on the day we accepted an offer Paul rang and said he had found a house, and had put an offer in. It was a quaint miner's cottage in the coastal town of Deal, but I didn't see it myself until the day we moved in at the end of August. I totally trusted his judgement and he didn't disappoint me. It was perfect, only a twenty-minute commute for Paul to Connaught Barracks where he was a Company Quarter Master Serjeant (CQMS) with A Company. Paul would never ride his bike home wearing his military clothing. He gave strict instructions never to hang his Army stuff out on the washing line to dry. We were to keep his identity secret, and no one should know what Paul did for a living.

He also asked me not to tell any friends I made with neighbours or at Christopher's nursery, that he was a soldier. I was to just say he was a logistics manager, which wasn't entirely untrue. It wasn't hard to comply but the reality of the threat to us didn't hit home until a week after our move to Deal. On the 7th September, we heard the awful news that the wife of a British soldier, stationed in Germany, had been shot. 26-year-old Heidi Hazell was sitting in the family car at her home. She was approached by a member of the IRA who was wearing British Army battle dress. He opened fire with a Kalashnikov automatic weapon, shooting her fourteen times, at point-blank range. The IRA subsequently gave the warning to civilians to 'keep well clear' of military personnel.

Paul had previously encouraged me to always reverse park, as to make driving away quickly possible. He had always insisted we close the curtains at dusk before putting lights on too. After the murder of Heidi, Paul's advice had more meaning to me and the reality of living off camp, without any security, began to sink in. The following evening, after Christopher was settled in his cot, Paul sat down with me and explained that the intelligence was that there were several IRA cells were operating in and around Dover, and I was to be circumspect in everything I did. If I were to drive to Connaught Barracks or visit the married quarters patch, called Burgoyne Heights, I was to deviate my route each time and not create specific behavioural patterns. Paul's concern for his family was completely understandable, for during that year alone the IRA shot eleven soldiers dead, including a young Lance Corporal who drove the school bus for British soldiers' children. In a petrol station in Germany, they shot dead an off-duty member of the RAF, as well as his six-month-old daughter in her car seat. A further three soldiers were killed in a bus bomb, and five barracks were bombed including one in Osnabruck.

Despite the threat from the IRA, I was to quickly settle into our new home, enrolling Christopher into his new nursery and registering with a new GP and midwife. Whilst walking Christopher to nursery on the morning of 22nd September at around 8.20 am, I heard a loud boom. It reminded me of sunbathing in my parent's garden as a girl, when I would watch Concorde leave from Heathrow, fly over us, and hear the sonic boom as she passed over the coast. I dropped Christopher off at nursery and returned home for the morning. Walking away from the sea and town centre, I did not notice the large pall of smoke that had begun to cover the town. So, it wasn't until I was walking back to the nursery that I saw the smoke and realised something was wrong. The other mums waiting at the gates were in shock, some crying, others holding each other. I approached a couple whom I had chatted with previously, they both turned and in unison cried out 'there's been an explosion at the Marines' depot!'

The Royal Marine Depot was one and a half miles from our house and the boom that I had heard was a devastating 15lb time bomb being detonated in the School of Music building. Ten Marine bandsmen were trapped and died in the collapsed building. A further young Marine's body was recovered from the roof of a nearby house. Twenty one suffered serious life-changing injuries and one of these young men died later in hospital. Most of the casualties were teenagers. The IRA claimed responsibility for the atrocity. One week after the bombing, the staff and students at the School of Music marched through the town, thousands of us watched and applauded as they maintained gaps in their ranks to mark the positions of those unable to march through death or serious injury. Further investigation showed that security at Connaught Barracks had been so tight that the IRA had given up their plan of attacking 2RGJ, and had turned instead to the School of Music. Our Riflemen on guard duties, and in particular Corporal Larry Wall, were later commended for their vigilance and rigorous safekeeping of the camp and quarters.

I spent more and more time at Burgoyne Heights during the next few months, making new friends with other wives. One of Paul's company clerks at the Light Division Depot had married one of his close friends from their days in Minden. Jock was now back with 2RGJ, and a Corporal. His wife Debbie had left the Women's Royal Army Corps and they were living on the patch with their one-year-old son, Paul's Godson. Debbie and I became very close, and it was decided that when the time came for the baby to be born, we would drop Christopher off to her on the way to Dover hospital. The baby's due date came, and I felt perfectly fine, no twinges, nothing, and as it was glorious for that time of year, we packed up a picnic and took Christopher to Ramsgate beach. We spent the whole day there and at 5 pm I said to Paul we should pack up and head home to get Christopher bathed and into bed. But when I stood up, I experienced a sudden pain, then another and another, then my waters broke. The colour drained from Paul's face as I crumpled up in contraction after contraction. Paul threw everything into the bag, picked Christopher up in one arm and hauled me up to the car. He wanted to go to the nearest A&E, but I was insistent we return to Dover as I wanted Debbie to have Christopher, plus I wanted my community midwife, Stella, to deliver my baby.

By the time we had arrived at Jock and Debbie's house, I had started to push. Paul leapt out of the car, undid Christopher's car seat, and handed him over to Debbie. I began giving instructions to Debbie about his bedtime routine, between panting, when she yelled at Paul 'get her to the fucking hospital, Paul!' Stella met us at the door with a wheelchair, and Paul practically ran pushing me down to the delivery suite, through the doors and lifting me onto the bed as Stella delivered Jake at exactly 5.55 pm. Debbie and I spent the rest of the year with all three of our boys, exactly a year between each of them. They were to grow up together and develop into lifelong friends.

After Jake's birth, Paul was extremely busy as CQMS. He was providing logistical support to his company prior to a six-week-long deployment to Canada (Exercise Pond Jump West). Paul went away when Jake was six weeks old, and I really began to struggle. My sister visited with her children from Devon and helped, but they were both in school, so she couldn't stay long. In June I attended a wedding alone at Dover Castle. It was the marriage of the other serjeant that had been propping up the bar at the Rifle Ball in Minden on the night Paul and I met. Jimmy Mitchell, known to everyone as Jimmy, was a good friend of Paul's but had been on a posting away from the battalion with a Territorial Army (TA) unit in London. There he had met and fallen in love with one of the TA soldiers, Alison. She was petite and beautiful, but when the photographer was not having much luck getting the attention of the wedding party, specifically the Groom's friends, my eardrums nearly burst as Alison emitted the loudest wolf whistle I'd ever heard. She commanded, in an extremely loud and pronounced Waltham Forest accent, for us to gather around. We didn't need a second telling.

Paul's time in Canada was dragging for me. Four weeks down and two to go, and after a week of barely any sleep, I was putting the bags of rubbish out for the bin men to collect when one split, spilling its contents all over the path. As I was picking the rotten contents up whilst trying to keep a 2-year-old away from it, the postman delivered a postcard from Paul. The picture was of a group of tourists laughing and paddling a white-water raft. On the back, Paul's distinct tiny and neatly printed writing described the adventure training they were doing. How he'd seen a bear, been climbing, and was generally having a great time. I scooped Christopher up, went back into the house, sat down, and cried. It felt so unfair. At that moment the phone rang, and it was my nursing friend from Plymouth, who had been my bridesmaid. I poured my heart out to her. She was about to take a week's annual leave and the next day she drove up to Deal, and put me back together. It was just what was required to get me through the last days before Paul returned home.

The IRA continued its aggressive campaign on the mainland. On 20th July, they detonated a bomb inside the London Stock Exchange and Britain felt under siege. However, our attention was being drawn to the Middle East. In August, Saddam Hussein invaded Kuwait and the USA launched Operation Desert Shield. On 14th September, the United Kingdom and France announced the deployment of troops to Saudi Arabia. Any fears of Paul being sent were mildly reduced knowing that the MoD had planned to move 2 RGJ to Omagh in Northern Ireland. For the last twelve months the battalion had been refining their counter-terrorism skills; to change that skill set and find someone else to replace them in Northern Ireland would take a gargantuan effort. But the niggling doubt would occasionally surface and bring with it a hint of fear.

We had taken leave in August and had a holiday cottage in Cromer, Norfolk. On our return, we received an invitation to have dinner with friends who lived at Burgoyne Heights. Jacqui encouraged us to bring Christopher and Jake, so I bathed Christopher and had him ready for bed when we arrived, and lifted him asleep into their guest bed, then joined the other guests at the table. I was introduced to a couple with a baby twelve weeks younger than Jake. She was asleep in her Moses basket and Jake slept in his carrycot beside. Her father was the corporal who had been commended for maintaining the tight security of Connaught Barracks, the previous September – Larry Wall, and his wife Jill. Larry was known to everyone as Wally, and he was a fellow Chelsea supporter who Paul had played football with for many years. Jill was also a nurse; she had been in the Queen Alexandra's Royal Army Nursing Corps when she had met Larry as her patient. Jill and I hit it off immediately. Not only because of our professional connection, but it felt like I had known her in a previous life or something. I was so pleased to hear that they too were coming to Omagh, our next posting, as I'd recently heard that Jock was not taking his family to Northern Ireland.

By the Autumn the battalion was earnestly preparing for the move to Lisanelly Barracks, Omagh, County Tyrone. With the whole Army suffering huge cutbacks under 'Options for Change' the battalion would be stationed there for three years, and not the two previously planned. Still, it was better than being sent to war in Kuwait. We were to move in January, so by Christmas I had packed the majority of our MFO boxes (*Movement Forwarding Office* boxes are wooden crates that are made up of four pieces of plywood and screws, occasionally can be made from cardboard). The wooden boxes would be put together and filled with all our belongings, ready to be shipped to our new quarter. I had gone to visit my parents when Paul called the house phone. He explained that as 2 RGJ were packed and trained up, ready for our posting to Omagh, it was looking likely that we may not move to NI, and instead, the troops could be sent to the Gulf. After I hung up, I lay on the sofa crying, my mother came into the room to see what was wrong, and I explained. I expected a hug and words of consolation, but she showed me no sympathy, and in no uncertain words told me to 'man-up' and not give Paul further things to worry about. It wasn't the reaction I had hoped for, but this was the woman who had been bombed out of three houses during WW2, had lost her younger brother aged fifteen to bomb damage clearance, and whose husband had survived D-Day. It was exactly what I needed to hear.

By 17th October 200,000 American, 15,000 British and 11,000 French troops were stationed in the Gulf region. But in December, the MoD had confirmed we were definitely moving to Omagh after Christmas, and my thoughts turned to the logistics of travelling with a ten-month-old baby and a toddler. Paul would take our car over with our Jack Russell, Jessie. This would mean him driving up to Stranraer in Dumfries, catching the ferry across to Larne, and then the drive west to Omagh. He felt it safer for the boys and me to travel across with the other families on an RAF flight to the military airbase in Aldergrove, which was attached to Belfast International Airport. There had been no let-up from the IRA attacks, bombings, and shootings. The Unit Families Officer Captain Tony Manley, known to us all as 'Spanner' (his nickname apparently came from his ability to fix all things mechanical), had given briefings and demonstrations about what to expect, and the boys and I were booked to move on 10th January 1991.

Around 250 families were moving with the battalion. We were coached from Dover to RAF Lyneham in Wiltshire. I took both car seats, a nappy changing bag with spare clothes, and packed food for the day. After being checked in we were given a briefing by an RAF Staff Sergeant, who explained that all their Boeings were being used to fly personnel out to the Gulf and that we would be flying on a Hercules C130 troop carrier. This news was greeted by whoops from the older children and groans from their mothers. There was plenty of crew to help us up the ramp and into the colossal belly of the aircraft. The centre was piled high with cargo secured by netting, and there was just enough room to sidestep to the side of this man-made mountain to where we would be seated. The metal sides of the aircraft had steel poles running along at knee height, and a network of straps to form a kind of hammock seat. A crewman secured the two car seats with me into these straps, and I clipped both Jake and Christopher in. At least now my ten months old and toddler were restrained.

The back door closed slowly, and it became dark, a crewman squeezed past us handing out a pair of yellow or red ear defenders for each person. Thankfully both the boys were ready for their nap, and they didn't resist when I placed the ear defenders over their heads. Putting mine on, I sat back and tried to relax. The boys nodded off and the Hercules rumbled away; it wasn't long before I had joined the boys for a nap. It was at least an hour before I was woken by another crewman, squeezing by to give out the inflight snack of a packet of two custard creams and a carton of apple juice. Looking at my watch I was excited, everything was going to plan. The boys would be waking up shortly, but we must nearly be there.

I tapped the arm of the crewman and he bent over, pulled off the ear defender, and gestured for me to talk into his left ear.

'Are we nearly there yet?' The crewman laughed and replied into my right ear:

'We haven't even fuck'n taken off! The Black Box isn't working.'

I felt panic rising, 'shit', what was I going to do? They will be waking up any minute. Then to my relief, the engines cut and the back door began to lower. Whatever the problem was, they couldn't fix the plane.

Although this was a regular occurrence for those who flew 'Air RAF', for me it was all very surreal. All the families were coached to hotels. I felt quite lonely that night and dreaded going through the whole process again in the morning. Alison was still in London and not joining us until later in the year. Jill and Larry had decided to drive over with their baby, and Debbie, of course, wasn't coming. I lay awake for a long time thinking and realising that even though I thought I knew what life as a Camp Follower would be like, I never could have imagined its reality. The following day both the boys slept during the flight and when the Hercules landed at Aldergrove, several coaches were there to meet us. We pulled through the gates of Lisanelly Barracks around 11 pm, and Paul met us on the parade square to take us to our new home. He tried to prepare me, by saying things like 'just remember it will be much better when we have pictures up' and 'our redundant furniture will make a huge difference'. I walked through the door and burst into tears. It was old and tired, with what looked like a 1960s kitchen, including an outside toilet! But he was right, we made it our home.

Paul was excited, he had picked up his next promotion, and received his Warrant signed by Her Majesty The Queen. He was now a Serjeant Major or Warrant Officer Class 2 (WO2). But at that time, the Army and the Regiment were undergoing huge changes, and there was a shortage of Sandhurst trained officers, so he was made Platoon Commander of 16 Platoon.

Life immediately got busy. Firstly, there was the unpacking and attending endless security briefings on what we could and could not do. We always had to drop into the Intelligence Room and check if there was anything we should be updated on before leaving camp. There were strict 'no go' areas, basically Republican areas, and maps were posted for us to become familiar with. If we drove anywhere, we had to take an alternative route the next time we visited that place. Enniskillen was the only cinema we could attend. Despite the town's appalling history of being attacked, such as the Remembrance Day bombing on 8th November 1987, it remained popular. We became experts at being unseen and unheard. Even on the phone, we had to be vigilant as conversations might be heard by a terrorist. We were never to give out dates of movements, leave dates or anything that could give the terrorists the intelligence they needed to plan and execute an attack on troop movements. We developed our own coded language. If I wanted to know what time Paul would arrive home from patrols on the border he might say '4 hours after the time of Jake's birth', or if trying to tell my mother the date of our return for leave, I might say 'the day of Christopher's birth plus 3, in the month that Dad was born'. We were to have no calendars pinned up with dates denoted just in case a maintenance worker was under threat to gather information for the IRA.

I couldn't drive the car straight away as we were awaiting our new Northern Irish plates, so my first venture out was on foot. Wrapping the boys up into their double buggy, we visited the Intelligence Room for the latest update and booked out at the Guard Room. From the barracks into town was a downhill walk, and halfway to town was the medical centre. There were only two GPs who would allow dependents of British service personnel to register, so the boys and I were waiting over two hours to be seen. When we left the practice, I clocked a man in a dark green jacket and jeans standing across the road, leaning against the play park's fence. Something familiar about him became apparent, but I couldn't place it. I carried on into town, going into several shops, including Wellworths and the bakers. Each time I came out of a shop, the same man was across the way. I had decided to walk back home, calling into the butchers on the way. I was just asking the butcher for a pound of sausages when a dark blue Sierra pulled up beside the shop. A giant of an RUC Officer climbed out and stood in the butcher's doorway, he had to be 6' 5' at least, but unlike Lofty, he was easily 5' wide as well. Everyone in the shop simply froze.

Out of the Ford Sierra, two RUC Officers tumbled and immediately apprehended the man who had followed me around the town. They bundled my 'dicker' into the car. The RUC officer who was blocking the doorway turned and declared 'I think it's time for you to go home'.

Well, there we were, life in Omagh was like nothing before. Christopher knew that we had to use a mirror on a stick to look for 'baby mice' under our car. The reality was that I could not park up and leave the car for a single moment without checking the IRA hadn't planted an incendiary in our absence. We were on a four-month cycle. Paul's platoon spent four weeks patrolling the border, four weeks on guard duty protecting the barracks, four weeks on active duty pursuing the IRA, followed by four weeks leave. The boys and I would spend our time living in Omagh, staying with my sister and her family on Dartmoor, and with my parents.

I couldn't work in County Tyrone Hospital as it was in the Catholic area and too high a risk, so Spanner asked Jill and me to run a camp creche. Jimmy and Alison joined us with their new baby daughter a few weeks later, but I had barely seen Paul since our arrival. On 11th April, our 4th wedding anniversary, I walked down to the camp shop. Pushing the double buggy out of the swing doors, I saw a soldier hunched in the corner of the foyer with a rifle leaning against him. He was completely camouflaged from head to toe. He was wearing a helmet and writing a card with a box of Ferrero Roche chocolates. Christopher shouted from the buggy 'it's my Daddy' but I took no notice as he would shout this at most of the soldiers on camp. Then I recognised the shape of his shoulders, the outline of his jaw and Paul looked up, with that big grin. He stood up and handed me the card and chocolates, 'happy anniversary wombat' he said. 'I promise this will get better'. I wasn't convinced but what could we do but carry on. I just stood and watched him jog away and climb back into a Lynx helicopter and disappear into the sky.

Paul was on his month of border patrol when Jake developed a high fever one night. I called the 'out of hours Doctor' but he refused to come on to the camp. The IRA had a campaign against firms and individuals supplying services and materials to the British Army, and he was too scared of reprisals. But Jake worsened, Paul happened to call as Jake started to convulse, I knew it was a febrile convulsion but couldn't get his temperature down. Ten minutes later there was a loud knocking on the door; it was Jock. Paul had called the Serjeant's Mess and managed to get hold of him. I called Alison and she ran over to sit with Christopher. We wrapped Jake in a blanket and I jumped into the back of Jock's car with him. Stopping at the Guard Room, he signed out a 9mm Browning pistol because we were going to County Tyrone hospital. We were admitted onto the paediatric ward, and they managed to bring Jake's temperature down, but Jake would not lay in a cot. You could cut the atmosphere on the ward with a knife. The nursing staff and other parents glowered at us; it was clear that we were unwelcome. The only time Jake would stop crying was when he was being cuddled. Jock walked up and down the room cradling him all night long. As I sat in the chair watching Jock nurse my baby son with a pistol holstered to his chest, I wondered if this was worth it, should we have stayed back in Deal, but it was too late now, and to return to our house would feel like giving in to the terrorists.

A few weeks into the tour, Jill and I were running the creche. We were becoming very close as we shared our experiences as nurses, our fears, and dreams for our children. Jill disclosed her fears about the state of Larry's health, both his physical and mental wellbeing. They had met in the Queen Elizabeth Military Hospital, Woolwich. It was the classic romance, Larry had been admitted on to the urology ward where Jill was a Staff Nurse, he was diagnosed with bladder cancer and having been operated on, the cancer was removed. During the following weeks that Jill nursed Larry, they had fallen in love. They had married, and Jill quickly fell pregnant with their daughter, but Larry always feared the return of his cancer. This doubled with the intensity of the work he was involved in; his mental health had started to suffer.

The Catholic estate behind Jill's row of quarters targeted the houses, lobbing bottles and bricks over the fence, crashing down onto their roofs. It got so bad that Spanner organised for the grass in their garden to be taken up, and paving stones put down so that Jill could sweep up the glass, and her daughter could toddle around the garden without the fear of stumbling on the hidden glass. Larry was ensconced in the murky world of intelligence gathering and without us knowing, he was becoming more and more poorly. Intuitively, Jill's parents visited to see if they could help. During one of the warmer days, they decided to take a trip to Omagh Town centre. On their return to camp, and just as Jill pulled up at the gate, an angry crowd charged the Guard Room and began throwing glass bottles at everything in their range. Glass rained down inside the man-made choke point. Jill's father was sitting beside Chloe who was ten months old and strapped into the baby seat. He was leaning over her as the bottles threatened to smash through the car windows. It seemed like an eternity before the Quick Reaction Force deployed from the Guard Room to protect Jill as she accelerated out of range of the young Republican thugs.

Paul and I lived in a quarter that formed part of a terrace row that paralleled the back gate of the camp. On the far side of the perimeter fence was the town's largest Catholic housing estate, with a large hill where the estate occupants could stand and jeer. The security fence was solid metal, with double razor wire. Every hundred metres or so, there would be a watch tower, known as a sangar, protecting the perimeter fence. Riflemen watched everything that moved, ready to use their weapons if necessary. One evening, whilst Paul was deployed in Strabane, I was bathing the boys when gunshots rang out. I knew it wasn't fireworks because of their timing and cadence. There was a crack and a thump as the back wall of the quarter vibrated. I pulled the boys out of the bath and carried them down the stairs and into the lounge at the front of the house, and realised that the phone was ringing. I lifted the receiver; it was Jimmy shouting

'Get down. Stay down!'

Jimmy had been in his garden when he heard the screeching of metal against metal, and immediately knew something didn't sound right, then two gunmen on the hill fired high-velocity rounds at the sangar.

The bullets that missed the sangar hit the back of our terrace of houses. An hour later the phone rang again, this time it was Paul. So unflappable, he simply said

'I hear you've had some excitement.'

Jill and I had become increasingly worried about Larry. He hadn't slept for 6 weeks, he had been running on the treadmill every day to try and tire himself out, and Jill had spent several nights talking with him on the phone, trying to keep him thinking straight. Then her grandfather had passed away and she had returned to England for his funeral. On the morning of 6th June, I awoke at nearly 5 am to what sounded like stones hitting our bedroom window. I drew back the curtains and cautiously opened the window. Outside the front door was Spanner. My heart sank to the deepest depths of my stomach. Why else would the Families Officer be knocking on one's door at 5 am unless he had some dreadful news?

'It's not Paul, it's not Paul.' Spanner whispered loudly.

Relief flooded over me, but then my mind kicked into gear.

'Who then was it?'

Spanner whispered, 'It's Jill's Larry, he's been hurt.'

Spanner had to tell Jill about the horrendous news over the phone and arrange tickets for a flight back to Belfast City airport. Alison took the boys from me and after signing out a 9mm Browning pistol from the Guard Room, Spanner drove us to Belfast City Airport to meet Jill and their baby girl, who was 3 weeks away from her first birthday. As he drove, Spanner updated me, explaining that whilst on his intelligence duty in a border outpost, Larry had attempted to take his life by shooting a single round into the centre of his abdomen. The bullet had exited cleanly, and he had survived. He had been taken to the Military Wing of Musgrave Park Hospital in South Belfast, where 5 months later the IRA would plant a bomb killing two soldiers. Whilst I looked after Jill's little girl, she disclosed to Spanner that she had just found out they were expecting their second child but hadn't told Larry. They decided to tell him in the hope that it would be an incentive for his recovery.

September brought changes for us. Paul was appointed Company Serjeant Major, B Company. During wartime, B Company were known as Fire Support Company and consisted of the most senior Riflemen in a battalion. Support Company had four main components: Mortar Platoon, Reconnaissance Platoon, Anti-Tank Platoon and Machine Gun Platoon. It was larger than the rifle companies and consequently busier. On 14th November, a Lynx helicopter carrying a patrol made up of members from Anti-Tank Platoon suffered a bird strike while operating above Gortin Glen. The small aircraft suffered total engine failure and crashed whilst trying to make an emergency landing. As the airframe slammed into the hillside, the main rotor struck the rocky ground, breaking into shards of flying debris.

Onboard were the pilot and co-pilot, and eight members of Paul's company. Corporal Matthew (Mad Dog) Maddocks, aged 38, lost his life. Matthew had been in the battalion for nearly fifteen years and was loved by everyone for his quirky sense of humour and slightly crazy outlook on life; he was a larger-than-life character. The other nine occupants all received injuries in this tragedy, Rifleman Steve Pendleton losing a leg and also his sight. Soldiers', Sailors', and Airmen's Families Association (SSAFA is a charity that offers support to serving men and women, veterans of the British Armed Forces and their families) called and asked me to support a family of one of the injured. In recent years, the Army welfare system has transformed beyond all recognition. But in the '80s and '90s welfare was self-generated. Duties of notification and counselling were left to the wives of Warrant Officers or field officers (majors).

Paul and his company commander, Major Nick Haddock, were first on the scene with the Quick Reaction Force (QRF). Later, when I asked Paul how he could believe in a God when this happens, and the only man on board with children is killed, his reply was.

'I believe in God because, looking at the wreckage, no one should have survived.' Paul replied.

SSAFA organised for the families of the injured to be flown out to Northern Ireland and we hosted the parents and girlfriend of one of the injured Riflemen. I had spent the afternoon changing bed linen, cleaning, and making a casserole. The boys were bathed and in their PJs, when the doorbell rang. I answered the door to a large, portly SSAFA Sister, who in a broad Scottish accent, asked me if my mother was home. I explained that I was Mrs Harding and invited her, and the three people with her, in. They stayed with the boys and me for several days, visiting the hospital and talking with other families in the Families Centre. Thankfully the young Rifleman recovered, and they could return home to England with him for his recuperation. However, things did not ease up. Corporal Maddocks' widow and children remained in their married quarter; I visited them regularly to try and offer support, and worse still Larry was deteriorating.

After several home visits by a mental health nurse, Larry had been returned to work, this time with the Regimental Police, in the Guard Room. Again, Jill had become increasingly concerned for him. He had been to have a check-up scan of his bladder and he was convinced the tumour was back. He was feeling a burden on Jill and believed she, their 18-month-old daughter and their unborn baby would be better off without him. Jill had expressed her deepest concern that her husband was becoming increasingly ill and should not have access to the weapons held in the Guard Room. She was assured that Larry was being looked after. Arguably this was an attitude of its time, and certainly would not be the case today.

On 12th December, Jill was on her way to go shopping when she saw Larry walking between offices on the camp. She pulled over to talk to him, and as they parted, Larry said the strangest thing:' Life's over'. Jill did not know what he meant, and she thought perhaps he'd got his 'brown envelope.' Like many other servicemen of the early 90s Wally was half expecting an MoD redundancy letter that came in a brown envelope. The anxiety of waiting for the postman to bring an end to your suffering affected everyone. After fifteen years of loyal service, to be thwarted by a faceless civil servant was insufferable. The arrival of that brown envelope would have ended Wally's career and forced whole life changes on Jill.

He said 'no, life is over'. Jill said 'its OK, you'll be off for Christmas, Thursday, and you'll be at home, and you'll be with me, it will be OK'. He said 'you know I love you, don't you ?' He told Chloe the same thing and kept going back to the car to kiss them both. Jill said 'I'll see you tonight'.

Jill knew something was seriously wrong and decided to put off her shopping trip, and drove up to our quarter to talk about Larry. But Alison and I had already left for town to do our Christmas shopping. It had been a great trip as we both nailed exactly what we had gone for. My boys had been desperate for the playmobile fort, cowboys and all, and I had bagged the only one in Wellworths. As we returned to the front gate of the camp, we could see the Regimental flag was flying at half-mast and our elation vanished. Slowly we drove through the gate. The Rifleman on duty recognised me and with an ashen face and grim expression, asked me to go straight up to B Company Office. As we pulled up, Paul ran out of the company office. Holding me tight, he whispered into my ear that Larry had shot himself, and we had lost him. Consumed by shock, I collapsed to the floor and fainted. My next memory is sitting on the sofa in Jill's lounge; she was due to have their second child in 6 weeks. I was consumed with grief and anger that Larry had been left to his own devices. But, I managed to get a grip. I learned from the Padre that this time Larry had taken a pistol and shot himself in the back of his head. None of us could imagine the pain and anguish he must have been in, and the bravery it took to take his own life in such a way. He would have known that Jill would view his body to say her goodbyes, and this way his face was not damaged.

Anger does not come close to what I felt, but I knew I had to put it to one side and just love my beautiful friend and her baby girl. I would bathe Chloe and promise her again and again that I would make things right, that she would never want for anything. The misery of a military loss is beyond total. It's not just the loss of a dear friend and brave soldier, it's the loss of a family. When a soldier in a married quarter dies, his family needs to leave the camp within 90 days. The income stops, the schooling stops, the way of life stops as the family return to their pre-military existence. Worse still, it is the very people that they have come to love that enables this death of a thousand cuts. Thankfully though, my Army family were there; Jimmy and Alison helped Paul with childcare, I hardly saw my boys, nor Paul during the following week. Alison cooked my family their meals, did their washing and bathing, as well as looking after her own daughter.

Jill's parents flew in from Newcastle. Spanner and I picked them up from Belfast Airport and my heart broke for them, but I have rarely known such a strong couple. Jill's father became the rock that Jill clung to. I spent that week with Jill and her family, trying to help her manage the collateral damage of Larry's death, praying she would go to full term. Once Jill had been able to view Larry's body and say her last goodbye, and arrangements made for him to be flown back to England, Jill's father took his wife, daughter, and granddaughter back to their home in Durham.

Jill and Larry's quarter needed to be packed up and the contents shipped back to England. Fortunately, Jill's father owned an old chapel that he used as a workshop, and we decided that all of Jill's possessions would be stored there as she would be living in her old family home. Paul and a friend, Norman Gregson put together 25 MFO boxes and Norman's wife Jayne and I began the arduous task of packing our friend's quarter. Jayne and I cried and laughed as we took apart Jill's home room by room, photos and mementoes sparking memories of happier times, but I felt sick every time I thought of Jill opening these boxes one day in the future. I decided upon a plan that hopefully would help her.

We got a notebook and numbered each page, marking each MFO box with the same number. We then packed all of Larry's things into specific MFO boxes that only contained his belongings, then noted in the exercise book which boxes these were. One lunchtime, Paul came by with some sandwiches and a drink for us. He was taken aback when he found us staring into two open boxes. As he entered the room I looked up and said, 'and I thought you were king of the T-shirts!' We had just finished packing two boxes of hundreds of Larry's T-shirts, brand new and still in their cellophane. At least we knew Jill could choose her moment to open these boxes knowing their contents.

Jill's son was delivered 6 weeks later. I cannot imagine the agony she must have been in, seeing the other fathers visiting their newborns and partners on the ward. Jill and her children remained living with her parents for a further two years. Larry had been buried in their village graveyard behind their home, and she could see him and visit him as and when she needed to. We would visit as often as possible, sometimes staying in nearby holiday villages. Having left Queen Alexandra's Royal Army Nursing Corps (QARANC) to marry Larry, Jill returned to study nursing at Durham University. She graduated with a degree in Health Care a short time after. Focused on building a new life in the Northwest, she had a house built in a nearby village and began her next chapter.

I missed Jill immensely as the August Bank Holiday Monday arrived. Little did I know, but the hole left in my life by Jill's departure was just about to be filled by the most unlikely arrival. It started with a bizarre phone call from Jayne. A strange dog had turned up in her back garden. Stranger still, it was attacking her freshly laundered washing. It was jumping up at the clothesline, biting at the towels and swinging on her freshly laundered bedding. Both her husband and Paul were out on patrol in support of the Police, so Jayne called the Guard Room, but their response was to tell Jayne to ignore it and it will go away. The Riflemen on guard duty, being typical dog lovers, had previously fed it sausage rolls and crisps then sent it packing. Sensing Jayne needed help, I walked down and hooked this wayward pup onto a lead, and marched it back to my house and called the local dog pound. But being a Bank Holiday, it was closed until Tuesday morning. So, there was nothing I could do but feed the poor mutt, shut him in the kitchen and take our dog, Jessie, up to our bedroom to be with me. I then panicked, 'what if Paul returned from patrols tonight?'. I wrote a note explaining: 'Stray dog was in the kitchen, not to worry. I'll sort it out tomorrow'.

I couldn't sleep for wondering if this poor dog was pining or trashing the kitchen. Then the familiar sound of the Lynx coming into land rattled the windows – the patrol had returned. Twenty minutes later I heard Paul's key slide into the lock as he let himself in. Holding my breath, I crept out of bed and across the landing. Like a child creeping down the stairs at Christmas, I negotiated the first five steps so I could just about peep over the bannister far enough to see into the hallway. Paul, on his haunches, rifle resting on the floor beside him, was cuddling the stray. The dog was doing his best to lick the cam cream off Paul's face. Paul looked up and saw me; grinning he instructed 'you need to find this wee man a good home!'

The next day I dutifully drove to Omagh's dog pound and registered our stray. Walking back to the car, checking for bombs, and driving away was awful. I could not stop thinking of his short little legs and big brown eyes. Then on Friday morning, the house phone rang and a strong Tyrone accent declared that all dogs brought into the pound were put to sleep on Fridays by 4 pm. Omagh town did not have the facility to keep lost and stray animals over the weekends, and I had until 1 pm to reclaim the stray I had brought in.

Upon arrival at the pound, my stray was leashed and waiting by the door. The idea did not escape me that this might be a weekly ploy on behalf of the dog warden, but I was just relieved to have our stray back. I took him directly to our vet who lived way out in the countryside. He was the only vet that had the nerve to agree to treat animals belonging to British Army soldiers. A young Irishman with the harshest of Ulster accents, he had studied in England and knew his stuff, inside and out. Lifting my 'wee man' (as he was now becoming) onto the table, the vet drew in a sharp breath and muttered; 'not another f***ing son of Archie.'

Everyone knew 'Archie', whether you were a 'local', a transient British soldier, RUC Officer or Priest. The infamous 'Archie' was a Basset Hound who roamed freely throughout the town. He was renowned for sleeping in shop windows where the sun's rays warmed the display and his bones. Throughout the day, he would follow the sun's trajectory knowing where the warmest spots to snooze were, until eventually, the shops closed. The vet diagnosed, unequivocally, that my stray was a Basset X Corgi, or as Jake would later call his dog a 'Borgi'.

So, our 'Borgi' was neutered, vaccinated, and treated for infestations, before I brought him home. Then 4 weeks later I heard the Lynx helicopters landing once more, and left another note taped to the kitchen door. This time I explained that I had personally found 'that' stray wee man a very good home and, peeking over the bannister, I spied a 'roughty, toughty' platoon commander, who had spent weeks tracking down IRA arms smugglers, holding tight the ugliest stray dog imaginable. Heinz slotted seamlessly into the Harding way of life, and for a further 14 years, answered to the title of 'Jake's dog'.

The Christmas of 1991 was hard. Alison and I had to pull together even more than before. We ached with grief for Jill. Out of a sense of duty, we attended the 'Wives' Christmas Party' but left after the meal, as it was too painful. In the new year, fourteen local contractors began repairs to the road at the bottom of our garden. I would make them tea and sandwiches every day. They were hard-working, honest men. Cheeky and lovable all rolled into one, they would not have been out of place working in Chelsea or Glasgow. Christopher loved to watch them whilst dressed up in his little hard hat and high-viz jacket, with his Tonka digger, and they would pat his head and chat to him. By now he had quite a Tyrone accent which impressed the young workforce.

On the evening of 17th January 1992, I collected the empty cups and gathered the cleared plates before wishing them a good weekend. It was late Friday as they climbed into their white Ford transit van. An hour later, seven were dead, and seven badly injured. The van driver would die in the Royal Victoria Hospital four days later. They had done little more than try to earn a living. But taking the same route too regularly in Northern Ireland is hard to avoid if you are a contractor working for the Security Forces. On this occasion, the IRA detonated a roadside bomb at the rural Teebane crossroads. The blast was heard 10 miles away.

By February 1993, it was our time to leave Omagh. It was a confusing period of time for me. On one hand, there was a feeling of immense relief to be leaving the bombings and murders behind, on the other, the regret and guilt of leaving Alison and the memories of Jill and Larry. But there was nothing I could do, other than pack more MFO boxes and build a new life back in Winchester, where Paul had been appointed Regimental Quartermaster Serjeant (RQMS) of the new Army Training Regiment. Leaving the restrictions of Northern Ireland was like being reborn. Life was so different, we still had to be security-aware, but it was much more relaxed, and I could visit Jill and her children much more often.

Chapter Five

Winchester to Iraq
Mrs Paula Harding

Basking in the splendour of such a glorious city as Winchester was all we could wish for. The beautiful Cathedral and wonderful country pubs were a welcome distraction from the hardships of the previous two years. Life was great, it was hard to imagine it getting better. But just as the feeling of comfort had delivered the final waves of euphoria, change was knocking at the door once more. Paul came home full of excitement, clearly something had pleased him. With that big grin of his, he announced his promotion to Warrant Officer Class 1 (RSM) and we would be moving to Oxford where he would be taking up the post of Regimental Serjeant Major of the 5th Battalion, The Royal Green Jackets (5RGJ), a Volunteer Regiment. It seemed like only yesterday, but there we were once more, packing MFO boxes and moving to Slade Park Barracks. It was our 6th house move in seven years of marriage. Despite the brief love affair with Winchester, Oxford, the city of spires, proved to be just as wonderful. I returned to college as a full-time student whilst Christopher and Jake settled into a lovely school and nursery.

I was even closer to Jill, Zac, and Chloe. Alison had moved with our parent battalion, which had now been re-numbered after a round of Government cuts and called The First Battalion, The Royal Green Jackets (1RGJ). The battalion had left Omagh and was now ensconced in Dhekelia, in the Eastern Sovereign Base Area of Cyprus. Alison, Jimmy, and their daughter Bethanie were safely out of the troubles at last. Our Oxford posting was for two years, and whilst there was some envy at not being in Dhekelia, at least I could take the boys out for holidays and stay with Alison and Jimmy.

Blissfully unaware that trouble had been brewing in Cyprus, we had no idea that after three years of lockdown in Northern Ireland, some soldiers had begun to abuse the hospitality of their hosts. After a year of sun, sea and alcohol, discipline was edging out of control, and on 16th September, three Riflemen lost control of their senses and brutally murdered a Danish tour guide. It was an unforgivable, horrific crime that brought shame to the United Kingdom, let alone the Regiment. The battalion was unravelling, discipline had relaxed and the draconian measures used to prevent a recurrence had a damaging effect upon unit cohesion. Our time in Oxford was cut short, and Paul was required to move to Cyprus, and bring the situation under control. By the time Army Personnel Centre had rounded off their processes, we arrived in mid June, with just over six months of the posting remaining in Cyprus.

It was like being back in Northern Ireland. All movement for every serviceman and their families had been heavily restricted. Police stopped and checked everyone who looked like a Rifleman. It was a ghastly time for the families. There was a huge sense of shame and embarrassment, as well as anger from other units on the island who blamed the battalion for ruining their tour. The front gate of the base had become a macabre stop for the tour buses, as local protesters kept vigil and vented their anger at all who came and went. But we were determined to make the most of this time in the sun and I enjoyed our days on the beach with Alison and her daughter.

The six months flew by. We just about squeezed in Christmas in the sun before returning to the UK. As a festive treat, we had taken the boys sledging in the snow-covered Troodos mountains. Bizarre as it was to leave the hot beaches of Dhekelia, to the crisp frozen slopes of Mount Olympus, we had a wonderful day. On our way home, we passed an overturned car lit up by the flashing blue lights of Police and ambulance vehicles. I said a silent prayer, hoping that no one was hurt on the eve of Christmas, but that prayer was not answered. We had bathed the boys and had them sitting in front of a log fire ready to put out a mince pie and whiskey for Santa when there was a knock at the door. Paul went to answer and came through with Nick Haddock, who was the Duty Officer. He was pale, I just knew that the traffic incident was the reason for his call. One of our Riflemen had been driving home with his toddler when the little boy had undone his restraint. When the man had turned to clip it shut, he had lost control and overturned the car. He had survived and been taken to hospital with a broken arm, but the toddler had been thrown from the vehicle and tragically died of his injuries. Personnel Services Branch 2 (known as PS2) had not been developed in 1995; instead, Battalion Headquarters would arrange for the Duty Officer, and invariably their wife, to accompany the Padre to inform and stay with the bereaved. Nick's wife, Annabel, was now expecting their fourth child and Nick had called to ask me, instead, to accompany him and the Padre to sit with the child's mother. Returning home late that Christmas Eve, I sat on the chair in the boys' room until dawn, staring at them both, dozing, and praying that God would always keep them safe.

January 1996, and the battalion moved to Kiwi Barracks, Bulford. Paul had done a fantastic job in re-establishing discipline and morale, and whilst we will never forgive the Riflemen who disgraced the United Kingdom, we had left Cyprus ready for the new challenge of life in an Operational Ready Brigade. Our married quarter was on the edge of Salisbury Plain, and we decided not to enrol Christopher and Jake into the camp school, but into a village school a little further afield. Whilst in Cyprus, Christopher had experienced taunting by older boys whose fathers had received a reprimand from Paul. It was a tough call. I had become an integral part of the battalion and spilt blood and tears in its defence. But Paul was now the RSM. Maintaining values and standards was Paul's main role, but it was unfair that our children should suffer abuse from the children of the very soldiers Paul was serving so well. It made eminent sense to put a little distance between the children.

The Balkans had been suffering the ravages of war and genocide for five years. As part of an Operational Ready Brigade, the battalion quickly found themselves preparing to deploy to Bosnia as a NATO peacekeeping force to prevent further ethnic cleansing. Thankfully the tour was cut short after just 17 weeks, and the battalion was home in time for Christmas. Life was good in Bulford; the boys were happy at their tiny village school, and I returned to work. Just when it seemed things could not get any better, in July 1997 the icing on the cake came when Paul was promoted to the rank of Captain. It is one of the greatest achievements for anyone to be awarded a Queen's Commission, but to earn it from the ranks is remarkable. Paul earned a Late Entry (LE) Commission, only one of three people in the Regiment that year. I was overwhelmed with pride. I knew that Paul was good at his job, the way people spoke about him, and I just knew he had won the respect of all he served with. As thrilled as I was to move to the Officer's Mess, it was heart-wrenching to leave my friends in the Serjeants Mess.

Paul started his new life as the Unit Welfare Officer, with the battalion he had originally joined twenty-two years previously. After a short course at Bristol University, he enjoyed two trouble-free years looking after the welfare of some domestically challenged Riflemen. Then, as was the tradition back then, he became the Mechanical Transport Officer (MTO) and returned to operations, long exercises and deployments. First came Kenya, from October to December 1997, heavy rainfall and flash floods led to thousands of deaths across the country. Sadly, Rifleman Blackledge was amongst the fatalities. He died attempting to rescue a fellow Rifleman from a swollen river. It was the first time for a few years that the battalion had experienced a loss of any kind.

We had become very comfortable in the Southwest of England. The Army had resized several times and the days of moving units all around the world (known as Arms Plotting) had finished. For all the money in the world, it looked as if Paul would remain in Bulford until he was 55. Desperately keen to secure a good school for the boys, we searched high and low for our forever home, before eventually settling for a beautiful house in a village north of Winchester city. The schools were perfect for the boys, the countryside suited our outdoor lifestyle, and the dogs loved the never-ending supply of rabbits to chase. When Paul announced he was taking up the role of Regimental Recruiting Officer and would be working out of Sir John Moore Barracks, Winchester, it was a dream come true. We made the most of our time together, almost living like a normal married couple. Gone were all the deployments, exercises and married quarters, hello country pubs and lazy afternoons with kids and dogs running riot in the fields next to our house. But, no sooner had we become comfortable with our Winchester lifestyle when Paul announced the battalion was to move to Weeton Barracks near Blackpool, with him as Quartermaster (Technical). Before we could get our head around the speed of change, Paul had deployed to Sierra Leone. Even when he returned, getting home was proving troublesome. The firemen went on strike, and he was now in charge of all Technical Equipment, which meant he was chasing fire engines all around the country.

No sooner had the firefighting finished and the battalion was sent to Iraq in September 2003 as part of Operation Telic 2. Fortunately, Paul had been selected for Staff College in Shrivenham, and would return after only two months in Basra. Paul was elated by the news of his selection for Staff College. Not only did it come with a promotion to Major, but it was an indication that the Army was considering him for promotion to Lieutenant Colonel. It would mean that before Paul could make himself available for consideration for such a cherished promotion, he would have to perform the duties of an Army Staff Officer at one of the many specialised Headquarters. Luckily for us all, Paul had secured a job at Worthy Down, Winchester.

It was his first real staff job. Professionally known as an Initial Grade Two appointment, he was responsible for the development of a new computer programme that would improve the efficiency of compassionate case management. The system was at its development stage and he would write the policy and procedures for informing families, or next of kin, in the event of an accident or death. Paul never enjoyed being stuck behind a desk, he wanted to be outdoors with the Riflemen. As dull as it was being chained to a desk, he was highly aware of the importance of his duty. The Army had been at war ever since the Twin Towers were attacked and casualties were increasing in Afghanistan and Iraq. The long days and late nights would eventually make such a difference to the families of the bereaved. If nothing else, we were both enjoying a rare spell of stability.

Jock and Debbie's son and daughter were now attending The Duke of York's Royal Military School (DYRMS) in Dover, Kent. It was boarding only, and Jake had started asking me if he could go there too. During the tour, Christopher also decided it would be a good place for him to study for his A-Levels. He already knew that he wanted to study engineering at university. For the next two years, we lived life for the weekends. I loved being back as pillion on Paul's new BMW K100, biking down to the school to watch the boys play hockey and rugby, or driving over with the dogs to break them out of the grounds to go camping was just wonderful. The quality time we spent together could not have been better. Despite the harmony and leisurely pace of his job, we knew it would have to come to an end if Paul wished to go further in his career.

In June 2006, the boys' school career at DYRMS culminated in 'Grand Day' and we joined Jock and Debbie to watch the parade and presentations. However, we didn't bring the boys home with us as they flew the following day to Johannesburg for a three-week hockey tour. The rest of the summer was spent relaxing and waiting for exam results. Thankfully, they were excellent. They secured both Christopher's place to start his Masters in Civil Engineering at Exeter, and Jake to take his A-Levels at Peter Symonds College, Winchester.

The Royal Green Jackets reduced from three battalions to two during *Options for Change*, and whilst 1RGJ had moved to Blackpool, 2RGJ had moved into Kiwi Barracks, Bulford. In October 2006, if Paul needed any further evidence that he was being lined up for greatness, he was assigned to 2RGJ as Company Commander, Fire Support Company. Of all the privileges to bestow upon a LE officer, to give him command of 90 Riflemen is the greatest. Paul would take charge of the most senior and experienced soldiers within the battalion. Like all Army units, the company was given a single letter to indicate its role on the battlefield. On this occasion, tradition had used the letter 'S' Company-Fire Support. Although its main role is to provide fire support to rifle companies during battles, it also provided intelligence, surveillance, target acquisition and reconnaissance (ISTAR) for the rest of the battle group. In turn, this placed Paul as the Commanding Officer's principal planning officer during operations. In simple terms, Paul was overjoyed to be given this command.

Chapter Six

Africa to Iraq
WO1 Garry McCarthy

For the first month Zimbabwe was exactly as it had been described, a busman's holiday with adventure and promise. First up, Best Man to my Coldstream Guards housemate, Roger Taylor, as he married his beautiful wife, Jane. Less than a week later, another beautiful Jayne arrived, in the form of my fiancé. For three weeks, we toured the country and met the real people of this beautiful land. From the splendour of Elephant Hills hotel to the historic Victoria Falls, Army life didn't get much better than this. The job came with a domestic helper who catered for my every need. My days of washing, ironing, and cooking were long behind me. My weekends were free to spend as I saw fit. There were trips into Harare and further afield, including Bulawayo. Yet, as spectacular as the travelling was, nothing compared to sitting on the porch, sipping a Mojito cocktail, and watching the sun disappear behind the mountains that surround my small house.

At the start of the second month, with little more to do than write lesson plans and check in with my platoon commander, I took my Nissan Patrol car up the mountains to Border Camp Nyanga. The gravel track wound its way through townships and farmland, through valleys and plantations. It was the most soothing commute known to man. As usual, I sang out loud to Don McLean's American Pie and waved to the locals like some eccentric land owner. But, no sooner had the euphoria of my brilliant job set in, the good times came to a crashing end. The unmistakable silhouette of an Antonov AN22 troop carrier, with contra-rotating propellors, eclipsed my vehicle. The iconic Soviet plane was so low, I could almost read the writing on the undercarriage which had been lowered for landing. The smell of aviation fuel accompanied the unorthodox rumble from the engines as the aircraft reversed its thrust in the process of landing. In my disbelief this huge clumsy troop carrier lolloped to a halt on a makeshift airfield running parallel to the track heading to camp. For the next four months, the British Mission spent every waking minute training some of the most vicious tribesmen ever to walk the planet. Among the 50 soldiers I was responsible for was a 24-year-old Major General! Fascinated by the fact he had ascended to such a high rank at an age when UK officers would have just entered Sandhurst, I asked him to explain how he had made the rank so quickly.

'I killed more people than anyone else' said Ishmael.

He regaled story after story of the battles he had led. Although not conventional state-on-state fights that the UK prepared for, his tales of gunfights, machete attacks and dawn raids were horrendous and fascinating in equal measure. Not that this impressed me. Even in his abridged version of events, it was easy to see he was a murderous, evil individual, desperately holding onto power in the new world order of a UN agreement. If nothing else, his account of the war had me recalibrating my personal understanding. Zimbabwe had given me a taste of life outside of Regimental Duty. It was exciting and full of variety, offering much more travel than one would expect whilst serving in a large formation. My desire to make the most of my time in the Army was greater than ever. The tour had flown by and I had played my part in the successful formation of a new defence force for Mozambique. Within a week of returning to my battalion, my bags were packed for the next trip. Sandhurst was one of the last places on Earth I would have ever expected to serve. As a Royal Green Jacket, it was my given heritage to question anything needless or unnecessary. Sandhurst was full of conformists, and drill Sergeants that hated being questioned.

Conversely, Sandhurst was a year-long apprenticeship for those young men and women aspiring to lead people like Paul and me. Before they could understand the formula for good leadership, they needed to learn how to follow. My understanding of needless bullshit changed, albeit with a light touch. I saw the need for autocracy and dogmatic instructions, as well as the mind-numbing attention to detail, applied to the most menial of tasks. But if you wished to ascend to the dizzy heights of Second Lieutenant in Her Majesty's Army, there was a period of porridge to serve, and Sandhurst was it. If I could avoid getting into trouble for wearing jeans on a night out and calling people by their first name whilst playing football, there was every chance I could make a difference at Sandhurst and shape some of our future commanders.

Paul and I continued to cross paths as we passed from one conflict to another until eventually, we ended up in the same company grouping for the first time since 1984. In 2002 we had come together in the Quartermaster's Department of 1 RGJ based in Weeton Barracks just outside of Blackpool. Paul had moved from Mechanical Transport Officer (MTO) to Captain in charge of Technical Logistics (Quartermaster Technical). For my sins, I was one of two Regimental Quartermaster Serjeants (RQMS). Long gone were the carefree days of soldiering, playing football and riding motorbikes for fun. We were both fixed by the tedium of defence as a business. Saving the taxpayers' money, remaining efficient and complying with regulations monopolised all our free time. Occasionally the Firemen would go on strike and we would team up to deliver Green Goddess fire engines and fire crews to man them. But despite the busy nature of our world, we both missed the fun of soldiering.

Sat in my office, preparing invoices for broken hosepipes, Paul stood at the threshold of my doorway.

'RQ. The Adjutant wants to see you. I think he has found a use for your language skills'.

Captain Iain Moody was a legendary officer. A non-graduate from Zimbabwe, he was built like Mount Ziwa itself. I had previously caused Iain a heap of administrative pain after I refused to accept a promotion to the rank of Warrant Officer Class 1. In his view, I had been childish and silly. In my opinion, I had desperately wanted to cling to the adventures of world travels and new armies. Understandably he had little time for my petulant behaviour, as he would have been busy enough without dealing with a stroppy Warrant Officer. As I knocked sharply on his office door, he looked up from his desk and rolled his eyes at me. His tone was sharp, and he got straight to the point.

'Mr McCarthy. There is good news, and not so good news. Firstly, you are promoted to Warrant Officer Class 1, despite your recent refusal to take up the post of RSM Lisburn Garrison. The downside is you have been trawled for a job in Iraq.'

The phrase trawled referred to the method of identifying skill sets held by different members of the armed forces. The manning people at the Army Personnel Centre in Glasgow would do a computer search for people with specific qualifications and this would produce a list of names. The unit in which those people resided would be told to surrender that person for a deployment or write a penalty statement explaining why the person could not be released. I had to go out to Iraq immediately. My good friend, Company Serjeant Major John Mabb, was already on his way back from Catterick to take over my job. All that was left for me to do was get my rifle, check it was zeroed correctly and then go pack. And with a nod of his head, the Adjutant dismissed me along with the words; 'they need you there by yesterday, so you need to get cracking'.

I had been made aware that the Army could only muster up fifteen military Arabic speakers to deploy to Iraq. Although irrelevant to my predicament, it was still very odd the British Army could not muster up more Arabists. It is not like the invasion of Iraq caught us by surprise. The year previously, the UK took part in a 30,000 strong jolly old fun time in Oman where there were over fifty Arabic speaking volunteers. But now there was a real threat of being gassed, shot at or blown up, the number was fourteen, plus me. I made a short quip to the Adjutant as I departed, and he called me back to say:

'Oh, no. It's not your Arabic you have been trawled for, it's your Chemical Weapons qualification!'

It was tough breaking the news to Jayne. Our second child, Lauren, had just come along, and our son, Ross, had just started school. In hindsight, leaving them in Blackpool witn no friends, no family and no support was neglectful of me. Like many other riflemen, I had placed service to the Crown ahead of loyalty to my family. The next 24 hours flew by and before I could draw my breath, I kissed Jayne and the children goodbye, before returning to my office where the transport to Brize Norton was waiting. Paul handed me my weapons and issued a few words of encouragement. As I departed for Iraq, the battalion deployed to Salisbury Plain on exercise.

The war in Iraq was launched on the premise that Saddam Hussein had been stockpiling chemical weapons and was ready to use them on the civilised world. He had a 'previous' in the use of these evil weapons. In 1988 the Iraqi dictator ordered the use of nerve gas on the Kurdish community of Halabja, killing more than 3000 people. There was no questioning that the dictator was capable of ordering the use of chemicals once more. The fear of a WW1 style chemical attack on coalition forces was very real. The fear in the civilian and military community was palpable. Everywhere you looked, people carried gas masks and chemical suits. With the expected delivery of the chemical coming from long-range missiles, no one within 1000 miles of Iraq felt safe.

My journey from Blackpool to Camp Commando in Kuwait took 48 hours. The staging post for the conflict was bursting at the seams with soldiers and civilian contractors all waiting for the order to invade Iraq. In the meantime, the Battle Group Commander tasked me with reminding and revising the Duke of Wellington's Regiment in the art of chemical warfare survival; a simple enough task which was a pleasant distraction from the rumours and conjecture that gripped our idle days. With some help from Martin Ness, the Regimental Sergeant Major of the Dukes, I delivered a full day of chemical warfighting training. The day was full of practising gas mask drills, walking through fake chemical gas, explosion simulations, and treating casualties. As dusk arrived, the complete Battle Group consisting of nearly 1000 men gathered on the makeshift parade square. It was time for me to summarise the importance of the training we had undertaken.

My opening words were 'we all recall what happened at Halabja'. At that precise moment, the unmistakable whoosh of a missile about to strike interrupted my address. The sight of the missile coming into land on the camp was terrifying in itself, but as the detonation ripped through a few buildings behind where we stood, the full magnitude of the realities of war sunk home. For a brief moment, people stared at me in disbelief. They assumed it was all part of the training day. It was a plausible deduction, but once people saw the state of panic into which I had descended, they went scurrying for hardened shelter fearing another missile would follow.

Along with the other 5,000 members of Camp Commando, I was now hiding in concrete bunkers as the chemical warning sirens wailed nonstop. The concrete bunkers were little more than long tubes of prefabricated reinforced concrete. With over 100 of us squashed in like sardines, we sat patiently wearing gas masks and chemical suits. Heavy breathing muffled by the mask was the only other sound I could hear until someone shouted from the end of the tunnel. 'Mr McCarthy! Mr McCarthy!' Louder and louder, my name was shouted as the message was passed down the long tube until it eventually arrived at where I sat.

I knew it was my place to go and conduct chemical tests on the warhead. With my heart racing at a million miles an hour, and my suit filling with sweat, it dawned on me that if I simply shouted 'Mr McCarthy' and passed the message on, no one would ever know it was me!

With a huge sigh of fear and trepidation, I raised my hand and shouted: coming, before scrambling across the sea of bodies. In truth, it was good to be out of the concrete tube. The messenger handed me my Chemical Agent Monitor (CAM) and pointed me in the direction of the missile impact area. The missile had separated and landed on the camp shop, but failed to detonate completely. The main section of the body sat torn and twisted fifty feet away, the pale blue paint compromised its origins, possibly a Silkworm or Seersuka. Flash burns on the tail section indicated a partial malfunction.

Dressed in a heavy chemical protection suit, wearing a gas mask (this was known as readiness state three, or 3 ROMEO for short), the wreckage was examined. In all my years of training for just such an event, never did I think I would be standing over a missile waving a CAM. Even if I had, it would be hard to replicate the surreal environment at that precise moment. Sirens still bellowed around the camp, and despite the deserted appearance, the noise of running vehicles and machinery compromised this perception. It was reasonable to assume I was on my own as the CAM went through its start-up procedures. The digital bar danced around on the screen as it adjusted to the sandy environment, frantically trying to calibrate. Then, just as it settled down, it crashed. The screen went blank and the light sucking sound it made whilst sampling the air, stopped. With every passing minute, my stress levels soared. Fearful of a second missile, terrified of making a false diagnosis, supremely conscious that the camp's American and British occupants were dependent on what I said next, I felt the world was closing in on me. With the CAM unresponsive, and time dragging on, I went to plan B, the blotting test. As archaic as it was, by using chemical detection paper to confirm the presence of a toxic agent, I would at least be able to inform the operations room of its presence, or absence.

Griping a section of twisted metal that was once part of the missile's main body, I dragged a fresh piece of three-colour chemical detection paper across the full length of the underside. The three-colour detection paper would identify any chemical weapon residue present on the metal. But just to make sure I swabbed as much of the missile as plausible,

I decided to flip over a large section of the body. A combination of the slippy rubber gloves, my nerves and the clumsy chemical detection kit I carried, made the chunk of metal too difficult to handle. One final go, and just as it reached equilibrium, the weight and strain were taken from me. Glancing to my right, four locally employed civilians had come to help me. Wearing nothing other than their traditional dress, they looked at me dressed in 3 Romeo, and thought me mad. They were frustrated by the length of time it was taking me, and these busy drivers needed to leave camp. A brief chat, and a quick look at their eyes for any sign of symptoms, and the ordeal was over.

Sitting in the chemical warning centre, the inquest had begun. I was fully expecting someone to question my performance. But instead, an elderly gentleman tapped me on the shoulder and questioned me about my conversation with the men that had come along to help. He had watched me deal with the locals and identified my ability to speak the language. A few hours later, no longer was my job to react to the missiles. My new employer was from the Intelligence Corps and from now on, I would be hunting them. It was more than a stroke of luck (so I thought). For the next four months, I found myself at the forefront of every miserable incident of the war.

Despite numerous false alarms, our hunt for Weapons of Mass Destruction proved fruitless. But the knowledge of the Iraqi forces I had amassed needed a place, and a chance encounter with a fellow Rifleman in Diamond 10 of Basra International Airport, the command centre for the British Forces, saw me assigned to help the Special Investigation Branch (SIB) of the Royal Military Police (RMP) investigate war crimes (under the overall command of Lieutenant Colonel Eddie Forster-Knight). For the first time in my life, the realities of war hit home. Daily, the SIB would invite me to translate a conversation between the Police and eyewitnesses. Repeating the most evil of acts carried out by man on his fellow man was emotionally breaking. The SIB were relentless in the pursuit of the truth. They had little regard for who was at fault, they just focussed on delivering tangible evidence: whether it be the death of Terry Lloyd, Baha Mousa, or the execution of two Royal Engineers, the SIB endlessly gathered and collated the details of the horrendous acts of inhumanity dished out in a lawless society. The daily analysis of such emotionally charged information would inevitably have an impact on those who handled it.

By June, the RMP commander recognised that my reservoir of emotional tolerance was close to empty. Taking me away from the daily interrogation and interviews, he set me the task of helping his lead officer to deliver a newly trained Police Force. Right up until June this had been one of the most productive periods of the conflict for the UK. Training twenty Police officers, two weeks at a time, and building new stations was proving successful. Working out of Abu Naji Camp, for two months I and two other members of the RMP toured Maysan Province, selecting and training members of the Interim Security Force. The concept was simple: we would travel to a location where the RMP had already established a relationship, and reinforce our commitment to the Iraqi people with quality training and investment in infrastructure and equipment. We started at the Stadium in Al-Amara and then moved to Al-Gharbi, and Qal'at Saleh before finishing with the small Police force at Al Majar Al Kabir.

By the time we had made it to Al Majar Al Kabir, we had established ourselves as a very productive team, winning high praise from those charged with reconstructing Iraq. Major Simon Miller, who had been placed in charge of the operation, visited frequently to keep us on track. He had been present on the first day of training at Al Majar and sanctioned the use of the section that looked after the Police station. Despite the less intense nature of the task, it had been a difficult few months and before Major Miller departed, we discussed my need for a break. I was absolutely exhausted. Fully submerged in the language, only dealing with the evil aspects of the conflict, he agreed that this was to be my last task with the RMP. As he departed, the Al Majar-Al Kabir section and my team dutifully set about giving the Iraqi policemen the best of our efforts.

On 22nd June, we had completed the training, and all returned to Abu Naji camp in preparation for our return to Basra. The UK forces were at the start of the Relief in Place (RIP) and consequently, there was a never-ending list of checks and double-checks to be done. But life must go on and on the eve of our departure, we celebrated our endeavours with the rest of the RMP company who were celebrating the birthday of a young Lance Corporal. Morale was high and rightly so as we settled down into our sleeping bags that evening. We bade farewell to all those who had helped us, knowing we would be up and out of the camp at 0300 hrs in order to travel south under cover of darkness. The journey would be painless but tiring, and the team was quick to disperse, to get some much-needed rest once we arrived back at Basra. In a well-rehearsed drill, I cleaned my weapons, threw my kit into a washing machine, and hit the sack, in the space of three hours.

It felt like a nanosecond before I was woken up by a fellow Warrant Officer. It wasn't a gentle nudge, more a hefty tap on my torso demanding I woke up.

'Gaz, it is your team. They're dead. All six of them. Colonel Eddie wants you now'. (It is common to drop the word Lieutenant whilst referring to Lieutenant Colonel as the third party).

It is not uncommon for a sleeping soldier to have nightmares. In fact, the more hostile the environment, the more frequent and intense the nightmares. I had plenty of interrupted hours fearing my worst fears had come true. Surely this was just another. My head hit the pillow and I went back to sleep in an instant. I had spent all my time thus far working with specialised groupings; mentally I was exhausted. Surviving by my wits, and living day to day, fearing death with every passing minute, there is no hiding from such emotion, even during sleep. They become so great, your mind is numbed by the pain. So great was my exposure to evil that I conditioned the nightmares into a form of numbness that offered me sleep.

'Gaz! Gaz! Now. The CO is snapping! He wants you now.'

The outburst angered me as I struggled to piece together what was occurring. It wasn't a dream. Lieutenant Colonel Eddie Foster-Knight, the Commanding Officer of the RMP, was inconsolable, apoplectic, and traumatised by the loss of six members of his Regiment. As I entered his office in downtown central Basra, he had a face like thunder.

'Mr McCarthy. I need you to get back to Al Amara. I want to know who did this. I want to get to the truth. The Adjutant will arrange your movement. The team trusts you. Get back there and help them locate these bastards.'

There was little more for Colonel Eddie to say. A few hours later, clothes still wet having been dragged out of the washing machine, I hitched a ride on an empty Chinook heading north.

Exploiting the contacts I had previously made, it was possible to discover the basics of who did what. Aware that my knowledge of the area was probably more current than anyone else in the Battle Group,

I offered my services to the Operations Officer 1 PARA. He immediately saw the benefits of having me inside his team for their first return into the town since the shootings. Furthermore, it made better sense that I translate for Colonel Tom Beckett, CO 1 PARA.

As we surveyed the Police station, I repeated the story of one of the Policemen who claimed to have witnessed the whole event unravel. Colonel Tom was a measured character, he listened more than he spoke. It was obvious that he was hurting, his demeanour oozed a desire for justice. But as a seasoned soldier, I knew this was not going to be that easy. G Squadron 22 Special Air Service was poised ready to strike, but the difficulty of conducting such a kinetic operation the day before you are due to leave the theatre of operations would be fraught and divisive.

Several times, we sat in launch positions waiting for the order to strike. The intelligence we gained from our meetings in the town was, at best, uncorroborated hearsay. Acting on such information could be disastrous. I had previously been conned by an intelligence source. He had deliberately set out to blacken the credibility of a business competitor by accusing him of bomb-making. At Al-Majar-Al Kabir, there was a desperate desire for retribution, the pressure to attack would have been unbearable. Even as the King's Own Scottish Borderers (KOSB) were arriving to replace 1 PARA, many were still demanding a full-on assault into the town. As the stories of what happened started to leak out, it was hard not to seek revenge.

Many of my friends in the Paras were furious that we didn't return to the town and hunt down those who killed Sergeant Hamilton-Jewell (HJ), and his RMP section, as well as those soldiers in 1 PARA injured during the ensuing gun battles. But, it was the right thing to do. What separates soldiers from insurgents is the legitimacy of their actions. It would have torn the Commanding Officer of 1 PARA apart to withhold the order to attack. It takes a high-quality officer to lead a battalion of The Parachute Regiment into a fight, but it takes a world-class leader to know when not to. The urge to unleash the most efficient killing machine on the planet would have been overwhelming. We would have all gladly gone back into the town in a hunt for the killers. But it would be hard to see how anyone could act without bias given the anger we felt towards the villagers. Despite the obvious pains, retribution would do little more than perpetuate the violence. Furthermore, the backlash would be suffered by the newly arrived unit who were yet to be fully operational. Not returning to Al Majar Al Kabir to hunt down those responsible is the most courageous decision I would ever witness during thirty-seven years of service.

By September my parent unit had caught up with me in Iraq. At short notice, they had been deployed to cover the elections and, for the briefest of moments, I was back in the fold. They had taken up residence in Shaibah Air Field but had companies deployed across the south of the country. Paul was head of logistics and busy setting up the base camps. Taking a five-minute break from the misery of accounting for stores and equipment, we shared a coffee as I downloaded my miseries on him. Dispassionately he listened to my complaints as I recalled one miserable event after another. Secretly I was seeking sympathy, or someone to acknowledge my hardships. But after thirty minutes of soul searching and theologising, he glanced up and said:

'You know what they say scouse. If you can't take a joke, you shouldn't have joined the Army.'

Squeezing out of the bench chair that was thrust up against the table we were sitting on, Paul explained he was heading back to the UK to prepare for a tour of Northern Ireland which would begin as soon as the battalion returned from Iraq. Although not over-enthused at returning to school (Staff College) for a year, he chatted about the opportunity to be closer to his wife and children. As he headed back to the UK, I collected more ammunition and morphine and headed back to Al Amara Stadium.

Attack after attack on Al Amara stadium had me at my wit's end. I had been attached to D Company, The 1st Battalion, The Light Infantry (1LI), and the stability established in Iraq after May was truly gone. Insurgents appeared at every corner fighting for their piece of influence in a country that was now lawless, and in meltdown. I had been at it since the turn of the year. Reality and fiction had merged, and it was hard for me to see when this was going to stop. My luck was surely about to run out. To date, I had gotten away with little more than a concussion, and a neat scar on the forehead. With every day that passed, the odds of survival diminished. Even after we caught the most wanted man in Iraq, the elation was dampened by the need to take him by road to Basra. It was, however, to be my final duty in Iraq. Having arrived at Shaiba Airfield, the Commanding Officer 1RGJ tracked me down to congratulate me on being selected for a Commission, to be promoted from WO1 to Captain. Two days later, it was back to Blighty in preparation for another tour of Northern Ireland.

Arriving at Crossmaglen a few months later as a Captain was a dream come true. Having spent much time as a soldier pounding the streets of Northern Ireland, it was much more leisurely returning now that the vast majority of the troubles had subsided, even though there was still a realistic threat from the terrorists. Many of the battalion staff had changed and Paul had departed to undertake a year's tuition at the Joint Command and Staff College. Whilst he was not looking forward to the course, he was more than ready for an extended period of stability at home. In truth, he picked a good time to be away. No sooner had we returned from Northern Ireland, then we were heading to Kosovo on an emergency tour.

A conflict that had died down since our last visit, but still demanded much effort, I had progressed from a junior Staff Officer to Battle Group Logistics Officer and a baptism of fire was my reward. My first real glimpse into planning battles and executing strategic plans, it was an education of the highest order. In total, the deployment lasted 29 days and fell short of the criteria to earn a NATO medal by two days. It was now April 2005 the show pressure of not seeing my family for months on end was beginning to tell. Just as I was thinking it could not get much worse, the Commanding Officer summoned me at short notice. Staring out of the window, back towards me, quietly he asked if I had heard the news: two Riflemen killed in a serious road collision.

Normally, when tragedy strikes, the chain of command cuts off all communication so it can manage the information and ensure those who 'need to know' hear it first. It was unusual for the Commanding Officer to be telling me. Given that I was not in the chain of command or part of the welfare system, I sensed there was something else coming.

'Gaz, I need you to be the Visiting Officer. You are the only member of the team who has the capacity and right background to take this task on without getting it wrong.'

Of the two Riflemen to die, I was assigned to the family of the youngest soldier. Barely eighteen, he arrived at the battalion less than a month ago. Typically, he was the son of a single mother who struggled all her life to ensure her child received the best she could afford. Living in a small bedsit in Sheffield, paid for by social services, it was crime-infested, drug-ridden suburbia at its worst. The young lady had worked miracles to keep her son on the straight and narrow. Having come from a similar background, I knew first-hand how huge her sacrifices would have been. Cruelly, days after seeing her son graduate from Harrogate Military College, I stood at her door helping her to manage the funeral arrangements of her only treasure.

From the day her son died until months after the inquest, my job was to guide Ms Steel through the military, and at times civilian, processes whilst providing direct support in the immediate aftermath of his passing. Arranging the funeral, visiting his body, collecting his ashes, deciphering probate, working out pensions, repatriation of personal belongings. For the first three weeks after his death, the visits were daily lasting up to six hours at a time. There would be endless crying, a state of permanent emotional turmoil, accusations, suspicions, contempt and disbelief. Twenty-four hours a day, seven days a week, the assistance never stopped. Ms Steel had nothing, nobody, just her son. Her father was in ill health, her sister estranged, this was the worst case possible. For the pair of us, this was emotionally painful, psychologically draining, and physically sapping.

The Army had taken away the only thing she had in her life and with it her future hopes and dreams. She had every right to be angry, bitter, animated and resentful towards me. Every day she could have looked at me knowing I represented the institution that deprived her of motherhood, yet she welcomed me into her home and leant on me heavily to help her through the mangled wreckage of her life. Despite living and breathing her grief every day for the first four weeks, there was a feeling of shame and embarrassment as each day presented new questions that I just could not answer. When I visited, for the first ten minutes or so, she would be fine. We would start discussing something and for the next five hours, she would curl up on the sofa and sob her heart out. It was heart-wrenching, and I felt like little more than a cheap fraudster wallowing in another person's most intimate moments. The funeral had induced a breakdown, but no sooner had she recovered, it was time to attend the inquest. I was very conscious that it was my presence that was providing stability in her life. She had absolutely no one to turn to but me. And all the time I knew that very soon, I would also be gone.

After six months of emotional stress, the CO had seen enough. He called me into his office and explained the battalion was returning to Iraq and to save me from self-destruction, I needed to take a break from the front line. He was posting me to my home town to concentrate on my personal life and prevent it from falling apart at the seams. It was an astute call. Being the Visiting Officer to the young mother had savaged my private life. Having dedicated six months to helping another family manage its grief meant my own family shared some of the pain. There were no regrets, committing oneself wholeheartedly was little more than I would have hoped for if my mother found herself in the same position. But the CO was right. It had taken its toll. Emotionally, I had expended everything, one more day and I would have imploded.

I went to work for Lieutenant Colonel Peter Balls who had been tasked with merging the Light Infantry, Royal Green Jackets, Devon & Dorset and the Royal Gloucestershire, Berkshire & Wiltshire (RGBW). In what would be the biggest regiment ever to be formed, The Rifles would go on to be the most successful merger of modern times. Peter had given me several duties: dress and accoutrement design, personnel and manning strategy, and finally, recruiting. He was a master of tasking the right men to the right job. As cunning as a fox, and twice as clever, he outwitted the whole of the Army as he learned from the mistakes of other Divisions of Infantry, as they stumbled through the biggest change in the Army since the end of World War Two.

In the days leading up to the official announcement, we had yet to agree on our Regimental cap badge. It had not been a major concern until a brigadier from one of the county regiments submitted a formal recommendation for consideration.

'Quick Gaz, get in here. Have a look at this and tell me what you think?'

'Bloody hell, Colonel. What is it? I mean, I can see it's some kind of Royal Coat of Arms, but why the pyramids, castles, lions and unicorns?'

'This is the only recommendation we have for The Rifles cap badge. This is serious, it looks like Harry Potter's school crest. We need to come up with something today before this eyesore gets into the public domain, and some halfwit takes a fancy to it. Do you think you can come up with something simple? Something that represents our 'light' heritage, and reflects a Rifle Regiment identity?'

Three hours later, I returned to Peter's office petrified that my offering was not going to please him. As accommodating as Peter was, he was a tough taskmaster. He would always welcome your assistance, and just when you thought it was up to scratch, he would demand you did it better.

'I like it Gaz. That's everything we need. How did you make it?'

'You said simple. So, I cut two badges in half, glued the bottom of the Light Infantry badge to the top of the Green Jacket badge, and sprayed it silver!'

In a masterstroke of genius, Peter circulated the image of just a bugle with a crown to the generals representing their respective Regiments, and a major disaster was avoided. We continued to draft policies and concepts for the launch of the Regiment which was due in early 2007. After delivering the dress policy to the Adjutant General, and Army Dress Committee, Peter handed the final publications to Paul for further refinement. As much as it hurt to watch a year's worth of hard work be given to someone else to finish, I knew this was on the horizon. Paul would finish the document to a standard I couldn't achieve and set the conditions for the launch later in the year. Officially, Paul was now a Staff Officer, and as we discussed the rationale behind some of the decisions I made, I remained nervous that he wouldn't approve of my efforts. I was desperately keen for Paul to understand the contribution of Tommy Dalman's 'Ammo & Co'. Tommy and his team had worked miracles producing props and samples that shaped the final look of all our dress accoutrements. And with little more than a nod of approval, Paul was content I had not left him too much work to do.

Paul was now Officer Commanding (OC) Fire Support Company, 2RGJ, based in Bulford. It was a phenomenal achievement for a LE officer. It was not unusual for an ageing LE officer to be given command of Headquarters Company, but the privilege of commanding a fighting company was reserved for only the most talented LEs. Consequently, he was busy preparing for another tour of Iraq as we discussed the forthcoming launch of The Rifles. Having been Regimental Serjeant Major of 1RGJ, it was entirely appropriate that he wrote the discipline and dress regulations for the new Regiment. He had recruited the help of Captain Rob Cutler, a fellow LE officer and former RSM of 2RGJ. Between the pair of them, they would finalise the documents and return them to RHQ for endorsement. We agreed one final meeting after the formation of The Rifles, and the visit of the Duchess of Cornwall on Tuesday 6th February 2007. We would discuss procurement and outstanding issues that Tommy Dalman was still working on. The meeting never took place as Paul found himself busy hunting the Rifleman who had decided to scrawl the word BOLLOCKS down the side of the Bulldog armoured fighting vehicle that the Duchess took a test drive in. Despite the Sun newspaper publishing the picture in full colour, the Duchess laughed it off. Overtly smitten by the affection the battalion had for their newly appointed Royal Colonel, she wrote a humorous letter to the CO acknowledging her affections for the witty Rifleman.

For the next few weeks, life became busy for both Paul and me. The wars in Iraq and Afghanistan were putting a severe strain on manpower, and it was my responsibility to source and recruit replacements. Meanwhile, Paul had become fixed by the pace of the preparations, and the Brigade training under the overall command of Brigadier James Bashall. Such a busy period prevented the meeting from taking place. Dutifully, I waved goodbye to Paul as he headed out of the camp to deploy to Iraq a few weeks later, confident he would email me any questions or outstanding problems once life had settled down in Basra.

Chapter Seven

Iraq (Again)
Mrs Paula Harding

It was a glorious, warm evening in late April when Paul and I drove the half-hour westward on the A303 to the home of 4 RIFLES, Kiwi Barracks, situated 2 miles north of Amesbury on the periphery of Salisbury Plain. The setting sun was almost blinding, and as we coasted past fields beginning to erupt into life, we chatted about how Jake had just turned 17, and how it was possible that we were now parents to two young men? I remember it was a Wednesday; I had hurried home from work to shower and change so that I could accompany Paul to the 'tour briefing for all ranks and dependents' given by the Battalion's Colonel, Patrick Sanders, that evening. We were only just three nights away from Paul deploying to Iraq. I was simply dreading his departure, but I would never have said so. I was had been an Army wife for 22 years, and knew what I had signed up for.

Originally Paul was not going to be deployed, as his company was to be divided and do exactly what its name said on the tin: support the other parts of the battalion. However, a few weeks previously, he had come home buzzing and had asked me to stop what I was doing and to come and sit with him in the lounge. He had made a coffee, as usual, asked how my day was, any news from Chris, and so forth, but he could hardly contain his glee when we settled into one of the sofas, as he explained how that afternoon he had been called into Lieutenant Colonel Patrick Sanders' office for a meeting. Patrick had proposed that Paul take on the role of Chief of Staff of Basra's Provincial Joint Control Centre (PJCC), a small and very isolated outpost co-located with the Iraqi Security Forces in the centre of Basra. The appointment would mean he would be responsible for security, resupply, liaison, and the overall daily running of the organisation.

He looked me in the eye and asked:

"What do you think? Are you OK with that?"

IRAQ (AGAIN)

I wanted to scream and yell an emphatic 'No, no, no, no!' We had done our 'bit', he had done his duty to Queen and Country, we had survived countless separations, countless missed opportunities. I had done my time as an unaccompanied wife, and after 31 years of service why did he want to go to a war zone? But I looked at him and remembered I had never said my marriage vows with a caveat and time restriction, and so I just said:

'If that's what you want to do, you must go, you must go and do what you feel you have to do.'

We sat in silence for ten minutes or so. He never patronised me with a nudge and one of those insincere statements like, *'are you sure?'* Or a disingenuous *really?* Instead, he leaned over, kissed my cheek and said;

'Thank you, thank you so much.'

We then began to discuss his task in more detail. Paul explained he would not be out on patrol, but that he would be within the building of the PJCC, and carrying a personal weapon. He assured me that if he felt in danger at any point he would use it; in these circumstances it would be best to ask for forgiveness retrospectively, rather than permission.

And so, we were driving through the gates of the barracks, parking up and readying ourselves, for yet another pre-tour briefing. However, upon entering the NAAFI I stopped and did a double take. I had never seen so many Riflemen, their young wives and families, ensconced into the dated and tired building.

Colonel Patrick gave a clear and concise talk that evening. The room had fallen silent when he stood up to speak, and only the cry of a new baby needing a feed had broken the trance-like atmosphere. Paul and I held back a while, as Patrick and the Unit Families Officer (UFO) fielded questions from concerned wives about clubs and activities to keep their children busy whilst the men were away. Once he was free Patrick approached Paul, and we chatted with him for a while. I could sense his concern for not only his men, but the families they were about to leave alone for the next 6 months. Paul and I then slipped away to a quiet corner with our drinks, and we settled down to mull over the briefing. I had just one burning question, and I could not resist asking it:

'Patrick said 'when' we have casualties, not 'if' we have casualties. Is it really going to be that bad?'

He leaned forward and kissed my cheek, but said nothing at first. Taking both my hands in his strong grip he looked me in the eyes for several moments. I could see he was gathering himself.

'We will have casualties, and I am praying we do not lose anyone, but it is going to be the toughest tour yet as we pull out of Basra. I will have my personal weapon on me at all times, and I am in the safety of the Control Centre.'

I didn't push him any further, there was no point. I would just have to pray as well, and hope for the safe return of the man I adored, and his men.

That Friday Paul, Jake and I went out to our favourite Gurkha restaurant in Winchester for a pre-deployment supper. Earlier we had taken photos of Paul and Jake and the dogs in the garden, and I promised to get them developed and send them on to him. Paul ran through with Jake how to start up and maintain his BMW K100 during his deployment. After returning from the pre-deployment supper Paul and Jake said their goodbyes. I'd watched this scene over and over for 16 years, I felt a lump in my throat, and my eyes stung as I watched Paul wrap his arms around our boy, now the same height as his father, and say:

'I'm proud of you Jake, stay strong and we'll be out on our bikes in no time at all.'

The following morning Paul and I were awake early. Skipping breakfast, we were quickly on our way to Bulford as Paul planned to eat with his Riflemen in the cookhouse before boarding the transport. I drove, and this time the sun was chasing our backs along the A303. We didn't talk, Paul seemed to be in deep concentration and the lump in my throat prevented my vocal cords from uttering a single word. Silently we slipped into the camp, the Riflemen on guard duty didn't need to check Paul's I.D. I don't imagine a single soldier in the battalion didn't know his face. I followed the one-way system and parked up on the far side of the parade square. We just sat, in silence, for a few minutes doing nothing other than just holding hands. Eventually, Paul got out. He was in full desert combats and, after retrieving his bergen from the boot, he leant over the passenger seat and hugged me saying:

'Six months. This will be the last one'.

I begged him to be careful. He, of course, assured me that he would, and then he turned and walked away. I sat and watched his back retreating further away from me across the square and as he reached a door in the red brick building on the other side, he turned, gave me that huge grin of his, and disappeared inside. I sobbed all the way home but pulled over when I reached the outskirts of the village to compose myself. Jake would be waking up by now, and I needed to be his Mum. I went straight to the kitchen to make some breakfast for him, a sausage sandwich would cheer him up. As I went to get the orange juice from the fridge I noticed two new yellow 'post-it notes' stuck on the door. In Paul's neat and distinctive handwriting were the contact details of the Officer Commanding the rear party on one, and Paul's Scottish Widows life insurance policy number on the other. I stood rooted to the floor. Never, ever before had Paul mentioned his life insurance, taken out when Chris was born. The paperwork had sat in his metal filing case, out of our thoughts.

Later that day, I checked my emails and found one from Paul in my inbox. He had sent it to me just after I had dropped him off at the barracks. He implored me not to let his absence spoil my time with the boys, and if anything should happen to him, I was to pick myself up and not let his loss stop me living the life I should have. It was heart-wrenching and I just couldn't bear the thought of him not coming back to us, but again this was a first. Paul never left me notes, letters or an email like this. Telling myself he was just being sentimental and cautious, I printed his email off, cut it down to size, folded and tucked it into the back of my purse. Time to get on with this. My job was to stay buoyant, write lots of bluey's ensure our boys had all they needed to thrive, and look forward to Christmas with us all together again.

Jake and I quickly settled into a routine; I was working at Peter Symonds College where Jake was studying his A-levels. Paul had also played a part in college life. The previous year he had led the Duke of Edinburgh Gold group training expeditions in Snowdonia, guiding and mentoring the students, leading them up Glyder Fach to the cantilever rock. They had given him thank you letters and a framed photo of them all on the 'balancing' rock; clearly, he had left an impression on them. He had also given a lecture to the A-Level General Studies students, entitled "Can war ever be justified?'. I had sat at the back of the lecture theatre in awe as he talked about Kosovo, and the children his Riflemen had rescued. He had never talked about any of this at home, and I felt rather humbled. I saw another side to my husband as he drew the questions out of his audience, encouraging them to debate and think critically about the subject.

Christopher was coming to the end of his first year at Exeter, and I was looking forward to him coming home later in June. Most days Jake and I travelled to and from college together. He was coming up to his first-year exams and had started looking at potential degrees and universities. Earlier in the year he had gone to Belize for three weeks with his biology class and had developed a keen interest in wildlife and photography. One of the places he was keen to explore was Falmouth University. He had already earned a diving qualification with the Professional Association of Diving Instructors (PADI) and previously Paul had taken him to a training centre in Havant. This fuelled Jake's interest in Falmouth's Marine and Natural History Photography Degree. On my 41st Birthday, I woke Jake up and made our breakfast as normal. I had an empty feeling in my heart, wishing that Paul was home, but as we reached the exit of our village I spotted an enormous poster of my face with a banner attached, it read 'Happy Birthday wombat.' I turned to look at Jake in the passenger seat and saw Paul's grin beaming back at me.

The May half-term was an ideal opportunity to investigate Falmouth, so Jake and I drove down to Dartmoor, to stay with my sister and brother-in-law. Driving down to Cornwall for the day we attended the university's open day. Returning to my sister's, Jake and I were full of enthusiasm. I knew we had found the perfect place for Jake to take his studies on to higher education. I should have felt relieved, if not excited, that Jake would be so close to my sister and brother-in-law, but I couldn't shake off a sense of foreboding. It had been over a week since Paul had called. Ordinarily, he would ring every 3-4 days, and I was becoming increasingly concerned. The following evening we had just eaten supper and were loading the dishwasher when the house phone rang. My brother-in-law answered it, and reaching out he handed the receiver to me, and I was quickly left alone.

Paul sounded dreadful, utterly exhausted. I asked why he hadn't been able to call and without hesitation, he explained that the PJCC had had some 'visitors'. I was taken aback. I hadn't imagined the PJCC being a venue for dignitaries, I supposed the visitors must have been high ranking officers, or similar. I continued with my description of our visit to Falmouth, and we talked about Jake's grades for his UCAS application. Realising that he was struggling to keep his eyes open, I brought our conversation to an end and expressly begged Paul to go to his bunk and sleep. He didn't resist.

Life continued over the next 3 weeks as usual. The days were long, and our dogs, Monty and Bella, were enjoying long walks every evening. It was exam season in the educational world, so Jake was busy taking them, and I was busy helping my students revise, and stay focused. Chris would be finishing his Freshers year by the end of the month, and we had the Summer to look forward to. Seven weeks to chill, we had been looking at holidays, and I had begun to make plans to meet with some old friends.

The evening of 19th June 2007 was a Tuesday, it was bright and balmy – I met up with Jake after college ended, and we drove home together. The dogs were excited to see us, as ever, and that afternoon I took them straight out for a walk. As we walked up the back lane behind our house I bumped into Ken Gray, Paul's old boss. Ken was out for a run, but he paused and we exchanged a bit of news; Ken was, of course, keen to hear how Paul was doing. Jake and I had a spot of supper together, and then he went up to get some college work done and hang out with friends through the world of X-Box. I had just about given up hope that I would hear from Paul that night; it was around 10.30 pm and I'd decided to go up to bed when the telephone rang, and to my relief it was Paul. I lived for these calls, hearing his voice and telling him our news was simply the highlight of any day, or week even. I had written a 'bluey' to Paul every day and received some in return from him. I treasured these flimsy aerogrammes, to hold the same piece of paper that he had touched, and run my fingers over the page feeling the indentation his pen had made like some kind of secret love braille. I could read his writing over and over, but nothing beat hearing his voice. It was around 12.30 am, Iraqi time, and he sounded tired. We had been chatting for around 5 minutes, and I had just retold the conversation Christopher and I had had when he had called home the day before. He had told me that he had been dating a girl for around a month, she was a fellow student in the same year at Exeter. That night they were attending their Summer Ball, DJ and ballgown, just like a

Mess function, celebrating the end of their first year. Paul was chuffed with the news and said:

'Well done Chris!'

But when I replied there was silence, the line was dead. This did not feel good, I had gone from elation whilst chatting to him, to utter disappointment that our call had been cut off. The darkness of disappointment descended over me, this bloody conflict, I thought. All I wanted was a proper conversation with my husband. One where he wasn't exhausted, one where we could really talk, it was so unfair! Totally fed up, I poured myself a very large glass of wine, sat on the sofa by the phone and waited, and waited, but he didn't call back. At midnight I called it a night. I drained the last drop of wine and went to bed, ensuring my mobile was on charge, and the volume at its loudest, just in case Paul did call me back. Thankfully, the wine had a soporific effect and I did not lie awake worrying, or wondering what had happened, instead I fell straight into a deep sleep.

It felt like seconds later that I was woken by Monty and Bella barking, they were going crazy in the kitchen, at the front of the house, beneath our bedroom. I looked at the time on my mobile and my eyes focused slowly on the bright glow of 02:00 hrs. What on Earth could they be barking at? Our house was tucked away in the corner of the village, a no through road, without street lights. I opened my bedroom window and peered out into the dark over the sloping kitchen roof, to see what was in the street to make the dogs so agitated. They were used to foxes so I couldn't think why they were so perturbed, then I saw the outline of the large black saloon car and heard a voice say.

'Paula it's me, Pete.'

'No, no, no, no, no, please God, please God no!'

Throwing on a dressing gown I fumbled with the cord then I raced down the stairs and across the hall, flung open the inner hall glass door, then stood at the front door with my hand on the doorknob. In a split second my mind processed; what is Pete here to tell me? Whatever it is for Pete to be standing on my front doorstep at two in the morning it is going to be catastrophic, and like Pandora's box, once I open this door there will be no returning to the status quo of our lives. And then I was turning the handle and pulling the weight, I begged Pete:

'No. No please, no!'

He stepped inside, followed by another chap who seemed vaguely familiar:

'Pete, please no!'

Pete Bullard was the Officer Commanding Rear Operations 4 RIFLES, it was his name and number Paul had left on a yellow post-it note on our fridge freezer with the instruction that I should call him if there were any issues. There was only one reason why he would be standing inside my house at 2 am. Pete gently explained that there had been a sustained insurgent attack on the PJCC, and it was confirmed that Paul had not survived.

'No, no, no, please, could he be just injured! I don't care how bad, but not dead, please!'

Begging Pete, my knees buckled and I started to sink to the ground, then I heard Jake's voice from behind on the stairs.

'Mum?'

All I could say to my darling boy was:

'I'm so, so, sorry.'

Denial, shock, all those feelings you hear people talk about were coursing through my very being. Pete sat Jake and I down, together on one of the sofas and introduced Dean Murch to me. Dean was a fellow LE officer who had joined 4 RIFLES from what was once known as the Devon & Dorset Regiment. As is tradition for new LE officers, he was appointed as the Unit Welfare Officer. Having acted several times as welfare support for wives, widows and grieving families, I understood the reason for Dean's presence.

Pete explained that there had been an attack on a resupply convoy as it reached the PJCC, around 12.30 local time. Paul had left the control room and run towards the front gates as his men were under sniper fire. He had taken up position in the very front watchtower (sangar). There was a direct hit on this sangar by a mortar, and Paul had been killed instantly.

I asked Pete if they were absolutely sure it was Paul, and both Dean and he nodded, and said that there was no doubt. I could literally feel my heart tearing into pieces inside my chest. The emotional pain was excruciating and real. Somewhere in my head I thought 'so this is what a broken heart feels like'. All I could do was hold Jake's hand and say 'I'm so sorry', over and over and over.

Pete then explained that the press would be asked to give us 24 hours before revealing the news, to allow time for NOK to be informed. Paul had listed me, my mother, and his parents as NOK, and they had to be told first before anyone else could be notified. I explained that Christopher was in Exeter at university, and I must tell him before he heard it from anyone else. I also explained to him that my mother was being looked after by my niece in Devon, as my sister and her husband were on holiday in Greece. She was 82 years old and please could we leave telling her until the morning? Pete explained that Paul's parents would be receiving a call from two officers local to their home in Surrey any moment now. God, I thought, this cannot be happening, my Mum, Paul's Mum and Dad, how will they survive his loss?

Pete requested a photo of Paul for the press release. It was better to give them one, rather than unscrupulous reporters searching the internet to find one themselves. This wasn't making sense to me. I was trying not to panic, I wanted to go to the front door and run, run away and somehow go back to yesterday, and for this not to be happening. Pete again asked, and so I opened the lid of an old writing bureau where I had a few photos waiting to be framed, and picked up one of Paul, standing outside the Officers Mess in Kiwi Barracks. As I handed it to Pete, I had no idea that 24 hours later that image of Paul would be rolling around the printers of Fleet Street's tabloids with the story of how Paul gave his life in an attempt to protect his men.

I then reiterated to Pete that I must get to Exeter, and get Christopher home. Pete made some phone calls, whilst Jake and I just sat together. My 6'2", 17-year-old, darling boy, and all I could say again was 'I'm so sorry'.

I settled the confused dogs into their beds and Pete gently hurried us out of the house. Then we were locking the front door and climbing into the back of the black sedan. The plan was to drive back to Bulford Camp where Jake and I would switch to another welfare vehicle, and a driver would take us to Exeter University, 116 miles away. It was now 3 am and as we cruised westward, down the A303, the sun was just starting to appear behind us. I could still not believe this was real, how can the Earth still be turning, the words 'Paul's dead' repeated over and over in my head. My mind was silently screaming inside my skull: Paul was meant to be safe inside the Control Centre, not in a dangerous place such as a sangar; those days were over for him, he was a LE major, he cannot be dead, he was too strong, this cannot be happening.

We slipped off the A303 at the brand new Solstice Park. I remember looking at a giant dragonfly artwork, and Jake holding me tight to him. And then we were outside the Welfare Office in the Camp. We were transferred to another car with a driver, who looked pale with incredibly sad eyes. He opened the back door, and we slipped inside and buckled up. He then handed me a box of tissues, taking them, I thought 'how does he know we need these?' Then he was behind the wheel and we were back on the A303. Stonehenge slid by, rolling golden fields and miles of bright yellow rapeseed blurred through my tears and the speed we were travelling at. The driver was following his sat-nav as Jake and I sat staring out of the windows and the outskirts of Exeter grew larger on the horizon. Incredibly it was only 4.30 am, even with the changing of vehicles, we were arriving way too quickly. I took out my mobile and texted Christopher asking where he was. He did not reply, and 10 minutes later we turned into the grounds of the university and pulled up outside his accommodation. It was locked and in darkness. Then my phone bleeped, it was Christopher....

'Why?'

'Jake and I are outside your halls, please come back.'

My heart was lurching. Jake and I held each other tight, and then we saw Christopher running towards us, with all the aggression he would normally force into a rugby tackle, over the manicured lawns and across the neatly arranged flower borders. Full-on he headed towards us, in his dinner jacket, white shirt undone, black bow tie loosened and flapping around his neck. I knew that he knew. I knew his world was about to irrevocably change, forever. Christopher's eyes were wide and his look was wild, as he jumped the garden wall and crushed us both to him I blurted out:

'It's Dad, he's been killed.'

We crumpled into a pile of sobs and then, after several minutes, we fell silent as Christopher pulled away and turned to our lovely driver. Christopher held out his right hand and shook our driver's hand firmly, and uttered the words that I will never forget:

'Thank you for bringing them to me. Can we have a few minutes to ourselves?'

The driver agreed, he needed to refuel the car. He left us alone.

Christopher guided Jake and me up the two flights of linoleum clad Tudor stairs to his loft room, and there the three of us laid down on his bed, just holding each other, and silently dying inside. Eventually, we began to catch our breath and my boys simultaneously asked if it was confirmed, that there was no doubt? I had no choice but to say that we had to trust the battalion. I got up and started to throw stuff into a bag for Chris. He and Jake sat on the bed, arms wrapped around each other's shoulders, staring out of the bedroom window as the sun insisted on forcing my sons into the first day of their lives without their father. It was excruciating. We readied ourselves to face the next stage of this nightmare. Christopher locked his door, and we retraced our steps down to the gardens where our driver and car were waiting. Christopher climbed into the front passenger seat and Jake and I reclaimed our seats in the rear. A new box of tissues sat between us, pristine and untouched.

We were now three, Christopher reached back through the front seats and held Jake's and my hands the whole of the journey home. The words 'Paul's dead' were on a loop around my brain the full 90 minutes, whilst each of us uttered 'I'm so sorry' to the other two every few seconds.

As we turned into our quiet, rural no through road, I immediately noticed the large black car parked in front of our house. It was around 7 am, the road was coming to life, and my neighbours were starting to rise for a brand-new summer's day. Christopher climbed out of the front as the driver opened my door, I looked at my eldest son, just 19, and the pain squeezed my heart tight. Christopher looked dreadful, his eyes were bloodshot and I remembered he would not have had any sleep as he had been at his Summer Ball. Christopher opened Jake's door and they walked around the car together and shook our driver's hand. Pete was already waiting at our front door, and he took my key and led us inside.

The boys went into the kitchen to make coffee. Pete sat me down in the lounge and explained the Army had to ensure that all the named next of kin in Paul's records were told of his death before any of our other friends and family could be called. I could not bear the thought of a stranger knocking at my sister's home in Devon to tell my mother and niece the news. I expressed that I needed to call my niece and explain what had happened in my own words, she would then break the news to her Grandma. Pete made a call and then returned and agreed that I could

IRAQ (AGAIN)

make the call. My heart broke all over again at the thought of my darling niece and Mum going through this pain, but there was no other way to move forward, the Army protocol had to be adhered to. I made the call.

Once I had gathered myself, Pete explained that two officers had been sitting outside Paul's parents' home since 2 am, but it had become clear that nobody was home, their house was empty and locked up. I had no idea where they could be, and could only think that Paul's sister, Jo, might know as she lived near them. I suggested I give her a call; the problem was that she wasn't on the list of Paul's next of kin. Pete's mobile buzzed and he stepped out to answer the call; upon his return, he agreed that I could call her. But her house phone rang out, and I presumed she must have left for work, so I tried her mobile, again she did not pick up. I asked Pete to call the College and to leave a message that Jake would not be in lessons and that I would not be in work.

Pete explained that I needed to be allocated a Casualty Visitor Officer (CVO), who would help my bereaved family navigate the minefield ahead. The Army could provide us with someone immediately from Worthy Down, or if I was prepared to wait, someone was willing to take on the role from The Rifles, 'one of our own.' I asked:

'Who would be one of our own?' Pete replied:

'Gaz McCarthy, but he is in Liverpool for a conference. He won't get here for a few hours,'

Without a heartbeat of hesitation, I replied:

'We will wait for Gaz'.

I called Jo, again and again, every 20 minutes for hours, and left message after message begging her to call me back. By lunchtime, I was becoming desperate to call someone to come and be with the boys. But both my sisters and their husbands were abroad, one living in Spain, the other on holiday in Greece, and I couldn't get hold of Paul's sister. I needed back up, I was crumbling away inside, my chest hurt so much that even breathing was painful.

Then my phone rang, it was Jo. She was panicking, as one would imagine she would be after I had left so many desperate messages. All I could blurt out was 'we've lost him' as I burst into sobs of despair. Jo couldn't comprehend what I was saying, I had to take several long, deep breaths and repeated 'we've lost him' then 'Paul! We've lost Paul'. Pete took the phone from me, he was so gentle with her, asking where she was, and who was she with? Jo was on holiday in Portugal with her partner, they had just returned to their hotel room, switched on her mobile and picked up my numerous and frantic messages. Pete explained that her parents were not at home and that the Army needed to find them before the media broke the news. All Jo knew was that her Mum and Dad were on holiday in Sri Lanka. She did not know where they were staying, but at least we had a country.

This turn of events knocked me sideways. They had gone to Sri Lanka and not told me? This didn't make sense.

'What next?' I wondered. The boys and I just sat on one of the sofas in our lounge and the words 'Paul's dead' were on a loop inside my head. I just couldn't stop the repetition. Every so often I reiterated to Pete that I needed to call someone for the boys. It wasn't their fault their grandparents had gone on holiday without leaving contact details.

For the next hour, Pete seemed to be constantly checking on us between taking calls. Then he got the call informing him that the British High Commission, Sri Lanka, had found a record of my parents-in-law entering the country and were confident that they could trace them at the hotel they had entered on their landing cards.

Chris, Jake and I continued to huddle together on one of the sofas in the lounge, taking turns to apologise to each other for the grief and loss we were each going through. Then around 4 pm, Pete hung up on his latest call and sat down on the other sofa. He said the decision had been made that I could, at last, contact someone, not on the next of kin list. However, we would need to wait until tomorrow before contacting anyone else to ensure Paul's parents had their 24 hour period of grace.

I ran through the geography in my head again, Jill in Durham, Alison and Jimmy in Hertfordshire – both Jill and Alison had young boys. Jock and Debbie were in Wiltshire, 30 minutes drive away, and their teenage children were at boarding school. I knew for sure that Debbie would be in her office. I looked at Pete and said 'Jock will be devastated' as I made the call.

Debbie picked up immediately, I had never before called her at work so she instantly knew something was wrong. I had no other words in my head other than:

'We've lost him'

Debbie replied:

'What do you mean lost?'

I just said:

'Paul'

I asked her where Jock was, and she explained he was leading the Army Compulsory Drugs Testing team, several hours drive away. I then asked:

'Can you make the call to Jock, and then come here?'

I ended the call because I knew she would be on her way. An hour later the doorbell chimed. Pete answered it and I heard him explain the situation with Paul's parents to Debbie, and that no one else can be told. She calmly walked into the room, knelt down and wrapped her arms around the three of us. The boys in unison asked if Jock was on his way, and she said he was, but it would take him 3-4 hours as he was driving back from Catterick. It was now 5 pm, 18 hours ago I was talking to my husband on the phone and now I would never hear his voice again. The words 'Paul's dead' continued to roll around inside my disbelieving mind.

Pete had stepped back into the garden to take a call when the doorbell rang again. Christopher was making some coffee, and from where I was sitting on the sofa I could see him crossing the hallway, and so I followed him. Then he was opening the door and Gaz was shaking his hand, and almost pulling him into our home. I hugged Gaz and thanked him for coming, and habitually asked him how he was, as a voice answered inside my head, 'what a stupid question, Paul's dead!'. He followed me into the lounge and Jake stood up and shook his hand. He spoke to Debbie, she explained Jock was due around 8 pm. We sat down and waited for Pete to finish his call. I was staring at Gaz, I couldn't work out what was wrong with him. I nearly asked if he had hay fever, but as he wiped his eye with a handkerchief, I realised his eyes were swollen and bloodshot, like ours, from crying.

When Pete finished his call, Gaz joined him in the garden. They embraced and I was moved by how these two hardened soldiers I had known for over two decades were clearly in pieces, but holding it together for us. Then I could hear quiet voices as Pete brought Gaz up to speed, how they were waiting to hear that Paul's parents had been found, and that I had to wait until tomorrow before telling anyone else.

But, I had to tell my best friend from school. Maria, my best friend of 35 years, had been my bridesmaid, was Godmother to Jake, and I just had to tell her what had happened. She and her husband lived in Sussex, and although I knew that she couldn't do anything, it seemed ludicrous that Paul had been killed and Maria didn't know. We had shared everything in our lives, and I needed her to know, like I needed air to live. Debbie was now sitting on one of the sofas between the boys, holding their hands tightly. I slipped away upstairs and using my mobile I called Maria. After a few rings, her husband answered and I told him what had happened, and how no one else must know. He was devastated. He explained Maria was driving home after an appointment, and he would wait to tell her when she was safely home and with him.

I returned to the lounge to find that Pete had left, and Gaz was now talking with the boys. Christopher was earnestly asking him questions, when the doorbell rang again. I looked at the hall clock, it was just past 7pm, surely too early for Jock? But Christopher rushed past me and opened the door, and in swept Jock, ashen white and red-eyed he grabbed Christopher hard. Letting go of Debbie's hand Jake jumped up and ran to him, both the boys clung to him, breaking their hearts.

Jock brought them back to the sofa and, holding them close to him, sat them back down. Debbie eased me over to the other sofa, and we all sat in silence, not needing to say anything, just feeling the pain in the atmosphere around us.

Gaz was in the garden talking on his mobile when the house phone rang, and Jock suspiciously answered. I could hear Maria's voice coming down the line in sobs, asking to speak to me. Jock reluctantly handed me the receiver, and I poured my heart out to her, telling her about the knock at 2 am, the drive to Exeter to pick up Christopher, and how Paul's parents had gone to Sri Lanka without telling me. She wanted to drive to me straight away but I assured her that we were being looked after, explaining Gaz, Jock and Debbie were here. I reiterated that she must not tell anyone else yet. We sat and cried together, and she kept saying;

'I'm so sorry.'

By 9 pm there was nothing more Gaz could do, and we hoped that overnight the British High Commission would trace and tell John and Hazel. Debbie was going to stay the night so Gaz headed home assuring me he would be back first thing. Jock took the dogs out for a walk, and then he too headed back to their house as they also had dogs and cats that needed caring for. The boys went to Jake's room and climbed into his double bed. And I reluctantly followed them to what had been our bed, but was now my bed. I lay there, my grief all-consuming, my heart in agony. Begging Paul to come back, begging God to perform a miracle, bargaining and pleading with him between sobs, knowing deep down it was futile.

Chapter Eight

Notification
Captain Garry McCarthy

Sheffield was never dry. During my many visits to see Ms Steel, the sun never once made an appearance. Although it had been three years since the death of her son, it still felt like yesterday. The phone calls and texts asking for support and help had slowed, but if ever work took me to the North of England, out of respect, I would call to ensure all the bereavement agencies were still providing enduring support. Ms Steel kept a keen eye on The Rifles, mainly because this is where her son would be if he was alive today. Sat in her bedsit drinking lukewarm tea, the pain of her loss was ever-present. Words fell from her lips with little conviction. It was a brave face she presented, but the rawness of her loss was overpowering. In every corner, on every wall, in every room, there were reminders of her son. His graduation picture, front and centre standing proudly in her living room. Drawings from his school days still adorned the fridge, sports certificates pinned to a notice board and dust-covered trophies neatly lined up on windowsills. We would start to discuss her recent return to work, but mid-sentence, she would lose track and drift away into incoherence. Always deprived of sleep, watching her demise was heart-breaking.

There was no way for me to help. As every conversation innocently drifted towards what her son would be doing now if he was alive, I felt more and more inadequate. In the background, BBC News ran a story about the increasing number of casualties in Iraq. When she heard this kind of news, she could not hold back the thoughts that her son was due to be in Iraq with 2RGJ. Another round of tears and heavy sobbing and yet more tea. It was hard to know if my visit was helping or hindering. I felt pain like I never experienced before during the many visits, but there were no words to describe the enormity of her grief. On my long drive north to Catterick later that day, the importance of keeping the

NOTIFICATION

Regiment fully manned seemed meaningless. It was hard not to share some of the blame for the death of every young Rifleman that died in Iraq, by virtue of my appointment, for the previous year and a half. It was I who was responsible for recruiting them.

Arriving at Catterick late that evening I was greeted by Colour Serjeant Lee Nichols. He had been my deputy for a few months. A highly intelligent man, he knew when my day had not gone well. Intuitively, he would clear the diary and run the recruiting efforts single-handed, and give me space to recover. His contribution would never be recognised, despite the valedictory reports often submitted about his performance. His loyalty and commitment went unnoticed. Dutifully he recapped the events of 'day one' of our recruiting drive in the North East. He concluded by explaining it would help if I was able to attend the quarterly recruiting conference in Liverpool the following morning. It would mean an early start and another long car journey, but it was critical to protect our interests in Merseyside. The only consolation was the opportunity to swing by my sister's house, and check on my family. Thankful for small mercies, and the opportunity of an early night, Lee was left in charge until my return late the following evening.

0400 hrs is a good time to travel the country. It made sense to beat the traffic and sit it out in a city centre café ahead of the meeting. Liverpool was just receiving the commuter traffic as I turned into Dale Street looking for a parking space. Stuck at the lights outside the RBS bank on Dale Street, my phone burst into life and Colonel Peter's name flashed on the LED screen.

'Hi Gaz, how are you?'

'Good thanks, Colonel. I am just searching for a parking space ahead of the recruiting conference in Liverpool.'

'Are you stationary ?'

'I am at the lights, on my hands-free?'

'Can you pull over please, I need a chat. Call me back when you are ready.'

Recruiting is a tricky business at the best of times. The pressure of finding suitable candidates provokes a stressful environment. Numbers, statistics, data, trends, and more work! The demand to fill our allocation of recruits always dominated our conversations. If he was calling me at

0830 hrs, he was unhappy with something. It didn't take me more than 30 seconds to park up and call him back.

'Thanks, Gaz. Are you parked?'

'Yes. Absolutely. Free to chat for the next thirty minutes. The conference starts at 0900 hrs. I think I am all set to tackle the accusations of poaching recruits if that's what you are calling about?'

'Paul Harding has been Killed in Action.'

It was like being hit by a train. A long silence fell before Peter repeated the statement several times over, each time using different phrases. Paul was one of the most senior LE officers in our Regiment, he was invincible. It was like getting a phone call to say 'the world ends tomorrow.' It was irrelevant that we were friends, LE officers don't die in battle. By definition of their title 'Late Entry', they had escaped such misery by serving a full career as a soldier. They guide, mentor and lead. They don't die!

'Gaz, Gaz, still there?'

'Fuck. Yes sorry. How, when? Are we sure?'

Peter calmly talked for ten minutes or so, but nothing was sinking in. My mind was racing out of control. Thoughts of his family, thoughts of his Riflemen leaderless in Iraq – and, 'Oh my God!' How this would hurt his Commanding Officer. Patrick Sanders was the first officer to Command 4 RIFLES. The first man to take them into battle, he had an unrivalled love for the Riflemen, even when they embarrassed him in front of the Duchess. For anyone who has taken charge of soldiers, command can be a lonely place, the bigger the command, the lonelier it can become. In combat, there is a similar formula for emotional pain, the more you command, the greater the pain and worst still, it lasts forever.

I couldn't order my focus. The pain of losing such a huge character would have far-reaching consequences on morale, and we all knew it.

'Who has been sent to notify Paula? It has to be someone who knows her. Please tell me they haven't sent a random dude from the Brigade'.

My knowledge of the casualty notification procedure had been tested to the full in recent years. Once it was confirmed that Paul had been killed, the compassionate system would race into action to beat social media or regional news channels. The Commanding Officer would lock down all communications in order to contain the news within Iraq. The Joint Casualty & Compassionate Centre (JCCC) would trigger a call

NOTIFICATION

out procedure and contact the relevant Arm and Service. For the Army, it would be PS2 in Upavon, Wiltshire (Personnel Services, Branch 2). The casualty handling unit was a small team, headed up by Hugh Welby-Everard and his assistant Shirley. They had both watched their roles change beyond all recognition since the turn of the century, and the emergence of conflicts in Afghanistan and Iraq. They had to work extremely quickly to ensure that Paul's family were given the news by a qualified Notification Officer and quickly organise a Casualty Visiting Officer. I knew Hugh and his team would have been working through the night to ensure everyone was in place to deliver the support.

'Gaz, it's under control. Peter Bullard is the Notification Officer, he has been there since 0200 hrs. I think he has organised transport to Exeter University to break the news to Paul's eldest son before he hears it on the news.'

'I am devastated. How could this happen?'

'Gaz, it has. It is now a case of supporting his family as best as we can, and that's why I have called.'

The blood drained from my extremities and raced between my heart and brain. My inner ears thumped. The fear of what Colonel Peter was about to say triggered every oppressed fear I possessed. Emotionally, I had not recovered from the last time I was a Visiting Officer. Worse yet, my mood was still dark from yesterday's visit, not to mention the instant grief that was starting to take hold having learnt of Paul's death.

'You will know that Pete is not allowed to be 'Notification Officer' and 'Visiting Officer'. To be honest, he really shouldn't have done the notification. But for the fact he was a close friend of Paul and Paula, it's too big an ask. Also, Pete will deploy to Iraq in the next couple of days anyway.'

The courage required to notify a wife that her husband has been killed in action is extraordinary. The amount of courage needed to tell your friend's wife, is incomprehensible. Pete Bullard and I were the best of friends. His emotional intelligence and compassion were second to none. In the eighties, Pete had been my section commander. We had done operational tours together, shared good times and drunk ourselves stupid together. An exceptional soldier and consummate professional, he would wish to play his part by deploying to Iraq and serving alongside his fellow riflemen. But there was a good reason for Pete not being allowed to become the Visiting Officer. The horrific emotional impact of notifying a relative of someone's death is traumatic for everyone involved. For friends, all previous happy memories of long, fruitful friendships are overwritten with a new memory. One that starts with the phrase 'I am sorry to have to tell you this.' It becomes the single worst moment of your life and anyone associated with it invokes the horrors of that moment in time. The Notification Officer and eternal misery are inseparable. From that point forward, whenever the Notification Officer meets the relative, that moment in time is re-lived. Having delivered the dreadful news of Paul's death, every visit thereafter would do little more than re-live that awful moment, over and over again.

The decision for Pete to not follow protocol stems from a depth of friendship and professional respect that is found in very few professions. Pete knew the risks he was taking, he knew that Paula could potentially hate him for the rest of their lives. Pete was risking the loss of two close friends, but he would not have changed his decision even if the head of the Army insisted. Paul was one of Pete's best friends. In the days leading up to the deployment, Pete, Paula and Paul had shared a table at their annual Rifle Ball, enjoying champagne, idle gossip, crazy madcap fun and belly-busting laughter. The very last time Pete and Paul had spent any length of time together, was the night Paul had dropped Pete off at home after the function. Pete would have fought Hercules for the right to break the bad news to Paula. He knew that Paul would wish for the news to be given by a senior Rifleman. Someone who could comfort his wife and family with the love and respect she deserved. It was the only circumstance that had me agreeing with Pete's decision. Whilst I was in Iraq at the start of the invasion, I had given my wife instructions to ask for one of my closest friends to be 'Visiting Officer' should I be killed in action. I would have wanted someone who knew me and all my failings to support my family. Johnny Mabb, Wez Weston, Chris Lamb or Eddie Edwards, it needed to be someone who could connect with my family through recounting my life.

Colonel Peter offered a small list of suitable candidates available to take on the duty of visiting Paul's family. As the small talk faded, it was becoming increasingly clear that Colonel Peter was choosing his words with great care. He was deft and articulate, moreover, he knew me better than any other officer in the Army. During our thirty odd years of service, we had spent a lot of time in each other's company, and now we shared an office in Headquarters Infantry, Warminster. Above all, he had seen me at my lowest after dealing with Ms Steel, and my own challenges after two tours of Iraq. For many an hour, he had listened to me recount the stories of life as a Visiting Officer and the emotional strain of one year fighting insurgents throughout 2003. In fact, Peter and his family had spent enough time in the company of my family, that he intuitively cross-mapped my suffering and watched as it played out in my personal life. He would not be able to say to me that I was the only person capable of being appointed as Visiting Officer to Paul's family.

'Gaz, we have a few options for the Visiting Officer duty, but I have reservations about each of them. You know all the candidates well. What are your thoughts?'

If you wanted to be with someone during a crisis, it was Colonel Peter. He was an accomplished manager of soldiers and officers. He gently led me to the only solution without compromising our professionalism. He knew that this particular duty needed a volunteer. He had given me enough opportunities to opt out and left the door open for me to volunteer. He also knew I was highly likely to do just that.

'Colonel, Colonel, Colonel!' I carried on interrupting him until he stopped talking.

'This is a no-brainer. It's me. All day long it's me. Whilst I think the world of the other candidates, they have domestic challenges of their own. It can only be a Rifleman, and that Rifleman is me.'

'Are you sure Gaz?'

'I am sure. I will turn around and head to Winchester now.'

'Ok, thank you. I will pass your details on to PS2. They will give you the full details and the Visiting Officer's pack. Please call me after your visit.'

Hanging up, I sat in the car for fifteen minutes. Eyes closed, struggling to orientate my thoughts, an uncontrollable rage consumed me. It was a complete lie. In truth, I was clinging to my sanity by my fingertips. Every night I would see Sergeant HJ and his five blokes help me train the militia at Al Majr- Al Kabir. I re-lived every near miss, every dead body, every interview and interrogation. I was being haunted by demons who were haunted themselves.

TRIBUTE TO A HERO

Still restrained by the seat belt, I closed my eyes and screamed at the top of my voice. Every item within striking range was kicked or punched. The steering wheel, the dashboard, the window, the rear-view mirror, the pedals and the gear stick, I lashed out at it all. This was greater than the loss of a friend, the loss of another fellow Rifleman. This was the loss of an icon and something I couldn't process. To add to this mental anguish, the selfish fear of telling my family that I was about to be emotionally vacant for at least another two years as I commit myself to help Paul's family rebuild their lives. The mess of emotions rattling around my head like a marble in a tin were only eased as I thought of the pain Paula and her two sons would be suffering in the first few hours of being told. My energy ran out, as the physical pain of hitting everything in the cockpit of my car took hold. The tears streamed down my face uncontrollably. The sting and salt-filled bitterness brought a degree of calm to my thinking. It was a good thing to get this out of my system before making the four-hour trip to Winchester. So, with blood trickling down my shins having cut them on the bottom of the dashboard, my knuckles red raw, the car was turned around, and in no time at all the M6 was in sight.

For the next three hours, the phone rang non-stop. Firstly, the JCCC called to confirm my details. Then again to confirm more details, and again and again. In between the Unit Welfare Officer, Captain Dean Murch, called several times as he tried to keep ahead of the power curve. The closer I got to Winchester the more intense the phone calls became. Hugh and his team in Upavon ran through the critical requirements of the first visit. It was critical to understand the family dynamics and Hugh was quick to point out the pitfalls of getting it wrong. But no sooner had I put the phone down, it rang again. Each time the phone rang, it meant another stop, endless notetaking and analysing policy and process. In truth, the news was only just beginning to sink in. It mattered not how much information was given to me, the shock of Paul's death had shut down my intellectual functions. On the outskirts of Winchester, I decided to stop and consolidate all the instructions and compose myself. It was nearly 1500 hrs and there was nothing about the journey from Liverpool that I could recall.

Eyes red and swollen, nose rubbed down to the last layer of skin, there was no hiding the impact of the news. Emotionally, I was just holding it together, but my physical appearance compromised the personal turmoil being experienced. With less than five minutes to go before I knocked on the door of Paul's family home, the need to separate the moment from the requirement was imperative. The last thing the Hardings needed in their lives now was a man they could not trust or believe in. Our first encounter after Paul's death needed to be professional and courteous, above all, I had to hold it together.

Sitting in my Army issued blue Ford Focus staring at the front door, I recounted the twenty-odd years that Paula and I had crossed paths. In the bad old days before people like Hugh and his team in Upavon, it was someone just like Paula who knocked at the door of a soldier and delivered bad news. I could recall numerous occasions when she had supported a family during their bereavement. She knew that I would need to confirm Paul's personal details, confirm extended family details, and identify any family complexities that could cause friction.

Standing at the door with the sound of the doorbell echoing around the house, I panicked at the thought Paula may not recognise me. We had seen each other at a families open day less than four months ago, but we never spoke. It had been twenty-two years since Minden and despite attending several military functions together, I couldn't be sure she remembered me. It felt like an age before the door was opened by Paul's eldest son, Christopher. He shook my hand and welcomed me into their home. Paula greeted me in the hallway and instantly hugged me.

'Hello Gaz. How are you?'

She was genuinely concerned for me. Full of empathy, almost apologetic for interrupting my day. The memories came flooding back of Ireland and Cyprus. Paula had always been at the epicentre of supporting grieving families when tragedy had struck. I had a flashback of the support she gave to Jill Wall after Larry died. Larry and I had forged a fantastic centre-midfield partnership during our football days in Warminster, and his death came at a time when I was away from the battalion. Knowing that both Paul and Paula had been there to help Larry's family was comforting at a time of personal frustration. Now, here she was suffering the worst of all tragedies, her husband Killed in Action. Pathetically, all I could do was repeat the word 'sorry' and suppress the overwhelming urge to cry. Standing at the heart of this disaster, witnessing a family in grief is heart-breaking bordering fraudulent. I had no right to cry, no right to feel robbed or aggrieved, yet that's exactly how it was. Trying to keep my emotions in check was like trying to have a bath in a colander. The enormity of the loss the Harding family were facing was so overwhelming, that it could not be put into words, yet remarkably the family oozed calmness.

Pete Bullard walked around the house making small talk but subtly assessing the resolve of everyone present. It was the finest example of emotional intelligence being practiced. If Pete had identified someone he thought was not coping, he would have developed a support plan. Paula's close friend Debbie made more coffee and her husband Jock played on a PlayStation with Jake. It truly felt like the world was about to end. The shock of the news was masquerading as a surreal calmness, and at the centre of it all was Christopher. Composed and firmly in control, he asked me a plethora of questions about what happens next. How do we get father home? How do we recover his personal belongings? When will this happen? I braced myself for the question, 'how did it happen?' but to my relief, it never came. Christopher was as focused as his father always was. He was uninterested in trying to deal with stuff outside of his control but focused on setting the conditions for stabilising his family in preparation for the weeks ahead.

The coffee flowed as Paula, Christopher and I talked through the process of recording Paul's death. The options Paula faced once the Coroner released Paul's body, the financial support that was immediately available, and other aspects of military protocol. I dutifully took copious notes and double-checked everything Hugh had directed. His small army of helpers would be working late to ensure Paul was brought back to England in accordance with legislation and the Coroner's direction. Although there was little more information to give Paula other than the basic facts she had already received from Pete, I stayed to support the family until 2100 hours.

As dusk arrived, it was time for me to leave. I shook everyone's hand, hugged Paula for thirty seconds or so and promised to return early the following morning. Driving away in my little Ford Focus the phone again began to ring. There were over twenty-two missed calls on my phone and so many text messages, they were uncountable. Other than a courtesy call to Colonel Peter, there was no one else I felt the need to speak to. Although there was little to say to Peter, just talking about Paul's family had broken my thus far emotional resolve. My voice trembled and the repetitive throat-clearing gave the game away. Peter issued me with instructions to focus on the Harding family for the next week or so, and wished me a safe drive home.

Tear filled eyes, a face looking like I had just gone ten rounds with Rocky Marciano. My brain in neutral, not only could I not see the road in front of me, but I couldn't read the speedometer. Entering the fringes of Sutton Scotney, I ran straight into a Police speed trap, 35mph in a 30 zone. The fluorescent jacket of the traffic cop stood in the centre of the road snapped me out of my daze as he ushered me into a layby at the top of the village. He was half my age. Bumfluff limply flapping above his top lip in the cool evening breeze, the young officer questioned my morality as he pointed out my reckless behaviour before issuing me a ticket. He was condescending and arrogant, if I didn't know better, I swear he was goading me. It was the straw that broke the camel's back. Yes, I had broken the speed limit, but that did not make me a renegade. His lecture was poorly timed and delivered with contempt. He had tipped me over the edge and I let loose a tirade of abuse at him. It was more *'disappointed Dad',* than an angry driver. I was not contesting my misdemeanour, but more offended by the suggestion that I treated the life of others with such disregard. It was right that the traffic cop issued me with a fine and three points, but his lecture was misjudged. Had he taken a brief moment to assess the situation, look me in the eye and apply some emotional intelligence, I would have happily apologised and thanked him for keeping me safe.

Inadvertently, the young lad may have saved me from myself. I was in no fit state to drive and despite my foul mood, I accepted the speeding ticket but couldn't help myself having one more snipe at the young bobby; I am sure my words just bounced off his dogmatic automated demeanour. Out of respect for the authority of his position, I promised to drive with greater care. Less than one hundred yards later, in the centre of the small village of Sutton Scotney, I pulled up at a petrol station and slept for more than four hours. Despite arriving home at 0300 hrs, I crept upstairs and into my daughter Lauren's bedroom. Sprawled across the bed, blonde hair wrapped around her favourite teddy bear (AKA Pink Dog) I hugged her, and fell asleep at her side.

Chapter Nine

Home Coming
Mrs Paula Harding

Despite my body and mind being utterly and mentally exhausted, inexplicably, my mind was still running at a million miles per hour. I had remained awake all night sobbing into my pillow, the physical pain in my chest growing worse every minute. I wanted to be close to Paul, and now that wasn't possible, I needed something that smelled of Paul. Rummaging through his chest of draws I found his oldest Rifle Green beret. Still adorned with its faded silver Green Jacket cap badge, threadbare after decades of wear, it fell immediately into shape. I opened it and like a child with their comforter I lifted it to my face and breathed it in. I immediately felt connected to Paul, and it would be in my hand constantly for months to come.

The sun crept up and peeked through the curtains before 5 am. The morning after the Summer Solstice, Paul was dead so why was the Earth still turning? That word 'dead', how could it be associated with my Paul? 'Paul is dead', 'Paul is dead' was now on constant repeat inside my head, like a vicious earworm gnawing away at my brain. Round and round it went, it just would not stop. 'Paul is dead! Paul is dead! Paul is dead!' I lay there, eyes open but not seeing, it felt like a trance, as if I was losing connectivity with reality and just listening to the same words bounce around my mind like a marble in an empty tin.

Then the trill of the telephone in the kitchen below broke the spell. Chris's deep voice seemed to reverberate up through the wooden floor boards and slowly I emerged from my trance. The door creaked open and gradually Debbie crept across the bedroom floor towards the bed, gently coaxing me to take the phone call, saying:

'Come on babe, someone's on the landline for you.'

Forcing my body up and out of bed, I followed her downstairs and took the phone out of Chris's hands. His eyes were red and swollen and his expression confirmed the pain I knew he was in. His suffering broke my heart all over again. With my eyes closed, I put the receiver to my ear and whispered 'hello'. Pete's voice offered the briefest of pleasantries before explaining that the British Embassy had tracked Paul's parents to their hotel in Sri Lanka, and informed them of their only son's death. Sympathetically, he said the Embassy would be making arrangements to get them home as soon as possible. Thanking Pete, I hung up and joined Debbie at the kitchen table, where a mug of sweet tea was waiting for me. Paul had despaired with me over the years as I never drank tea or coffee, preferring a cold can of pop, even when camping in the snow. A brew was his priority every morning, and now I found myself conforming and accepting the soothing liquids on offer. Sipping from the steaming mug I closed my eyes and imagined John and Hazel sitting in a hotel room, in the middle of paradise, but in a living hell. A sharp pain stabbed my heart, like a kitchen knife being plunged between my ribs, all the way to the hilt before being twisted over and over. I gasped with the pain and sobbed:

'They've lost their darling boy, this will kill them'.

Pete's news meant that I could now inform my wider family and friends before the British Press were told, and the news broke in the British media. Debbie insisted I finish my tea before I started to make my calls, and as we sat there Jake and Christopher appeared in the doorway asking what news Pete had shared. I told them how their grandparents had been found and told. Debbie made the boys breakfast and mugs of coffee and encouraged them into the lounge as I began to work my way through the contacts on my phone. My biggest fear was that the photo I had given to Pete would appear in a news bulletin before I had been able to tell all of our remaining friends and family.

Every call was torture, I was in shock myself and the shock emanating back at me from the person on the receiving end was palpable. Every person I spoke with had the same questions: Were we sure? How? Was it instant? Who was with me? How were the boys coping? Can they come to me now? The love was tangible, the disbelief heart-wrenching. Both my sisters were abroad, my eldest living in Spain with her husband Lofty, my middle sister was in Greece, I was to learn later that the morning after Paul had been killed, my brother-in-law had nearly lost his life when the roof of the restaurant they were dining in had collapsed and that he had been taken to hospital with a head injury. By the time I had finished notifying as many people as possible, I had cried a river and felt exhausted. I retreated to my bed and again lay listening to my now familiar earworm 'Paul is dead'.

Jill Wall, Jimmy and Alison Mitchell were the first to arrive. They had immediately dropped everything, climbed into their cars and driven across the country to be with us. The first thing I uttered to Jill was:

'I thought I had imagined your pain. I now understand that I had no idea what you really were going through when Larry died.'

With that all-knowing look of experience, Jill replied with the words I will never forget:

'Thank God we cannot imagine that pain. No one would ever fall in love, and the human race would come to an end.'

Jimmy paced around the garden sandwiched between Christopher and Jake, arms wrapped high around their shoulders. With tears streaming down their three faces, Jimmy held them with a vice-like grip uttering sentences about how Paul loved them above everything. He repeated that Paul was the best of soldiers, and how they were the best of friends. Now, Jimmy would always be there for them, trying to fill the void, filling the role of the father figure. Alison looked ashen, sitting with Debbie and I on the sofa, with tears trickling down her face and repeatedly saying,

'I can't believe it, how can the world still be going on when Paul's dead?'

Breaking into this outpouring of grief and love, Gaz handed me a eulogy written by Patrick. He explained that Patrick wished to receive my approval before it was released to the press. It was impossible to read this in front of anyone. The intimacy of a husband's eulogy is not for sharing. I knew Patrick would be emotionally fragile having seen so many of his Riflemen die in combat so soon after arriving in Iraq. For him to seek my permission to release these words to the world's press, was to give me one more intimate moment with Paul.

I went up to our bedroom, got into bed, held Paul's beret to my face, took several deep breaths, and started to read. Patrick spoke eloquently and from the heart about Paul, describing him as a soldier and family man, and of the outpouring of grief amongst the Riflemen upon learning of his death. He spelt out how everyone looked up towards Paul, and how dozens of notes had been left on his desk describing what Paul meant, recounting the effect Paul had on their lives and how he was respected. I have never felt so humbled. To me, he was my Paul. A husband, a father, a son, and a brother. Yes, I knew what an amazing person he was, and how incredibly lucky I had been to have shared 22 years with him. But I had never given a thought about his effect upon others, I had taken that for granted. It was painful beyond comprehension to read, and I still couldn't believe that I was sitting in our bed and that he would never be there with me again.

Patrick described how shortly after the tour began, the PJCC was attacked by a sizeable, well-armed and controlled militia force who were intent on over-running any number of coalition buildings. On one particular evening, after Paul's building had been subject to a sustained attack, Paul's calm and inspiring leadership prevented the militia from capturing the PJCC. With a small group of men from 1st Royal Horse Artillery, and a few others from Brigade Headquarters, he led a Platoon from 4 RIFLES and fought off concentrated attacks lasting more than 4 hours. So intense was the fighting that Paul and his small group had fired over 9000 rounds in their efforts to prevent a major victory for the insurgents.

I later discovered that the remote location had run out of gun oil, and Paul had cleverly realised that cooking oil would work just as effectively, to lubricate their weapons and stop them from jamming at a vital moment. It was this clever piece of ingenuity that saved the lives of at least 100 people. Patrick later clarified that this had been the attack that had prevented Paul from calling me when Jake and I were staying in Devon, visiting Falmouth University. During our weekly phone call, Paul had just referred to the militia as 'our visitors', and I had innocently assumed they were dignitaries or VIPs, like he would normally host in Bulford, and not 200 armed extremists.

Patrick explained that, during the attack when he was killed, Paul had placed himself in the front sangar (a concrete observation post) the most dangerous and exposed spot, and the closest to the enemy. He wanted to ensure the security of the route, as a resupply convoy from Basra Palace arrived. Wanting to minimise the risk to his men, Paul had placed himself in danger. This totally resonated with me; Paul would never have thought about not being there with his men. I now understood why he wasn't safely tucked inside the building that night, but down in the front sangar.

I re-read Patrick's words. I made only one short amendment. Where Patrick mentioned Paul's loss to myself and my sons, I added a note in the column 'please include son and brother'. I felt it fitting to have his parents and beloved sister acknowledged. Paul came from a loving family. He loved his parents and sister in equal amounts, and I wanted everyone to understand his love had no boundaries.

I returned downstairs and into the kitchen where Gaz was sitting, nursing a mug of tea in silence with Jimmy and Jock. Alison and Jill were in the lounge talking with Debbie in hushed whispers. The kids were sprawled on the sofas in the snug, and I realised that they were all waiting for my reaction. I gave it back to Gaz and mentioned the slight amendment to include Paul's parents and sister. Gaz asked my permission for Paul's name, photograph (the one that I had given to Pete) and Patrick's eulogy to be released to the media? I had no choice, I was going to have to share my beloved husband with the rest of the world, everyone I could think of had been told. I was bound to have missed someone, but I had tried the best I could. Looking at Jock and Jimmy they both gave me an almost imperceptible nod, and I gave Gaz the go-ahead.

Gaz left the room and made a call. Upon his return, he asked everyone into the lounge. We sat on sofas, chairs and the floor and he explained that the Army was now releasing the news of Paul's loss. He explained that he was heading home but would be back in the morning. He then strongly advised us not to make comments or reply in any way to requests for information or interviews with the press, but to allow the Army media people to deal with any inquiries. It felt surreal to me, not only was Paul dead but he was now going to be posthumously made famous. The press had made a big issue of the 150th soldier to die in Basra, Corporal Rodney Wilson, the first fatality of 4 RIFLES. Paul was the 153rd soldier to be killed since the hostilities in Iraq had begun in 2003, but significantly, he was the most senior and longest-serving member of the Armed Forces to be Killed in Action, and the press would be primed for the story.

It is impossible to imagine how quickly news, good or bad, can travel. That night, after Jill, Alison and Debbie had fed everyone, we were sitting in the lounge, and as ever, Debbie insisted I drank another cup of hot sweet tea. The TV was on in the background, silent. Time froze as an out-of-body experience took hold. So utterly filled with grief, it felt as if I had been transported through a black hole and was now living real-time in a film of my own life. All my senses became disconnected and disorientated, I could not cope with any non-diegetic voices or music. The evil earworm of 'Paul is dead' gripped me again, and so started the continuous loop. It would stay with me for the following, exhausting 12 months, before gradually becoming intermittent, and then fading.

I was crashed back to reality as Alison sprung out of her seat and picked up the controls to turn the volume on. It was the BBC's news at ten, and the image filling the screen was the photograph of Paul, the very one I had given Pete. We sat in silence and listened as the commentary washed over us and the words hung in the air: 'A soldier killed in Iraq has been named as one of the Army's most experienced men, a Major who served for 30 years. Major Paul Harding was killed whilst preventing his base in Basra from being overrun by the Iraqi militia. He leaves behind a wife and two children'. I momentarily stopped my crying to digest every word said. It was like pressing the reset button all over again. The level of pain was incomprehensible. It must be true, 'Paul really is dead' the BBC have said so.

Another night passed with people sleeping where they could in guest beds and sofas. I lay awake all night silently crying into my pillow and wishing I could just die, to disappear, and for it to all be over. I wanted to make a deal with God, I wanted to be with Paul. But, the Earth kept turning and a third day arrived without Paul, it was going to be the hardest so far. It was Saturday 23rd June 2007, the first Saturday without Paul. I would count these milestones for months, the first day, first week, second week, third, 50th and so on. Every landmark was recognised and referenced as 'without Paul'. The youngsters were all still in their beds but Jill, Alison, Jimmy and I were up, expecting Debbie and Jock to arrive shortly. We were talking about Paul, I had been crying so hard, saying how I just wanted my life back, I wanted everything to return to normality.

Jill had been phenomenal. She had been loving, but without being sympathetic. Her unique style contained a hint of tough love, and a chunk of 'I know what I am talking about'. Albeit her words were always delivered gently and with tact, they were brutally honest. She told me straight that things would not return to normal. That is never going to happen Paula, she said. But she was just as quick to reassure me that I would get through this, that I would create a new norm eventually. It was agonising to imagine life without Paul, and for a moment we sat and enjoyed a comfortable silence, something you can only do with a true friend. That was until the doorbell rang and Jimmy led Gaz into the kitchen. He looked haggard, red-eyed and visibly trying to hold himself together. I was developing a sixth sense with Gaz, it was like I knew what he was thinking, or about to say.

Accepting a coffee from Alison, he joined us at the table, taking a deep breath he prepared us for the devastating news he was about to divulge, we had lost another Rifleman. Corporal John Rigby had died the previous evening in a field hospital in Basra, after being injured by a roadside bomb whilst on patrol near Saddam Hussein's Basra Palace. It was on the day of his 24th birthday, and he had been nursed on a life support machine for 10 hours, whilst his twin brother William (also serving with 4 RIFLES) held his hand. His parents Doug and Liz had had to make the heart-breaking decision, from back here in the UK, to have the machine turned off. We were stunned. I could not believe that I could experience any more pain than I was already feeling, but as one always has more love to give, so one can feel more pain; even more than I thought imaginable. My heart broke all over again as I thought about John's twin, his parents and sisters, and grief filled me all over once more. I was suffering death from a thousand cuts. Everywhere I looked there was immense pain and grief.

The next few days fused into a blur of friends and family coming and going. Jill had to return to her home in Durham, and her young son. My sisters and brothers-in-law managed to return to the UK, and my mother had been brought back from Devon. Cards and letters arrived in huge bundles. Our postman had to knock on the door to deliver them daily as they were banded together and were too many to get through the letterbox. The sheer amount began to swamp me, so Gaz supplied me with binders containing clear plastic pages to put letters and cards inside. Each one of the A4 size folders could take around 100 letters. I had filled 5 binders in the first two weeks, as friends, Riflemen of all ranks, and strangers sent us their condolences. Some envelopes were simply addressed with nothing more than my name, or my village, even just a postcode, but somehow the Royal Mail delivered them. Some of

Alison and Paula at the opening of Harding Close.

Christopher and Jake with Mrs Jones before the Tough Guy endurance race.

Grand Day, Duke of York's School, 11 months before Paul was Killed in Action.

On holiday with Debbie & Jock Fleming, Jimmy Mitch, Jill Clarey and Alison Mitchell.

Paul and Major Henry Worsley (OC Company) Bulford 1997.

Paul firing a Wombat on Ex Pond Jump West.

Paul with Jessie, the pup he gave Paula for a wedding gift in 1987.

The day after Paul and Paula were engaged Minden, West Germany, August 1985.

the most moving letters came from parents, partners and siblings of other servicemen and women who had also given their lives in the Iraq conflict. These were especially poignant as they truly knew the torment that we were going through. Although it was hard to find comfort in anything at that moment in time, these letters were to subsequently provide much comfort and support.

The newspapers over the next few days covered the story of Paul, his career and his death as a soldier. We knew the press would be snooping around so I insisted on keeping the blinds and curtains at the front of the house closed. Inevitably when journalists did call, Jock would answer the door or phone and politely explain that we had no comment to make and shut the door or place the phone down gently.

Paul's friend, Andy McNab, wrote a moving piece in his column, on Monday 25th June and another friend of Paul's, the world-renowned war correspondent for the Times newspaper, Anthony Loyd, wrote Paul's obituary. It mattered not a jot that I saw these stories appear in the black and white of the national press, it still did not feel possible that Paul was dead, or that so many people were talking about him so publicly.

As ever, Gaz subtly started to prepare me for the repatriation of Paul's body. First, he would introduce the thought, then he would reintroduce it as a topic, and before we knew it, we arrived at the detail relatively painlessly. All repatriations happened on a Wednesday, so a week after his death on Wednesday 27th June, Paul's body would arrive home on British soil. On this occasion, there would be a first. It would stand out from every other repatriation thus far because, on this flight, Corporal John Rigby would be accompanied by his twin brother, William. He would be accompanying both John and Paul on their final flight home. It is unprecedented to give a soldier leave to exit a theatre of operations to attend a funeral. But on this occasion, William had to travel with his twin, to share the emotional pain with his Mum and Dad.

The Army Media Service had given me a DVD of the ceremony held in Basra before Paul and John flew home. It took me years to watch, but seeing how respectful and lovingly the service was for Paul, just affirmed my love for him even more. On Tuesday 26th, as the sun set local time in Basra, the battalion held a service of repatriation for Paul and John, to acknowledge the Regiment's loss, and acknowledge their sacrifice. Equally important was the opportunity it afforded for their friends and comrades to say their goodbyes. Every soldier dies a little inside when a fellow soldier is killed; their resolve comes from moments like this. I watched as the Riflemen of 4 RIFLES formed up on the edge of the runway and said the Lord's Prayer together. It was immediately followed by The Rifles' Regimental Collect, a prayer specifically for the Riflemen of the Regiment. Father Danny, the Regimental Padre, then offered a short service of blessing. A nervous giggle sneaked from beneath my tears as I thought of the Catholic-Protestant divide between Paul and I, and just as our life began together, it ends, with a Catholic minister leading the way.

Possibly one of the most moving tributes ever to be paid to Paul was delivered by the Fijian Riflemen he had commanded. Gaz would often say that Fijians reserved their cultural greetings only for those they truly respected. Watching this unique group sing laments in their native tongue inspired, enthused and broke me, all in one go. John and Paul's bodies were sealed in simple wooden coffins, wrapped in the Union flag. Both equal in death, both treated the same, no rank or insignia, they were simply two gallant warriors, both of whom made the ultimate sacrifice. They were each carried and placed inside the cavernous space of the Boeing C-17 Globemaster that would bring them home. There were no seats, no passengers, no cargo, just Paul, John and of course John's twin, William, who sat with them for the duration of the flight.

Gaz collected me, Jake and Christopher, on the morning of 27th June. It still felt impossible to me that Paul had been lost to us a whole 7 days, and now we were travelling the 60 miles to RAF Lyneham, just south-west of Swindon to receive his body. Still unable to listen to the gabble of the radio, Jake had brought with us a CD from Paul's car collection. It was a brilliant idea Jake had, one of many he would come up with over the next ten years. Paul's music would distract us from the true reason for our journey, and give us something memorable to concentrate on during the drive. Jake sat in the front with Gaz, whilst Christopher and I held hands in the back of the large, black military saloon. As soon as we got underway, I felt sick. I couldn't warm up. I found myself shaking. Then, just like Paul would have done, Christopher unclipped his seat belt, slid over one seat into the middle, and cuddled me. I realised it was a sense of shock and trepidation that I was feeling, and tried to relax and concentrate on the music playing. Jake had chosen Blue Oyster Cult's album 'Agents of Fortune', and the next track that came on was one that Paul and I had sung together on many a car journey. The unmistakable guitar riff of 'Don't Fear the Reaper' began, and I lost myself in the lyrics I knew so well. The dark thoughts returned immediately, I wanted so badly for death to come and claim me. I imagined Paul coming for me as I died, taking my hand, telling me not to be afraid, and disappearing into the other side with him.

I understand how selfish it sounds, but the pain was crushing me. More than anything, I wanted my Paul back and if that wasn't possible the next best thing was to be with him. My thoughts ran riot; 'get the funeral done, and I can work out how I will join you, Paul'. I didn't stop to think of the consequence, how would anyone ever understand the depth of this pain I was suffering. But as I opened my eyes and slowly gathered my senses, I felt Christopher's hand in mine, his eyes staring at me, full of love and concern. And in the front, I saw Jake staring silently ahead, the outline of his jaw as distinguished as his father's. The pallor of his skin changed as the light reflected off the cars we passed, and I couldn't help noticing the other people in their cars going about their everyday business as if nothing had changed in the world. I knew I couldn't leave my children. The fight inside me would resist the urge to be with Paul, and I just prayed that it would be strong enough to succeed.

Gaz led us from the car to the viewing gallery where a variety of old friends were waiting. Still clutching hold of Paul's old Green Jacket beret, I hugged Jimmy, Alison, and Jock. As ever, Debbie had blended into the background, she was at our home and preparing lunch for our return. Standing at the back of the gallery, the Rigby Family had already arrived. We didn't need the introduction, I instantly recognised that exhausted look they all wore. The aura of desperation and loss was enough to identify who they were. We hugged each other, bonded by our grief and broken hearts. There was no need for words. Neither of us wanted to hear another condolence, another 'sorry for your loss'. The emotions were understood and the sympathies mutual. We were escorted onto the side of the runway just in time to see a dark grey spec appearing on the skyline. It was dry but there was a strong wind that blew directly toward the incoming aircraft. ZZ173 looked like a giant, grey Thunderbird toy, and with the wind direction stealing the noise away from us, it was silent as it grew closer and closer. For a few moments, the world stopped turning and I felt a cold chill pass through my body and flash into my bones. I whispered to Paul 'you are nearly home'.

The Globemaster touched down and it was only as it passed in front of us that we were able to hear the noise of her engines. She taxied past the grieving families, friends and dignitaries, and took a sweeping circle to turn 180 degrees, before coming to a halt. It stopped so close to us that we could see the pilots as they powered down the engines of this huge aircraft. The noise of her tailgate was unforgettable. The loud click of the locks uncoupling dwarfed the noise of the engines now idling. She began to unfold like a giant toy transformer, as the solid ramp slowly bowed down to reveal its cargo. The huge machine was designed to take heavy vehicles, artillery guns, or tons of cargo, but not the broken bodies of infantrymen.

The bearer party formed up, and I was immediately struck by their lack of headdress. Where had their berets gone? Why had they removed them as they marched up the ramp of the plane and disappeared into the belly of the plane? A lone bugler standing near the ramp sounded the last post, a sound that always brings a tear to my eye, on any occasion. Slowly and reverently the bearer party carried the coffin containing Paul down the ramp, then I realised why they wore no headdress. The six-man bearer party held Paul's coffin tightly high on their shoulders, three on either side. Arms linked beneath it, hands wrapped behind their partner's neck, their ears pressed to the wooden sides and holding their counterparts' shoulder. Behind the coffin one man marched slowly, issuing orders to the bearer party, calling out the pace, muffled and silent, authoritative but with compassion.

As they prepared themselves to move forward, I saw the young Rifleman at the front right of the formation give a reassuring squeeze on the shoulder of his partner, I could imagine the physical and emotional fears the young soldier was managing. At the same time, I felt a pain in my chest. I feared for all those young men carrying Paul. They looked so young, they would have known Paul in all his glory. Leading from the front of all the fitness tests, berating those not working hard enough during football or rugby games, giving encouragement from the sidelines if he wasn't playing, and on occasions, issuing a quiet reprimand. I wondered if these were the same men who carried Corporals Jez Brookes and Rodney Wilson a few days previously? Once again, I feared for their mental wellbeing. I know if I had been standing next to Paul watching this, I would have demanded he make sure they were well looked after, and I was also positive Paul would have reassured me that 'the Riflemen always come first'.

We stood in silence watching the repatriation ceremony for no more than 30 minutes. Only when Paul had been placed into his hearse and slowly driven off the runway did the second bearer party repeat the procedure for John. In a repeat of what was done for Paul, John's coffin was slowly carried down the ramp, this time escorted by his twin brother walking slowly behind the seventh man. I looked across at John and William's parents watching their twin boys coming home like this, having lost one of them on their 24th birthday, and just when I thought it was impossible to feel even more wretched, the grief I felt for this family consumed me. The pain was now layering on top of pain to the point that I had become numb.

Later that evening, sitting alone at home cuddling Paul's beret, I watched the evening news. The newsreader stated that Tony Blair had expressed his condolences in Parliament at the start of PM's Questions. Then in another surreal experience, I watched Paul and John's hearses passing through Wootton Basset on their journey to John Radcliffe Hospital. The town had come to a standstill, shops closed, hundreds lined either side of the high street as both hearses crept along the road at a snail's pace. Veterans and Royal British Legion branch standard bearers lowered their standards, whilst bystanders placed roses on the ever-decreasing available free space on the vehicles. Although I cried uncontrollably watching this spectacle, still trying to comprehend that my husband lay in one of those coffins, I was touched by the respect my fellow countrymen showed to Paul and John.

Paul's remains had been taken to the John Radcliffe Hospital for post-mortem procedures. I had given Gaz instructions to use a local funeral director in Winchester, a family business serving our community for decades. I had found them to be very professional when my father had passed away 7 years previously. Gaz took the responsibility of liaising with the funeral directors which saved me the heartache of discussing the finer details of Paul's funeral. After his first visit, we discussed what clothes I wanted Paul to be dressed in for his final journey. He asked if it should be a military uniform or a suit? Neither felt right, Paul was most comfortable in jeans, desert boots and a polo shirt, so I went to our bedroom and chose his favourite pair of Levi jeans, a bottle green polo shirt with the Royal Green Jacket cap badge embroidered on the left breast pocket, underwear, socks, and desert boots. Gaz then took the clothes to the funeral directors and returned for me the following day to go to the funeral parlour to discuss floral arrangements, and decide if he would be buried or cremated. Jock and Debbie were with us when he arrived. I had expected to go alone but Christopher came down dressed and asked to come too – happy that Jake would have Jock for company. They enjoyed playing games on the X Box, which had become a useful distraction for the moment. Once again clutching Paul's beret, Christopher and I left with Gaz.

The directors were so gentle and kind, expressing how they felt it an honour to be caring for Paul's remains. We discussed details of Paul's cremation, and then as I thought we were about to leave, he asked if I wanted to view Paul's body in the Chapel of Rest. I had been fearful that the manner of Paul's death would leave him disfigured or unrecognisable, and I think Gaz may have had the same trepidation because he suggested that he view Paul first, and offer his last respects. Christopher and I sat on the sofa in the waiting area as Gaz was shown through a highly polished wooden door and left alone on the other side of it. Christopher took my hand and we waited the few minutes before he returned and asked me if I was ready. I stood up, holding Paul's beret tightly to my chest. I let Gaz lead me through the same door and into a softly lit and very cold room with swathes of silk curtains and silk floral arrangements on pedestals. As we approached the coffin in the centre of the room, I felt my legs shake and start to buckle, then I felt Gaz's hands firmly on each of my shoulders supporting me as he asked if I was sure I wanted this. Gripping Paul's beret even tighter I took several calming breaths and approached the coffin once more. Looking in, at first, I thought it wasn't Paul, he looked plumper, I muttered something and looked at Gaz, then back at Paul. He clearly had make-up on, obviously to make viewing his body, now 10 days post-mortem, more acceptable.

'Is it Paul?' I asked Gaz, and he nodded.

'Touch his hair' Gaz said. So, I reluctantly reached out and stroked the top of Paul's head, and felt the short, cropped head of hair I had shaved hundreds of times over 22 years. I then looked more closely and noticed a new scar beneath his chin and remembered the wording on the Coroner's Interim Death Certificate, 'fragmentation wounds to head and neck'. I pointed this out to Gaz and he confirmed this was where he had been hit. Strangely I did not sob as I had been doing the majority of the past 10 days, I managed to push the urge down and remain in control. This felt like it was going to be my last ever moment with Paul, so I took several deep breaths, leant closer to Paul's body, and said my goodbyes.

We had spent less than fifteen minutes in the chapel, but that was long enough for the cold to cut me to the bones. Gaz and I returned to the waiting room and to my shock, Christopher stood up and declared that he was going in to see his Dad, moreover, he wanted to be alone with him. I had a powerful urge to stop him, to protect him, but he walked forward determinedly, and let himself through the same wooden door. I sat on the sofa and watched Gaz stare pensively at the door. The concern he had for Christopher was hard for him to hide. Although he would not admit it, he was worried about the lasting impact of viewing his father's dead body would have on Chris. For what felt like hours, but was probably less than five minutes, the receptionist behind the desk was absorbed in some administrative task, but she too kept looking up at the door. Then slowly the door cracked open and both Gaz and I stood up. We were all holding our breaths, hoping Christopher had come through the experience in one piece. When he reappeared, pale and with red eyes, there was an expression of acceptance and contentedness. Staring deep into my soul, he walked towards where I stood and hugged me for several moments in silence before he whispered in my ear:

'I don't want Jake to see Dad like this, let him remember Dad the way he was.'

When you don't think the depth of pain and despair can get deeper, reality bites down harder. The layers of pain piled on top of each other one by one, and even those events that were designed to ease the pain did little more than add to it in another dimension.

Chapter Ten

Operation PABBAY
Captain Garry McCarthy

The Regimental flag stood lifeless at half-mast as I arrived at my office. The flag's lower toggle brushed against the freshly painted pole, and the silver bugle folded neatly between the red lines that broke the black and green backing of the large flag. It had been 24 hours since the news broke, and it already felt like a lifetime had passed. The 4 RIFLES Battle Group were in a scrap of epic proportions. Every flavour of extremist plausible wanted nothing more than to kill members of the Coalition. The tour was officially less than 12 hours old when the first fatality occurred. After just six weeks, there had been six soldiers and one officer Killed in Action, and twenty-three wounded. A highly charged feeling of guilt coursed through every sinew of my body. Despite the evident fatigue from my two tours of Iraq, there was no suppressing the feeling that I really should be in Basra, suffering the same relentless onslaught as my fellow Riflemen. Both battalions of my former Regiment were serving in Iraq in 2007, and there was a queue a mile long of volunteers desperate to deploy and fight alongside them. Every waking minute of the day I wanted to deploy, even after all I had been through in 2003. It was less painful than the emotional desperation of 'Rear Operations'.

The conflict in Iraq had spiralled into a free-for-all, with every protagonist hell-bent on self-destruction or total annihilation. The moment Saddam Hussein had been de-throned, every flavour of fundamentalist or minority picked up arms to fight against each other. The race to fill the power vacuum quickly escalated into chaos. It was like the Wacky Races meets 'A Fistful of Dollars'. Gun fights on top of gun fights, and more death than Father Time himself could deal with. Predictably, the hapless planning of the Coalition forces did little more than make the situation worse. The lack of a coherent strategy made it easy to blame the security forces, they were easy prey. But in truth, every quasi-militia force had something to gain by shooting at anything that moved, but their favourite pastime was attacking the military. Carrying a gun, reminiscent of the wild west, had become a way of life for most men living in Iraq. In the cold light of day, I recognised that I was fortunate to be taking a break from the misery of war.

As ever Pete Bullard was busy in his office planning and executing rear operations. Remarkably he appeared calm and composed, but I knew that he would be working at 100mph, tirelessly supporting operations in Iraq as well as his own deployments around the UK. Invariably a long line of Riflemen would be standing outside the office complex he shared with his Company Serjeant Major. At 47 years of age, Pete was still as agile and committed as he was on the first day we met in 1983. He was the epitome of professional soldiering, physically very powerful, quick-witted and never caught unprepared. He was known for his dedication to the service and there were very few people who had given as much to the Regiment as Pete had. For three decades, Pete had stood between evil and the innocent and asked for nothing in return. Like many servicemen, he was driven by loyalty and integrity, comradeship and justice.

Entering his office my suspicions were confirmed. Pete was working at a frenetic speed. He was managing the deployment of Battlefield Casualty Replacements, hospital visits, welfare appointments, not to mention routine management of a large military camp. As Officer in Charge of Rear Operations, Pete would be working 18 hours a day, every day of the week. His phone would never stop ringing and not even for a second could he find personal space to relax or rest. It was akin to a life beneath the Sword of Damocles. He was the absolute centre of all activity as he commanded and administered the one hundred or so soldiers supporting the operational efforts in Iraq.

As I walked into his office, I instantly felt reassured. Pete's infectious style of leadership empowered everyone to do their best. No matter how much stress he was under, Pete seemed to stop the world from spinning and brought order to the moment so he could listen to what you had to say.

'Morning Gaz, take a seat. What time are you heading back to see Paula?'

'Maybe 11ish. I just need to get a feel for the critical dates such as repatriation, equipment return, pay and pensions from PS2. Once I have a few answers, I will drive up to see her.'

'OK. Do you know if she wishes to have a military funeral?'

'No idea Pete. Not something we have discussed yet.'

'Gaz, I know this will be difficult, but please be clear with your advice to Paula. If it is a military funeral, we will take full ownership of it and it becomes tricky for the family to change the format!'

It was the kind of focused comment Pete was renowned for. We had both buried enough of our friends and colleagues to know how it goes. If Paula opted for a military funeral, the system would place demands on Pete that are unimaginable. Expectations become national and it was crucial Paula knew what this meant.

Shortly before midday, I had arrived at the Harding home. Silhouettes flashed in front of the privacy glass of the hallway door as I rang the bell. Paula opened the door and hugged me as she welcomed me back. Ushering me into the kitchen, she quickly made herself busy distributing coffee to anyone in the house. Sitting at the kitchen table, Paula studiously analysed everything I had brought with me. A plethora of pension papers, compensation forms and action charts nestled neatly alongside the mounting pile of condolence letters. Gently, I offered my advice as best I could, always cautious not to deliver advice that appeared to be a fait accompli, but mid-sentence I stopped.

'Gaz. Gaz. Gaz! Are you alright?'

The doorbell rang and Paula stood up to answer it. Muffled chatter filled the hallway as she invited them in and closed the door. A heartbeat later, Jill entered the kitchen with her beautiful daughter and teenage son.

At the start of the day, I had made a promise to myself to hold it together. To suppress all my personal feelings, so that I could remain detached from the emotional pain being suffered by the family. It seemed the best way to serve Paula, Chris and Jake. But the arrival of Jill had kicked seven bells out of that plan. I had last seen Jill a few months after Larry (Wally to his fellow Riflemen) had died in Northern Ireland. Wally and I had been good friends ever since the day we met way back in West Germany at the start of the '80s. Carefree, with irrepressible energy, the pair of us lived the single life during the battalion's first return to England for nearly a decade. There was always fun to be had when I was out with Wally. Nights filled with drunken episodes and near misses, our favourite pastime was to chase single women around Warminster every

Friday and Saturday night. He was even funnier as we chased a football around some awful excuse for a football pitch in the wettest corners of Wiltshire. It would take him thirty minutes to sober up before he was of any use to his teammates, but once he was on form, he was just like his idol, Chopper Harris of Chelsea. Wally would scythe an opponent down like he was felling trees, then instantly accuse the opposition of feigning injury. In the '80's when yellow cards were seldom seen, Wally averaged one a game. Hilariously, he would always protest to the referee as if he had somehow been harshly treated. His brazen claims would have me in tears of laughter, mainly because he believed himself to be innocent.

When I first met Wally, in a pub in Germany, he was out on the town with Regimental legend Gary Driscoll, famed for upstaging Cliff Richard in a singing duel on the Centre Court at Wimbledon. Both Garry and Wally were dressed in dodgy suits and looked ready to hit the streets of Peckham to sell moody goods. They had become known as the Kray twins because of their sharp suits and demeanour, but in truth, they were closer to Del Boy and Rodney. Garry and Wally were two of the nicest men you could ever meet, the very people who make life interesting and colourful. They enjoyed their London links and chats about Chelsea hard knocks and football gangs, but they were just playing the angles that facilitated their love for soldiering and camaraderie. It is not easy to understand if you never had the opportunity to serve in the armed forces, but characters and personas are both mythical and magical. An individual's identity becomes a blend of fiction and fact, and occasionally both components were exploited to enhance reputation.

I had never come to terms with Wally's passing. I would often play football and miss his cockney accent berating me for trying too hard.

'Cut it out scouse! No more of that tippy-tappy crap! Just hit'em up in the air an get on wiv it!' Then he would laugh at me with his the fake laugh that he stole from Bob McCartney, another part of the London "hard knock" club.

To compound the issue, in the unique nonsensical way that only the Army of the '90s could operate, I was refused permission to attend his funeral. In the words of the platoon commander in charge of me as I attended the Platoon Sergeant's Battle Course in Brecon, 'you can't go, McCarthy, you have already been to one funeral this month.' To this day, it remains one of the most disappointing acts of leadership I ever experienced. It was narrow-minded and utterly bizarre to suggest there is a quota of funerals allocated per person.

In 1994, whilst posted to Cyprus, I had caught up with Jill when she visited the battalion. Chloe, her daughter, was just four, and Zac had just turned three. Thirteen years later, Chloe had blossomed into a stunning young lady, and Zac was the spitting image of Wally. His gait, mannerisms and quirky smile, it was like Wally had just walked through the door ready to play football. The flashback of my days with Wally untethered repressed emotions that had been locked away for nearly two decades. The feeling of being denied a lifetime of fun shared with Wally was all too much for me. My composure was slipping away as I became distracted by my own grief.

There could not be a better friend to help Paula right at this moment than Jill. If anyone was capable of understanding the pain she and her boys were suffering, it was Jill, Chloe and Zac. I recalled vividly how Paula had helped so many wives during our extended tour of Northern Ireland and now, here she was, being comforted by just one of those who had suffered the ultimate pain of losing a loving husband. The collision of so many highly charged emotions and memories liquified my rational thinking. With the house full of so much support for Paula, with her closest friends all standing resolutely by her side, there was little more I could offer at the end of day two.

During the two-hour drive home my phone rang incessantly. For the first few times, I ignored it. I needed to get home and find the time to recalibrate. I was sure that it would be one of the two Peters, keen to discuss our joint miseries. But at the traffic lights at the Solstice roundabout on the A303, I glanced down at the phone. To my surprise, the LED screen displayed 'Ms Steel 5 Missed Calls.' It was most unlike Ms Steel to call so many times in the space of such a short time. I knew instantly this was not going to be an easy conversation. I turned off the A303 and pulled into the car park opposite Stonehenge. Perched on a large cold stone at the rear of the security hut, I returned her call.

'Gaz! Gaz! It's all over, I am going to top myself. I can't go on, he was the only thing keeping me going!'

The pain was evident, the tears relentless. Words spurted out inaudibly as she faded in and out of signal range. I visualised her curled up on her sofa, dressed in her son's clothes, rocking back and forth clutching the phone in the most unorthodox manner. The phone fell silent and after two minutes the disconnection tone kicked in. Several frantic redials later, there was still no connection. My options were limited: the Police, the Army Welfare, the ambulance service. If she was serious about suicide, I had seconds to find the right solution. In a moment of genius, I thumbed through my notes from three years earlier and found my list of contacts. Ms Steel had a half-sister who lived nearby. Brenda, a divorced school teacher, was a very strong character. Surprisingly, Brenda had anticipated my call.

'It's Father's death, Gaz!' Somehow, her strong northern accent made it seem more emphatic, as if the word death wasn't clear enough.

'She has been holding onto him for support over the past couple of months, but he had been ill for some time. I don't suppose you could visit her? She always gets a lift when you visit?'

Driving to Sheffield at 1800hrs and then needing to return to Bulford for 0700hrs was a big ask. For a short time, I contemplated making the journey but knew that I could not concentrate on driving for such a long time in my current state. It took every ounce of my resolve to say no. Ms Steel needed close intimate emotional support, and whilst I was able to provide that way back in 2004, it was just impossible to do it now.

'You promised you would always be there to help Gaz!' Brenda reminded me.

It was like a hot knife had been plunged through the centre of my forehead. I had made that promise. It was issued with sincerity and honest intent, but little did I know what lay before me. Brenda repeated the promise I made. I repeated my apology. The emotional pain we were all suffering was beyond describable. An angry Brenda offered me a few brief insults before hanging up leaving me wallowing in self-pity, doubt and regret. I had tried so hard to help Ms Steel. I had given up every spare minute I had between 2004-2006, but as I would come to learn, this would never be enough. Two years is but a micro-second in the life of a mother grieving the loss of her son, or the wife and children grieving the loss of a father.

An hour had passed since I had chatted with Brenda. Now, in silence, bum numb from the cold hard stone, the events of the day wreaked havoc with my own stability. There was no hiding my fragility. My legs shook, my stomach cramped, and inevitably I let go of the contents of my stomach in three gut-wrenching bursts. The fear that I was not good enough to support Paul's family terrified me. There was an irrational fear of making it worse, not better. The wiggly worm had control of my thoughts and it was all that my mind would consider. I had not felt this demoralised since I was sat on the back of a C130 alongside the six coffins of my force protection team in 2003. Arresting the flow of the tears streaming down my contorted face, I prayed to God for the first time since the fatal battle of Al Majar Al Kabir. Everyone in touching distance of me seemed to be suffering, I was desperate for things not to get worse.

Day three, and I had arranged to see Paula fairly early in the morning knowing that the date for repatriation would be confirmed. Most pressing was the need to decide if she wanted Paul to be buried with Full Military Honours or have a quiet family service. At 0715 hrs I parked my car outside the Battalion Headquarters in Kiwi Barracks. No buzz of busy Riflemen, no noise of printers and computers kicking into life in the corridors, something was up. It's not a sixth sense, but it's unexplainable how a soldier can smell disaster. The cold air on a summer's day, the lack of laughter in the building, the feeling of death stalking you. It was inevitable that more bad news was in the offing. Pete's office light was on, as was the light in the company clerk's office. I looked harder at his office and saw the shadows of two people. Captain Dean Murch, the Welfare Officer, stood pensively next to Pete who was on the phone. Pete caught my eye as he looked through the window before turning away so he could guard the conversation he was having. Pete would be mindful of protecting everyone's security and would ensure information would only be disseminated at the right time. Irrespective of how long we had been friends, Pete never discussed sensitive information that I was not entitled to know about.

It wouldn't be much longer before the news broke. Corporal John Rigby had been Killed in Action. If ever there was a time to get angry at the injustice of life, this was it. An outstanding young man, hell-bent on making the country of Iraq a better place, stolen from this world by evil insurgents who valued nothing other than the need to bully, oppress and dictate their way through life. My immediate thought was for his brother. John's twin brother was serving alongside him. He would have been one of the first to know. The scenario of who told him and who told his Mum and Dad was too painful to imagine. On the back of the loss of Paul, this news would hit everyone like a wrecking ball. If Paul had been described as the embodiment of 4 RIFLES, John and his brother were the lifeblood. Infectious enthusiasm and unrivalled commitment, the combined misery of losing two of the most valuable players in such a short time had the potential to be catastrophic.

Paula had already heard the news by the time I had arrived at her home. Yet, even in her darkest hour, her focus was on trying to help someone else manage their grief. The empathy she held for the Rigby family seemed endless. Recounting the loss of several soldiers over the years, she understood exactly what John's mother and father would be going through. Paula had helped her fair share of military families manage their grief and intuitively knew exactly what to say and do. It was not that Paula and the Rigby family were united in their loss; this was unbridled love for her extended family. A love for all soldiers fighting nobly to free the oppressed and persecuted, a love for all those families that paid the ultimate price in the pursuit of freedom. This level of selflessness is unique to military families, their wives, husbands, parents and children.

Sitting at the kitchen table, I explained that Paul would be repatriated to the United Kingdom on the morning of Wednesday 27th June. The first thing Paula asked was: 'would John be returning at the same time?' It was difficult to answer the question. Not because it was a complex question, but more because my emotional lexicon had hit overload. Everywhere I looked, there were expressions of pain and sorrow, yet this lady stood resolute, in complete defiance of the misery the world was inflicting upon her. Sitting at her kitchen table, flanked by Christopher and Jill, she was the true hero of this tragedy. Conversely, I was unable to stop my eyes from welling up. The irrational feeling of being a fraud sucked the concentration out of my tiny brain. Again, I would find myself thinking that I should be with my fellow Riflemen, fighting against a vicious enemy.

All Riflemen love the 'derring-do' of soldiering. There is no desire to kill people, but there is an intoxicating desire to defend and protect the innocent from tyrannical dictators, genocide or pure evil. The mind-set of being a 'force for good' is the panacea for facing the most dangerous of situations. Trading your life for the betterment of civilisation is a gamble few people will ever understand. It's not frivolous, selfish or reckless, it's a professional acceptance that your role in life is to stand between good and evil and that you may need to risk your life trying to achieve it. It can happen in the blink of an eye. On one occasion whilst surrounded by fifty angry Iraqi policemen, my commander, Lieutenant Colonel Eddie Forster-Knight invited me to translate his words to the head of the Basra Police force during his weekly meeting. Colonel Eddie was a dynamic and direct-action man. He rode the streets of Basra on a military Harley Davidson more commonly used by despatch riders. Like Batman patrolling Gotham City, he cruised the streets on the bike looking to douse the flames of disobedience and disorder. Passionate about policing and infectious in his desire to deliver peace, he was adored by his subordinates.

After the usual prolonged exchange of pleasantries, Colonel Eddie jumped right into the crux of the issue.

'Mr McCarthy. Please express our gratitude to Brigadier General Tariq bin Turki for his service. Tell him that we have been instructed by the commanders of the coalition forces to remove all Brigadier Generals from their posts. From this moment forward he is no longer in charge.'

The complexity of constructing the sentence in Arabic monopolised all my powers of concentration. But that was not the issue I wrestled with. Culturally, you don't sack an Arab in front of his peers. The loss of face is unbearable, and the consequences are inevitable. It never crossed Colonel Eddie's mind to manage the situation before imparting the bad news, and now the words had left his lips, there was no going back. I gulped and tried to select my words with caution. But halfway through my sentence, the expression of the Brigadier General changed from welcoming to disbelief and anger. Worse yet, the crowd that surrounded the two of us became instantly hostile.

'Please ask him to hand over his pistol Mr McCarthy.'

The Brigadier slapped the pistol in my hand, as one of his subordinates had decided to translate the conversation so everyone in the hall could hear.

Thus far, I had been shot at, mortared, blown up, and stranded in a minefield. On each occasion, I visualised my own death and what the inquest would say. Each method of death was unpleasant, but now I faced being hung, drawn and quartered by an angry Arab crowd. Dragged naked tied to the rear bumper of a Toyota 4x4 and dragged through the streets of Basra for the world's press to see. I could hear the crowd demand our heads. The indignity of what we had just done was something a proud Arab would kill for. We had embarrassed him in his own house, in front of his children. There was nothing left now but retribution.

Colonel Eddie wanted to talk more. He invited me to discuss compensation and the final salary arrangements. But by this stage, I had tuned into the angry comments demanding our execution. Inside the large Police building, we were cut off from our small force protection party outside. The conditions were set for lynching and the fear of swinging from a lamppost battered and bruised was now a reality. Despite Colonel Eddie being the size of a small mountain and towering head and shoulders above those who surrounded him, he would be easily overpowered. We needed to escape before the Brigadier General gave the nod to his subordinates to kill us. I grabbed the Colonel by his arm, pulled him away from the Brigadier, and clicked back the hammer action on the pistol I was holding. Only after the first few steps did Colonel Eddie realise the danger. Shoes flew across the room and bounced off the back of my head, spit and snot splashed over us as we made for the door.

Making good our escape in a silver Land Cruiser, the Colonel looked at me and sighed: 'that was close. I think we will ask the other Police chiefs to come to our camp from here forward!' Sadly, that would not materialise. Once the news spread that Brigadier Turki had been sacked, the writing was on the wall for all Ba'ath Party members who were tentatively clinging on to the end of their reign. Violence rolled through the city like a tsunami and days later, the Mahdi Army, raised by Muqtada Al Sadr, were on the rise. Of all the scenarios I had faced, death at the hands of an angry crowd terrified me the most. Unquestionably this was the derring-do that inspired me to be a professional soldier. Even the horrendous possible consequences seemed a fair trade-off for the peace that would result from the sacrifice. But, despite the praise heaped on me by Colonel Eddie for remaining composed in the face of disaster, had it gone wrong it would have been my wife and my children who would live with the debt of war.

Paula had decided Paul should be buried with Full Military Honours, a decision shared by Christopher and Jake. There was no hiding their pride in their father's achievements. They had shared the trials and tribulations as he ascended through the ranks to reach the cusp of lieutenant colonel. And whilst Paul never sought praise or glory, it was only right that the country had the opportunity to acknowledge his sacrifice. The veterans, associations, and patriots of Great Britain would all be desperate to pay homage to Paul. His service had stretched nearly four decades and those wishing to be present at his service would exceed many hundreds. Despite not knowing all the details, the background planning would start immediately.

Paula and Jill were in mid-sentence when Pete Bullard's name flashed up on the screen of my mobile phone. Knowing that any conversation with Pete would be one of a sensitive nature, I left the kitchen table, walked past Jake and Jock who were enjoying a racing game on the PlayStation, and sat in the lukewarm sunlight at the bottom of the garden. Pete confirmed the death of John Rigby and that it was highly likely that he would be repatriated with Paul on the 27th. Having two soldiers repatriated on the same flight would stretch his resources to the limit. The battalion had been deployed for little more than one month and Pete, commanding Rear Operations, was spending most of his time juggling visits to Sellyoak Hospital in Birmingham, and the families of Corporals Jess Brookes and Rodney Wilson, both of whom had been Killed in Action in the first weeks of the deployment. He was a man under huge pressure. Trying to find the balance of supporting Colonel Patrick Sanders who was leading the fiercest of fighting in Iraq, whilst maintaining morale and cohesion back in Blighty, was both emotionally exhausting and thankless.

We exchanged no pleasantries before Pete explained that we needed to confirm who would attend the repatriation, as well as confirming that Paul would be buried with Full Military Honours. Having spent most of his resources furnishing several families with liaison officers and welfare support, I knew Pete was now facing the need to plan and execute another two funerals in close proximity. The pressure would have been immeasurable. Not only did he need to ensure each family got nothing but the best possible support, but he also needed to ensure that he protected the emotional welfare of the soldiers selected to conduct the funerals and repatriations. He was acutely aware that you didn't need to be directly engaged in combat to suffer the effects of war. Every man and woman serving back in the UK carried some burden. Pete did all he could to ensure the burden was shared appropriately.

But for Pete, there was no sharing. Anchored to every casualty, the families, the soldiers and the grieving, the system had little it could offer him as he absorbed the human collateral damage of war. Few would have known, and he would have never told anyone that his eldest child and son-in-law had been fighting in Iraq since the beginning of the conflict in 2003. As a serving officer and the father of a serviceman, parental and professional fears are inseparable. Like every parent, who had a child locked into a war, Pete would have visualised someone knocking at his door at 0200 hrs just as he had knocked on Paula's. Unquestionably, the strain on Pete would have been felt by Fran, his wife and their children. Collectively, they would have lived through every death, every casualty and every funeral. It would be naive to think that Pete's family were unaffected by what he was doing.

On the morning of the 27th at exactly 1100 hrs GMT, we stood quietly in a makeshift reception room on the edge of the runway at RAF Lyneham. Paula gently hugged members of John Rigby's family. Brigadier Jolyon Jackson, Major Eddie Edwards, and Major Richard (H) Hays, all of them lifelong friends of Paul, stood soberly in the shadows. In turn, they all hugged Paula and shook the hands of Christopher and Jake. There were very few words to be shared. Major Eddie Edwards, who was the senior RIFLES LE officer, asked me to keep him informed of the family's welfare. Ever the Regimental stalwart, Eddie would regularly work 24 hours a day to look after the welfare of every Rifleman he ever served with. All regiments have a father figure, for The Rifles, Eddie was it. He had returned from Iraq only a few days before Paul died. I recognised that vacant look in his eyes as he reiterated the fact that the Hardings must want for nothing.

Bloodshot, wide-eyed, tired but determined, Eddie spoke on behalf of every Rifleman in the Regiment. On this occasion, Eddie made sure that both Jimmy Mitchel and Jock Fleming, both retired Riflemen and close friends of Paul and Paula, heard his declaration. For Eddie, it was most important that this commitment was heard by veterans and associations. His voice transcended all ranks and regiments. Irrespective of your history, Eddie demanded unity across the five pillars of the Regiment as we received Paul and John back home.

At exactly two minutes to 1100 hrs on the morning of the 27th, the Globemaster appeared serenely out of a grey sky. Its clumsy shape defied logic as it crept slowly in our direction at a height of one thousand feet. Briefly, the nose of the aircraft appeared to dip and rise before flares were fired from the rear of the beast of the skies. It was the RAF's salute to our heroes, a demonstration of unified gratitude for the servicemen they carried home. Everyone was transfixed by the majesty of this large aircraft as it banked to the left and circled the station before landing. A short taxi to the apron and the loadmaster would lower the tailgate of the aircraft, and hand over command to the bearer party.

At the rear of the C17, waiting to walk up the tailgate, WO2 'Batty' Batcock and his six handpicked Riflemen formed the repatriation party. This was Batty's fourth repatriation in as many weeks. On each occasion, he followed his own Regimental protocol. It started with Lieutenant General Nick Parker thanking the bearer party for what they were about to do. General Parker was a natural-born leader, and with his son serving in Iraq with 4 RIFLES at the time, it would have been even more poignant. Despite his very senior position within the Army, he was firmly at home chatting with the Riflemen. Whilst this may sound strange, many senior officers are brilliant at what they do, but some can't hold a two-way conversation with soldiers. But General Parker knew the stress the bearer party would be suffering and sought to ease that strain with gentle encouragement and support. He would tailor his words for that moment and inspire people as Churchill had once inspired a nation. His very presence would have galvanised Batty's party, but his words of support would never be rivalled by other leaders.

Batty would then march to the aircraft and stand amongst the coffins before taking a private moment to come to terms with the heartache of what they were being invited to do. Quietly, avoiding eye contact, Batty would then request Lance Corporal Kelvin Price to say a prayer on behalf of the bearer party. Pricey was preparing to leave the military and pursue a life in the church. His gentle nature, humbled by his junior rank, would afford the bearer party a moment to grieve in private before stepping into the gaze of the world's media. Batty would wait until he was certain that his team had summoned the resolve to walk down the tailgate of the C17, and remain composed. It's not uncommon for soldiers to well-up or cry silently during situations as difficult as repatriations.

There is no ridiculing a soldier who is baring his soul for someone Killed in Action. There is just total respect, total understanding, total love. Although Batty's young team needed to grow old to understand the emotions they were experiencing, he knew their vulnerability and managed the moment with deftness, empathy, and professionalism. For the first time since the arrival of the aircraft, Batty would fix eye contact with every Rifleman. He would gently nod his head and the party would move to their rehearsed start positions on either side of the coffin which had been placed on trestles by the aircrew. Staring deep into their souls, he needed to be certain they had their emotions under control. Then, and only then, would he give the order:

'One pace inward march!' The bearer party would stand tight up against the casket and clasp their hands around the bottom edge of the coffin. Feeling for the routed edge of the base, the party would search for a firm grip, three Riflemen on either side. They would rub the underside frantically to ensure no sweat or moisture could cause a slip once the next command was issued.

'Up!' Batty commanded with dignity, and the team would elevate the coffin chest high. This was the point of no return. From here on, the Riflemen would not have an opportunity to show their emotions again.

'Inward-turn!' In one swift move, the bearer party would lift the casket shoulder high and turn inwards to face the foot of the coffin. The casket would come to rest on the shoulders of the bearer party for a brief moment. Then the final part of the drill movement. The Riflemen would reach underneath the casket and grip the shoulder of the Rifleman on the opposite side. The spare hand would then be thrust up against the side to form a vice-like grip around the casket. It was the most important stage of the procession. If anyone failed to secure a strong hold on his opposite number, the coffin could slip out of control, whilst being manoeuvred out of the aircraft. Batty would take one good long look at his team. This was the moment he needed to be sure of, for every step hereafter, they would be in the eyes of the world's media. He had to be certain they were ready before he removed the trellis that previously held the casket in place. One final check to ensure the Union Flag was seated correctly, and that their exit was clear.

'Slow march!' Stepping off using the foot on the inside of the casket ensured stability as the bearer party walked down the length of the aircraft. Batty would make his way to the front of the casket and place his hand at the foot as it descended the ramp of the Globemaster. He would do this to prevent the weight of the coffin from running away as the bearer party negotiated the shallow slope ahead of the small step onto the runway. Protocol demanded that a serviceman exit the aircraft in rank order and feet first.

Repatriations are military operations that are run with precision. Code named Operation PABBAY, there was no room for error when it came to honouring the return of fallen soldiers. The world's media would report each repatriation, and crowds of veterans and Regimental associations would gather in the town of Wootton Bassett. Great efforts were made to know as much as possible about every member of the soldier's family attending. Mini biographies are drafted to ensure military dignities don't accidentally get names, places or events mixed up. Customary for all military events, there would be rehearsals and written instructions. The level of detail is nothing short of phenomenal. Checks for checks and then, more checks. To get the slightest detail wrong here would allow the national news outlets to capitalise on it, and spin it to harmonise the story with their political viewpoint. That said, this was not the reason for the diligence. It was professional pride, honour and respect.

As the bearer party neared the funeral hearse, Batty halted his team. This time, he gave the orders in reverse. He would command his team to 'inward turn'. The bearer party would release their grip on the shoulder of their opposite number and relocate their hands on the base of the casket. Slowly they would lower the fallen soldier onto the hearse's trestle.

Batty would stand still. For a moment, he and his team would fix their eyes on the coffin and say a silent prayer. With the bearer party standing to attention, Batty would pause briefly and salute.

'Inward turn.' The command from Batty would be the signal to form up again, and return to receive Corporal John Rigby.

Together, both soldiers were driven in the direction of Wootton Bassett, en route to the Coroner's Office at the John Radcliffe Hospital in Oxford. No sooner had the hearse left the front gate, than Paula, the boys and I left as quietly as we arrived. It had been a tricky day as Paula managed the expectations of Paul's Mum and Dad who were inconsolable at the loss of their only son. But when it comes to the military assisting the family of the deceased, it can only focus on one primary contact, and in Paul's case, it was clear cut. Paul had been married for longer than he had lived at home; his Mum and Dad would receive as much support as we could afford, but Paula and her sons were absolutely the main effort. Inevitably this could cause friction, but being thankful for small mercies, I was acutely aware that Paul had been brought up in a loving home full of practical decisions and stability. Thankfully, he instilled the same values in his own family.

There was little said on the short journey home. Occasionally, someone would break the silence with thoughts of the funeral. Every question imaginable was offered. Where it should be held? Was it a burial or cremation? What role would be filled by who, and what day would best suit those who would inevitably need to travel the length of the country to attend? The long list of potential attendees flowed. Occasionally, Paula would think of someone she had not spoken to since the news broke. In her organised way, she made a mental note of who still needed to be told. Politely I declined the offer of coffee as we pulled up outside their home. Work was piling up back at my office in Kiwi Barracks, and with the house full of concerned family and friends, they needed a little space having spent a full day surrounded by uniforms.

Thursday the 28th of June, and the difficult task of refining the details of Paul's funeral needed conciliation. An early meeting with Pete Bullard was short and sweet as we both faced another turbulent day. If Pete's office wasn't full of visitors, one of his phones was ringing off the hook. Several large 'whiteboards doing seven questions analysis' used for planning surrounded Pete's desk. They were crammed with timelines, deployments, returning troop details and the planning details for imminent VIP visits. The briefest glance at one of the whiteboards filled me with trepidation. The magnitude of his duties would never be understood by 'old school' officers who had experienced rear operations of the '90s.

'Gaz, we must be ready for hundreds of mourners', declared Pete after I offered my first assessment of VIPs attending Paul's funeral.

Pete was the officer in charge of planning and executing all military funerals for soldiers who died during his time as OC Rear Ops. He would put troops to task, and ensure welfare support had linked in with designated Visiting Officers. The size of his task was monumental. Pete had one primary staff officer and one Welfare Officer assisting him. Captain Bernie Bambury was his right-hand man for operational planning and strategic communications, whilst Captain Dean Murch dealt with family welfare. But the ace up his sleeve was Warrant Officer Class Two Andy (Batty) Batcock. With nearly 20 years' service, he was Mr Versatile, Mr Dependable. To have a man like Batty in your organisation was like having ten extra people. It was an incredibly strong team that had been assembled to deliver Rear Operations. Captain Bernie Bambury, charismatic and cerebrally agile, made light work of the turgid staff officer duties which gave Pete freedom of movement and the ability to visit the seriously injured in Selly Oak hospital. It was crucial that Bernie ran the routine commitments at Kiwi Barracks, by providing all the data, statistics, reports and returns routinely demanded of them by higher command. As unglamorous as his role was, Bernie was the oil that kept the machine running smoothly, allowing everyone else the space to achieve more.

Sitting at the kitchen table, with coffee, condolence letters and the occasional official form to complete, Paula and I discussed possible venues for Paul's funeral. Local churches, the chapel at Sir John Moore Barracks, and even the possibility of Paul's home town were debated. Then from inside the living room, someone shouted "the bloody Cathedral ought to do it"! Paula dismissed it immediately. She didn't wish to cause a fuss.

"Winchester Cathedral! They do funerals for Kings, not common folk from South London!' You don't think they would say yes do you, Gaz?" Paula giggled as she replied sarcastically. The notion of Paul, the world's most humble person, a man who gave everything and wanted nothing in return, sharing the privilege of his final journey with the past Kings and Queens of England. But we agreed, I should visit the cathedral, and ask the question.

Winchester is the ancestral home of the Royal Green Jackets, and its forefathers. According to the Very Reverend James Atwell, Dean of Winchester Cathedral, who welcomed me with open arms, 'holding Paul's service at Winchester Cathedral was the embodiment of his calling.' He was most insistent that the City of Winchester share in the celebration of Paul's life and give thanks for his service. Almost as if he was booking a wedding, he flicked through the calendar, then looked up from his comfortable wingback chair and stated 'Friday 7th. I hope this will be suitable?'

By now everyone was used to my phone ringing. They would watch me disappear into the garden to conduct my conversation. This time it was the Coroner's clerk. She had called to inform me that Paul's body had been released to the nominated undertaker in Winchester. Gently I explained this to Paula and allowed her some time on her own before she broke the news to the boys. We needed to discuss what clothes Paul should wear and finalise the formalities of the cremation. In her usual 'up and at em' way, we were outside the undertakers one hour later. With all the empathy in the world, the undertaker managed Paula's requests with sincerity and respect. He knew the military would do the planning and execution of the service, but still, he was keen to show his gratitude to Paul.

Chapter Eleven

Death of A Hero

HONOURS IN CONFIDENCE
Citation
MAJOR HARDING
Place: PROVINCIAL JOINT COORDINATION CENTRE, BASRA
Date of action or period covered by the Citation: 23/05/07 TO 20/06/07
How employed: CHIEF OF STAFF

Major Harding as COS was responsible for the day-to-day running of the Multi-National Force (MNF) aspects of the Provincial Joint Coordination Centre (PJCC), an Iraqi Security Forces C2 node in the centre of Basra. Exceeding what was expected of him, he also took on the role of DCOS, coordinating the logistic functions, and, with his superlative soldiering skills, tactical advisor to the REME CO. 80 UK soldiers were based at PJCC supporting monitoring, mentoring and training the Iraqi Security Forces (ISF). The start of TELIC 10 coincided with a 10-fold increase in attacks by militia against the British presence in PJCC, including the commencement of attacks by mortars, hitherto not experienced at this location (and for which there was no warning system). Due to the isolated position, and the severe threat to vehicle movement in the city, resupply convoys were minimised to avoid casualties.

Major Harding's ability to multi-task was inspirational in this unusual and unfamiliar environment, as was his supreme skill in all aspects of soldiering. That he found the time to get to know all of the soldiers, saw him idolised by all ranks. There are 2 shining examples of his influence: On 25th May PJCC endured a 4-hour battle with up to 200 Militia who were intent on killing or capturing MNF soldiers. The battle was the most intense in the city since the invasion in 2003, and PJCC troops expended nearly all of their ammunition stocks. When not fighting himself, Major

Harding expertly coordinated the defence and ensured the ammunition resupply and casualty treatment were optimised; he found innovative solutions to solve unexpected problems (e.g. using cooking oil to replace rifle oil). PJCC troops were not mentally prepared for this battle, and it was due to their admiration for, and dedication to him personally, that his presence inspired inexperienced soldiers of all capbadges (who were engaged in their first contact) to fight so hard, and successfully repel the well-organised and determined attacks. On 2nd June one of the rooftop sangars was hit by a mortar round and a soldier was seriously wounded. Major Harding organised his evacuation and gathered a group of volunteers to move the casualty to meet the CASEVAC helicopter. During this task the compound came under another mortar attack, aimed at the evacuation party and the helicopter; his inspiring presence and leadership steadied the men under fire and ensured that the casualty was swiftly evacuated, thus saving the young man's life. His personal example stood out as a beacon during a difficult, dangerous and confusing period. Moreover, his compassion and persuasive leadership quickly ensured that the soldiers were reorganised and reassured after the attack, and immediately ready to again defend the compound.

Major Harding always performed beyond what was expected. He was unflappable, and an oasis of calm during periods of chaos and danger. He was the consummate professional and his influence was everywhere, be it encouraging young soldiers, or advising the CO. Without his contribution I have no doubt that there would have been more casualties and morale would have suffered in this close and uncomfortable environment. Sadly, on 20th June he was killed by a mortar round. Despite having only served 4 weeks in PJCC his influence, example and leadership inspired, and continued to inspire after his death, as the soldiers tried to match his ethos and aptitude as a soldier. I have rarely seen such devotion and affection for one man. His contribution to the success of the mission was significant and worthy of formal recognition.

Date: 31/10/07

Chapter Twelve

In the footsteps of Kings
Mrs Paula Harding

Protecting Jake from the emotional pain was important to me, but there was no avoiding the need to discuss laying Paul to rest. For our own personal closure, we would need to say our final goodbyes. My anxiety had mounted over the weekend, knowing that Gaz would call early Monday morning with a need to inform everyone of the arrangements. Bizarrely, with the thoughts still running riot around my mind, Gaz arrived at the house. Clutching tightly to a mug of tea, we sat at the kitchen table running through the possible options. Firstly, I suggested the chapel at Sir John Moore Barracks. Christopher had been christened there in 1988, and our close friends Karen and Steve (Ginge) Starkey had been the first-ever couple to be married there. The chapel had great sentimental meaning to both Paul and me. Sir John Moore Barracks was our first posting as newlyweds. It was also where I had been presented to Her Majesty the Queen during a royal visit. The camp held a special place in my heart, and I suggested to Gaz that we should hold the funeral there.

I could tell Gaz was not convinced. Despite our short time in each other's company, I was becoming familiar with his mannerisms. Gaz was concerned that the small chapel might not have the capacity for the number of mourners wanting to celebrate Paul's life. For a moment I thought that he was pulling my leg; the chapel wasn't that small as I recalled. Of course, it was only right that we discussed St Peter's Church, where we had been married, along with a few local churches. Then a voice called out from the lounge.

"Winchester Cathedral. That's where it should be held"!

I giggled at first. I thought 'is this a joke?' After all, apart from Kings and Queens, the Cathedral was restricted to the rich and famous, people like Jane Austen and Josephine Butler, the 19th-century campaigner against human trafficking. But Gaz agreed. He said how it could be a consideration due to the number of mourners he expected. I couldn't believe that we were seriously considering Winchester Cathedral as a venue for Paul's service.

We had spent many a happy hour in the Cathedral. One of Paul's favourite military duties was the privilege of 'Turning the Pages' of the Regimental Book of Remembrance. Once a month The Rifles (or previously The Royal Green Jackets and The Light Infantry) would assign an officer of the Regiment to turn a page of the great book. The officer would be dressed in all his glory, medals shining, sword belt clinking, George boots crunching against the ancient cobbled stones. Accompanied by the cathedral staff, the officer would slowly turn the page of the Book of Remembrance and read out the names of the fallen that appear on that page. Powerful and emotionally inspiring, the event is well attended, and whilst it is not quite as popular as London's Changing of the Guard, it is a military event with huge kudos. I had watched Paul walk that aisle in his No.1 Dress tunic and medals many times as he executed his duties, nearly as many times as I had seen him walk the boys into a pew as we took our seats on Christmas Eve, or other traditional events and performances. We couldn't seriously be considering Winchester Cathedral, with the longest nave of any gothic Cathedral in Europe, to host the funeral of the most modest person I had ever known, surely not?

The following morning Gaz arrived in his usual quiet and unassuming manner. As had become the pattern, we made ourselves comfortable at the kitchen table, drinking coffee and sweet tea. Compassionately, he asked if I wanted a Military Funeral for Paul. Without hesitation, I said yes, knowing full well that the 'green machine' would take over the arrangements and use a format that dated back to the Tudor age. Paul had spent all his adult life a warrior and peacekeeper, from the atrocities of Kosovo, Bosnia and Sierra Leone, to defeating terrorists in Northern Ireland. In my eyes he had lived the life of a soldier, and deserved the funeral of one. Slowly drinking his brew, Gaz told me he had contacted the Dean of Winchester Cathedral. He explained the Dean was wholeheartedly supportive of celebrating Paul's life and final commitment at the Cathedral.

I was speechless, humbled into silence. My emotions were completely jumbled, proud, depressed, honoured, robbed, miserable and elated. I had never imagined this scenario for a single second. Sitting at our kitchen table, where we had shared thousands of family meals, imagining my husband, from his humble background in South London, son of a Soho bus driver, a grammar school boy, with no blue blood in his veins, would share his final journey with several of this country's late Kings and Queens. This was beyond surreal. Gaz explained that not only did he expect hundreds of mourners to gather, but amongst many others, there would be The Lord Lieutenant, The High Sheriff of Hampshire, The Mayor of Winchester City, Lieutenant General Nick Parker, and many other generals, as well as, astoundingly, Field Marshal Lord Bramall. I thought 'this is crazy.' How will we organise this? Gaz could see my reaction. He patted my forearm and said:

'This is going to be OK. Pete Bullard is on it. Between us all, we will organise everything. The Dean has suggested 6th July. Is that OK for you?'

Of course, I knew right away I was going to say 'yes', but the speed of everything was so overwhelming, even if it was understandable. I mentally processed our time scale, 9 days to plan and organise everything. I looked at Gaz and said, 'Yes we will do it.'

The following 48 hours were intense, but they gave Chris, Jake and I a purpose. I was running on empty, completely exhausted and extremely cranky, I snapped several times at my boys. Then a moment of calmness would descend, and I would sob, consumed with guilt. But instead of skulking off into their sanctuaries, Chris and Jake would envelop me in bear hugs. The power of their love would defuse the ticking time bomb, and recharge my batteries, for a few hours at least. They would laugh at the photos of Paul and me scattered around the house. Pictures of us both from the '70s and '80s, before we met and some of our favourite family photos from the '90s. At one stage they came across a stack of British Forces Post Office Blue Airmail letters: these letters we had amassed over the years were many. They carried the most intimate exchanges between a husband and his wife, which gave the boys plenty of opportunity to poke fun at my soppy nature. But the blueys proved our love for each other and our love for the boys. After the mildest of teasing, we all cuddled on the sofa. The warmth of their body heat offered some comfort, but the feeling of their love was inspiring.

I knew that our boys comprehended the depth of my pain, and that meant everything to me.

Christopher and Jake had agreed to write the programme for the Order of Service. They wanted to produce a biography of Paul's life, and fill it with happy memories. Slowly, word by word, they pieced together the story of their father. Sitting on the computer, they produced a small booklet with pictures and quotes that we had all loved over the years. We had recruited the help of Jonathan Gough, our Padre in Omagh. Way back in 1991 he had supported us stoically throughout those incredibly difficult years. It was all we needed to create a high-class program that we could offer to the mourners on the day. With a jacket of Rifle Green and silver embossed etching on the front and rear, the program celebrated Paul, the son, the brother, the husband, the father and friend.

I had a good idea of what music and hymns, readings and poems I wanted for the service. With the help of Jonathan, who explained how the order of the funeral service would flow, I was able to piece together a plan. Gaz asked who I would like to invite to deliver the readings. There were so many life-long friends to choose from. I sat and thought about the mentors and friends that Paul had shown love and admiration for over the years. But at the same time, many of them would be all consumed by their grief and sense of loss. I didn't want to put more pressure on those who were already sharing our grief. Most importantly, I wanted to enable everyone to remember the essence of Paul, and acknowledge just how far his life's journey had taken him. We had to get this right.

Firstly, I requested Nick Haddock to write and read Paul's eulogy. As his former company commander, he knew Paul well. Yet they were more than comrades; they were good friends. When Nick visited us to discuss his thoughts, he shared one of his memories of a time spent with Paul in Omagh. Nick and Paul had to spend several hours sitting together in a covert vehicle, waiting to relay news of an arrest operation back up the chain of command. They discussed a book Nick had been reading that featured the poem; *'The Life That I Have,'* written in WWII by Leo Marks. During WWII, famous poems were used to encrypt messages. This was, however, found to be insecure because enemy cryptanalysts were able to locate the original from published sources. Marks countered this by using his own written creations. *The Life That I Have* was an original poem he composed on Christmas Eve 1943 and wrote in memory of his girlfriend Ruth, who had just died, in a plane crash, in Canada. On 24th March 1944, the poem was issued by Marks to Violette Szabo, a British agent of Special Operations Executive (SOE) who was eventually captured, tortured and killed by the Nazis, despite the end of the war being days away. Paul had remarked to Nick that Leo Marks' poem said it all. *'The Life That I Have.'* So profound was this comment that I knew it would have to play a part in his service.

Andy McNab had been friends with Paul at the start of their careers, and had written a beautiful obituary about Paul on 22nd June. Andy had won the Military Medal on a tour of Northern Ireland whilst serving with Paul, and I thought it would be a nice gesture to invite Andy to do one of the readings. Nick Cottam, now a Major General, had been the Commanding Officer in Omagh. He had won the complete respect of all his Riflemen, and I know that Paul would have followed him anywhere. But it was the support of his wife, Susie, that had won our hearts; an incredibly caring lady, who engaged with the families with unbridled passion. The readings were finished with a personal poem written, and delivered by my closest friend from school.

The hymns to be sung were easy to choose: we would sing songs from our wedding. Paul had chosen 'Onward Christian Soldiers' and I had chosen 'Jerusalem'. They would be divided by 'Make Me a Channel of Your Peace', originally a prayer attributed to St Francis. I chose this because Paul had been God's peacemaker, bringing hope where there had been despair. The final song was 'I Vow to Thee My Country.' Simply put, Paul had literally carried out this promise. He had always put his country before anything else and paid the ultimate price for this pledge. Then from our personal collection, I added one of our favourite songs, 'The Nearness of You.' Written in 1938 by Hoagy Carmichael with lyrics by Ned Washington, we had often sung along to the Nora Jones version in Paul's car. My colleagues at Peter Symonds College where Jake had been studying, kindly organised the song to be sung by students studying music.

It did not take Christopher and Jake long to have the Order of Service printed. It was nothing short of spectacular. The cover jacket was perfectly crafted, and the content captured the essence of Paul. I was so proud of them both. To have the emotional strength to write the Order of Service for their own father's funeral, at such a young age, took courage beyond any I had ever known. The thought of their pain kept me awake at night. I was hardly sleeping and seemed to be crying all the time. The dreaded earworm 'Paul's dead' was still on its loop within my head. I was so fearful of getting this wrong. If he was in heaven looking down on me, I wanted to get everything spot on and ensure our boys would look back at this event and know that the three of us had given their Dad the final journey he deserved.

Jock, Debbie, Jill, Alison and Jimmy all arrived 3 days before the funeral. Jimmy and Jock went with Chris and Jake into town to buy new shirts, and to get haircuts. Standing at the door I waved them off, still overwhelmed by the bravery both were displaying. The letters kept arriving, at least 10 a-day. I would scoop them up, take them into the kitchen and put them on the breakfast bar. Slowly throughout the day, I would summon up the strength to open two or three at a time. So strong was the outpouring of grief contained in the letters, sent by friends, acquaintances and strangers, it would have been too traumatic to open them all in one sitting. But there was no escaping the news: at a special Party Conference in Manchester on 24th June 2007, Tony Blair had formally handed over the leadership of the Labour Party to Gordon Brown, who had been Chancellor of the Exchequer, under Blair's three ministries. Blair tendered his resignation on 27th June 2007, and Brown assumed office during the same afternoon. The day before Paul's funeral I received a letter of condolence from both Blair and Brown, these along with all the others were duly filed away.

An hour after I finished reading the letters from Blair and Brown, Gaz picked Chris, Jake and me up and drove us to the Cathedral Close. One of the finest medieval Cathedrals in Europe, once the seat of Anglo-Saxon and Norman Royal power, Winchester's magnificent Cathedral is the resting place of Saxon Royalty and Bishops. A juxtaposition of ancient stonemasonry and 21st-century law enforcement, police handlers and their service dogs were everywhere, searching the grounds, outbuildings and the inner sanctum of the Cathedral. Gaz took us to the café, sat us down in a quiet corner, and brought over drinks and cakes. He had explained during the drive into the city that we were going to have a run-through of the service. It was important to declare anything we wanted to ask or mention without hesitation. It would be our only opportunity to see where we would be walking and sitting and to rehearse our part of the service. I was chilled to the bone. Despite it being a hot July afternoon, I had come to realise that, when I allowed my grief to consume me, I would feel extremely cold, shiver and struggle to keep my composure. Having been unable to drink or eat the refreshments Gaz had bought, I asked if I could have a sweet tea. Gaz immediately got me one. Sipping it, whilst taking slow deep breaths, I summoned the strength to walk through the Order of Service.

We were met at the entrance by Lieutenant General Nick Parker, and Canon Jonathan Gough. As they walked the boys and I down to the front pew, Jonathan explained how we would follow Paul's coffin, and as the bearer party placed Paul by the altar, we would take our seats in the places set aside for us. General Nick then explained that after the last hymn, but before the buglers played the 'Last Post', Christopher and I would be escorted to the altar where Paul's coffin would be on a trellis. General Nick would then remove Paul's sword from the top of his coffin, with one hand grasped around the heel of the sheath and the other at the hilt. The sword would then be presented horizontally to Christopher. General Nick explained to us, that traditionally the sword would be snatched from the hands of the presenter, as a display of ascending to *Head of the Family*. We would all then follow Paul's coffin out of the Cathedral flanked by both boys, Jake to my left and Christopher to my right, with his father's sword in his right hand. Conforming to the legacy of a fallen hero, Christopher would be ready to protect his family from would-be assailants. It was all part of the military funeral ceremony that dated back to the days where the eldest son of the fallen warrior took on the responsibility of protecting the household. I looked at Christopher, just 19 years old, and thought to myself 'this is not what I had expected'. But I saw resilience in his eyes, and without hesitation, he gave a short, single nod and confirmed he understood. General Nick turned to me and explained that a folded Union Flag would then be handed to me. It would affirm Her Majesty, Queen Elizabeth's gratitude for Paul's sacrifice, and my loss. As we stood there digesting this, Jake touched my arm. 'What do I do, Mum?' he asked. 'Do I have something to carry?' Without hesitation, I replied, 'you will have Dad's medals', and turned to Christopher for confirmation. Christopher instantly agreed; 'yes Jake, we need you to take Dad's medals'. And so, it was. Paul's coffin would carry not only his sword but his medals.

The house was full on the morning of 6th August but unbeknown to me many more friends and family had occupied the local hotels. My hairdresser, the son of one of my work colleagues, had kindly come to the house to dress my hair. I just couldn't face going into town again like a normal day; how could life be normal when Paul was dead? It just seemed ridiculous. Cheekily, Jock came into the kitchen and asked if he could have a trim. When I was finished, I sat at the kitchen table with yet another tea and watched as Jock's hair was cut. At the end of his cut, the hairdresser asked Jock what products he used. For the first time, I felt a glimpse of real humour ripple across my face as Jock looked flummoxed. 'What are products?' Jock asked. I loved him even more than before.

Gaz arrived as planned with our driver and black limousine. Jock and Jimmy were making the final touches to the boys' ties and shoes, and then the five of us followed Gaz out to the car. Silently we took our places. It was less than a 15-minute drive to Sir John Moore Barracks. Passing through the gates, the gates I had driven through a million times since 1986, I felt tears pricking the back of my eyes. The security guard was dressed in his combats and boots, and I realised that I would never see Army combats drying on our washing line again. Nor would Paul's boots be stood on an open newspaper, covered in copious amounts of black Kiwi polish and 'elbow grease' ever again. In the blink of an eye, I had changed from Army wife to civilian. My entire adulthood had been ensconced within the military life. Endless tours where the men were away for 6 months at a time. Summer Balls, Christmas Balls, Ladies' Nights, Families' Days, Children's Parties, Wives' Club events, leave dates to look forward to, the next posting to prepare for, all gone overnight. I went to bed on 19th June 2007 the wife of an invincible warrior, a distinguished Major serving in the British Army and woke up a full-blown civvy. The life I had known for 22 years had changed forever on the 20th. No more postings, no more Wives' club events, my norm was blown out of the water.

As our driver pulled up outside of the Officer's Mess, I headed straight for the ladies' toilets. I needed to compose myself and reapply my mascara before I climbed the large staircase leading to the Mess bar, where my boys had been surrounded by Paul's well-meaning comrades. They looked like rabbits caught in headlights, but everyone's attention had turned towards me as soon as I had stepped into the room. A wave of love mixed with grief and compassion hit me full-on, but within minutes we were being guided gently back down to our car as Paul's hearse arrived. We exited the Mess to see an entourage of vehicles. Our car was now situated in a small convoy, headed by the hearse, containing Paul in his coffin, tightly wrapped in the Union Flag with his sword, cap and medals arranged on the top. Once again, our party of our two sons and Paul's loyal friends slid into the limousine, and we pulled away in silence.

We left the barracks for the last time together, so many memories. I smiled to myself at the thought of Paul, a fresh-faced serjeant, coming to my rescue at that first Ladies' Dinner Night, when the two belligerent wives had given me a dressing down in the ladies' toilets. And Christopher's baptism in the brand-new chapel as well as the traditional breakfast afterwards in the Serjeants Mess. We then drove down the Andover Road, past the spot where, pregnant with Christopher, I had run out of petrol, then run the battery dry, before Paul ran back to camp and commandeered a Land Rover to drive us to Romsey and captain Hampshire FC to victory. On into the city, through red lights, flanked by a Police motorcycle escort. In between the now constant narrative of 'Paul's dead' ran the question, 'What would Paul think of this? What on Earth would he think if he could see this?'

Our convoy of shiny black cars crawled around the city's one-way system leading into the Cathedral grounds. 1375 years old, it had borne witness to the full circle of life; in the year 1100 the funeral of King William II, and the coronations of King Henry and his Queen, Marguerite in 1172. The marriages of King Henry IV to Joanna of Navarre in 1403, and Queen Mary of England a.k.a Bloody Mary (the first Queen of England) to King Phillip II of Spain in 1554. I clung to Paul's beret, breathing his scent deeply, knowing I was going to have to leave it on the leather seat behind me when the time came to leave the safety of our car.

The blanket of bright green grass that normally hosted various picnics of summer students, shop assistants lunching and tourists soaking up the atmosphere was concealed by hundreds of people. I looked around the grounds and wondered why there were all these people, standing around, not walking, just staring. As the car turned, I was able to focus on some of the solemn faces watching us. We held hands and wrapped our arms around each other's shoulders. Then I recognised my fellow staff members and students from Peter Symonds, as well as Jake's tutor group. I asked Gaz 'What are all these people doing here?'. I couldn't quite make out his expression, for once he didn't have an answer. Then he exchanged a few words on his mobile and seemed to relax; 'They are here for you and the boys, to pay respects to Paul. The Cathedral is full and so they are standing in the grounds.' I looked at my boys, pale and staring out of their windows and muttered: 'It's OK. We are loved so much, they are here to give us strength'.

Our convoy slowly came to a stop at the West Door. In front of everyone, there was Alison. I looked into her eyes and saw the tears rolling down her cheeks, but she still steeled a smile and blew me a kiss. I looked over my shoulder at Jimmy and Jock and they gave me that imperceptible nod that I was quickly becoming familiar with. I took a deep breath and squeezed my darling boys' hands as the doors were opened. We withdrew ourselves from the protection of the limousine and into the waiting crowds. The press and TV reporters stood discretely behind a barrier, restrained by Police officers. We stood silently and watched as Paul's coffin was slowly and reverently lifted out of the hearse by a bearer party commanded by Serjeant Major Andy Batcock. My heart went out to him, how many times had he done this now and how much grief must he be holding in? He had known Paul since 1985 when they were stationed in Minden.

On top of the coffin lay Paul's sword, his medals and flat cap, which had been tacked down to prevent it from falling off should it be caught by a sudden gust of wind.

As the bearer party began to descend the stone steps into the cathedral ahead of Chris, Jake and I, the Regimental Bugler standing to attention to our left, lifted his bugle to his lips, and taking a deep breath, prepared himself to announce the arrival of Paul. Tradition demands the bugle call of the Officer Commanding Support Company is sounded ahead of his arrival. Historically used to communicate across long distances during the Peninsula Campaign, they were used to usher Wellington's skirmishers into battle or regulate rifle shots. It was the catalyst to the Regiment earning the accolade of 'Chosen Man'. However, as the Rifleman raised the bugle to his lips, his mouthpiece fell out and landed on the flagstones at our feet. He looked mortified, quickly picking it up and replacing it into the bugle, he stole a glance in my direction. Poor boy I thought, he looked so young to me. I smiled and nodded, 'It's OK' I whispered at him, as he completed the call perfectly.

Just as we began to enter the Cathedral, Paul's cap seemed to move and began to lift. Before anyone had the chance to arrest the fall, it fell at my feet. There was no wind, and Gaz, Jock, Jimmy and I looked at each other in disbelief, then one of the guards promptly stepped forward and replaced it back on top of his coffin. We followed slowly down the grey stone of the nave to the altar. All I could see was a sea of people filling the Cathedral. There was not a hair's breadth between them. Everyone seemed to be fixed on me, watching my every move, my every expression. I began to feel that chill in my bones. I searched for a distraction and chose to focus on Andy Batcock's broad shoulders. He sombrely steered the bearer party towards the altar. Each time he took a step, I took a short breath. Keeping time with his steps helped me remain composed.

We were seated at the front on the right, across the nave from HM Lord Lieutenant, the Mayor, High Sheriff and Lord and Lady Bramall. Behind us were all my family, Paul's family, and all our friends. I could almost hear every single heart breaking, and whispered sobs, yet still the words "Paul's dead" repeated inside my head. As planned, Nick Haddock delivered the Eulogy. He spoke eloquently and humorously about Paul, reflecting on the love we had for each other. Humbly, he described Paul as a soldier and friend, but most importantly he recounted the pride and deep affection he had for his boys. General Nick handed Christopher his father's sword, Jake his father's medals, and the Union Flag to me, as rehearsed. Together, we turned and followed Paul and his bearers retracing our steps towards the West Door, along the 170m long nave. This time, the walk seemed to take hours, not minutes. It gave me the space to study face after face as I passed the sea of pews. So many red eyes, so many grieving faces: 'My God' I thought, 'Paul, you were really something special.'

There seemed to be even more people in the Cathedral grounds as we emerged into the July sunlight. We slipped silently into our limousine for our final journey with Paul. The convoy wound its way out of the city, where shoppers and bystanders stopped what they were doing, stood still and paid their respects as we drove past. None of us talked. I think we were still blown away by the sheer number of people in the Cathedral and its grounds. They clearly wanted to pay their respects to a local fallen hero.

Paul's cremation was the opposite of his service. A very private affair with just our family, and close friends. Christopher and Jake had wanted to be bearers for their Dad, and so with 4 of Paul's closest friends, they carried his coffin from the hearse into the crematorium. I followed, placing my hand on the polished wood of Paul's coffin. My chest was full of agony caused by grief. I could not hold back the tears anymore. Seven years previously, I had done exactly the same for my late father. Standing in the crematorium, his loss came flooding back to me. After a short service, the red velvet curtains slowly closed around him, and he was gone.

I felt exhausted, the lack of sleep and trying to stay composed had left me feeling completely drained but there was one thing I was determined I wanted to do. I had told Gaz that I wanted to say a few words of thanks afterwards, to everyone, and he said it was probably best to do it in the Serjeants' Mess, after the food had been served in the Cookhouse (I had asked Gaz if we could put on a 'range stew' so that everyone could come together and share memories, and stories). We arrived back at Sir John Moore Barracks and entered to see hundreds of people. I knew that Paul was always a Rifleman in his heart, and he would have wanted every person showing their respects to feel welcome, whatever their rank or position. As we entered, the sea of people parted, and then enveloped us. The boys were surrounded by men, young and old, all showing them the love they held for their father. The stories of Paul and his remarkable career flowed from every corner. It was just the perfect outcome to the trauma of saying goodbye to him at the crematorium.

Once everyone had eaten, some people began to drift off. It was no surprise to see Paul's very oldest friends and comrades from Tidworth, Minden, Omagh and Cyprus moved back to the bar of the Serjeants Mess, so my family and friends went too. After a brandy for courage, order was called, and I took a few moments to try and explain just how appreciative I was of my family and friends, especially Jock and Debbie, Alison and Jimmy, and Jill. I described them as my guardian angels because that was exactly what they had been during the past 17 days. I then went on to thank Gaz for all his support and guidance, to which someone shouted, 'he's not here, he's sorting out the Cookhouse!'

'Well,' I thought to myself 'why am I not surprised?'. Gaz, never one to look for praise, knew my plan but was busy doing something necessary, no doubt. I found out later he was thanking the cooks and staff at the Cookhouse for their hard work and service.

By 5 pm I was feeling completely drained, and so Gaz drove me home, promising to get the boys back later. They were hanging out with the other youngsters, who were giving them comfort in their own way. The house was silent. I was home alone for the first time since that dreadful night when Pete Bullard knocked on my door at 2 am. I sat in the lounge and sobbed without holding back. I thought I would never stop. It felt good to just cry without worrying that someone would hear me, or that it would be pointless trying to comfort me, which in turn would make me feel worse if that were possible? I was at the kitchen window with a cold flannel to my face, I had become an expert at soothing swollen and sore eyes when I saw Gaz pull up, and the boys unwrapping their long legs from his car. I went to the door and saw Jake was carrying the large-framed image of his father that had been placed on the altar at the cathedral. He looked washed out. Behind him was Chris, supporting his brother with a hand in the small of Jake's back. Then both of them looked at my feet. Following their gaze I saw a large rectangular dish wrapped in aluminium foil just sitting on the top step. Picking it up, and waving Gaz off, I led Chris and Jake into the kitchen; we unwrapped the foil to find a piping hot lasagne. I never found out who left us that meal, but it was one of the most wonderful acts of kindness I have ever known.

The following morning, I was up at 5 am. I had hardly slept, spending the night between quietly crying into my pillow and ridiculously begging Paul to come back. Putting on my bathrobe, I stole a peek into the boys' rooms. Seeing them asleep, I crept downstairs and into the lounge. It was warm already as the sun again was rising against the back of our house, forcing me into another day, and later a dreaded night, without Paul. I opened up the French windows allowing the dogs (Monty and Bella) to roam the garden. I saw that Jake had propped the portrait of his Dad up against a table. I went to the other end of the lounge, away from the French doors, and sat down on the sofa. Bella ran in from the garden and sat upright beside me. Sitting on the rug with her chin resting on my knee, her eyes fixed on mine, it was as if she knew. As a Staffordshire Bull Terrier crossed with a German Shepherd, she was a large but incredibly gentle dog. But she had the habit of chasing every pigeon that ever dared to land on our lawn or patio. Looking at the portrait of my wonderful husband, I felt completely overwhelmed, and without thinking, said out loud; 'Paul, what will I do now?'. At that very moment, a small bird flew through the French windows and circled the room, before landing directly in front of me on the rug. Bella looked down at it, and then back at me. The three of us sat there for several seconds before the bird flew back out into the garden. I slid off the sofa and cuddled Bella tightly, not knowing what to think.

By lunchtime, my mother, sisters and the rest of my family had arrived. They had brought lunch and drinks with them but by mid-afternoon, I felt as if someone had pulled a plug and every drop of energy had drained from my body. I felt dreadful as everyone had travelled from afar, but the events of the past 18 days had caught up with me. I felt responsible for their pain in some way but knew that we were all helpless and just somehow, needed to just get through the following hours, days, weeks, months and years. They knew I was struggling and slipped away gracefully allowing me some time alone with Christopher and Jake, knowing the next day would bring a whole new challenge that I never thought would ever come.

Chapter Thirteen

The Regimental Family Gathers
Capt Garry McCarthy

The following day Pete Bullard and Andy Batcock had arrived in Winchester to walk through the funeral service. They would conduct a reconnaissance of every aspect of the Cathedral. Gate width, door height, number of steps, trip hazards. They would time the event and walk the routes, liaise with the Police, the council, and the MoD. There would be no blade of grass untrodden, no stone unturned, no risk of failure or embarrassment accepted. The funeral party would rehearse the event endlessly. They needed to learn the idiosyncrasies of the old church and condition themselves to be devoid of emotions on the day. This would be the third funeral in a very short period of time for Batty's team of pallbearers. In private, Batty shed his fair share of tears, as did several members of his party. Pete intuitively knew that, despite Batty's commitment and professionalism, for his own mental health he would need to franchise out funeral duties if the number of deaths continued at the current rate.

Prudence had me encouraging Paula, Christopher and Jake to conduct their own rehearsals. It was critical to condition themselves for the environment ahead of the service. We walked down the entrance steps and through the Cathedral's large oak doors. With each step, I explained what Pete and his team would be doing. Like the conductor of an orchestra, Pete would be queuing up VIPs to deliver readings and sequencing movements with surgical precision. We sat in the front row as rehearsals were conducted by several members of The Rifles family, including Lieutenant General Nick Parker.

As General Parker explained the procedures that the service would follow, I witnessed Paula at her mothering best. Amongst the debris of a catastrophic personal disaster, somehow, she had seen the imbalance of responsibilities divided between her children and immediately jumped in to restore parity. I pulled my sunglasses down over my eyes. Paula's words had torn me apart. A mother's love is unstoppable, irrepressible, unconditional and more powerful than any force known to man. Her desire to ensure Jake had a fair and equal part to play, a spiritual extension of Paul's memory had tipped me over the edge. My eyes filled, my oesophagus contracted, and I choked. Momentarily I thought the dark Oakley glasses would mask my lack of composure, then Jake, in all his innocence said.

'Gaz it's not sunny in here, why are you wearing your shades?'

On the morning of the 6th, we made our way to the Officers Mess, Sir John Moore Barracks. This would be our start point for the funeral. Experience had taught me that it was important to protect every precious memory held by the family. Their home was a sanctuary of pure memories. To bring the funeral cortege to the house would be to rewrite the history of the home forever. Every touchpoint that held memories of good times needed to be avoided when creating new events that would be remembered. Sir John Moore was the ideal venue. It was a place Paula knew well and felt safe in the surroundings, but she would never have to see it again after the day had finished.

Escorted to the Cathedral by Police outriders, the closer we got to the main entrance, the greater the number of mourners. The size of the crowd was phenomenal. It was like the whole of Winchester had turned out to pay their respects. Police on every corner, veterans filling the Cathedral grounds. I recall feeling cross that they were not seated before Paula, Christopher and Jake arrived. How rude! How dare they keep us waiting? I was a heartbeat away from shouting something at the top of my voice before I was told that the Cathedral was full, and the people standing around outside were those who could not fit inside.

We left the Cathedral one and a half hours later. The crowd had grown and once again, we were escorted by Police outriders. Totalling six, they remained with us and controlled the traffic all the way to the A303, en route to Basingstoke crematorium. Family and friends packed the chapel. Regimentally, it was a distinguished group of officers and soldiers: Bob Maddocks, Jimmy Mitchell, Steve Starky, Eddie Edwards and the world-famous SAS soldier, Andy McNab. Several people stood in the wings and watched as the heavy blood-red curtain closed on Paul's coffin.

Christopher and Jake held Paula tightly. Just the smallest evidence of a tear shed. It was impossible to understand how the three of them kept it together, whilst all around them grown men, hardened warriors, career soldiers and officers, were openly weeping. Eddie Edwards was known for his composure and calm demeanour, but even he struggled to contain his emotions. The tell-tale signs of blurry red eyes and a runny nose compromised everyone's disposition and yet, the day was nowhere near over.

We returned to Sir John Moore Barracks and assembled initially at the Cookhouse. In keeping with Paul's love for soldiering, Paula generously made provision for a hot meal for all, in the form of 'Range Stew'; the staple diet for soldiers whilst undertaking marksmanship training on the firing range, the all-in stew was loved and hated in equal measure. You loved it because the portions were always generous. You hated it because it was probably the messiest meal you would ever eat out of your mess tins.

The chefs had catered for 800 but estimated they had fed over 1000 people. The numbers were incredible. The support for the family was tangible. Everywhere I glanced, there was a veteran reminiscing and paying homage to soldiers past. For Christopher and Jake, it was an opportunity to reaffirm their friendships with Chloe, Zac, Bethany, and Stephanie, their closest of friends. For the briefest of moments, there was a respite from the emotional turmoil. Paula was surrounded literally by an army of supporters.

The sight of so many people rallying around the family was truly heart-warming and inspiring, but I knew tomorrow, it would all be gone. For everyone but the Hardings, life would return to how it was yesterday. Yet Paula, Christopher and Jake would still need to find the resilience and resolve to cope with their loss. The family would mask their pain, read the condolence letters, correspond with government agencies, and replace a life they had once planned to construct with an unwanted new beginning.

Then, at the Warrant Officer's and Serjeants Mess, by the kind permission of the Regimental Serjeant Major, the mourners gathered at the bar to reminisce and recall the life and friendship of Paul Harding. But for now, at least until the darkness fell, it was time to get Paula and the boys to take comfort from the love that filled the Serjeants Mess.

THE REGIMENTAL FAMILY GATHERS

Hundreds of people, stood side by side, acknowledging the remarkable life and achievements of a unique Rifleman. The love and support for the family was irrepressible. United in grief, unified in their love for a fallen Rifleman, it was so powerful you could feel it pulling you into a black hole of confused emotional entanglement.

As the afternoon turned into early evening, the need to make good our escape was signposted by the increased rate of beer flowing amongst the veterans and senior Riflemen. The funeral arrangements had been planned and executed by Pete Bullard faultlessly. He had orchestrated everything with perfect military precision on the back of delivering a similar operation in support of Corporal John Rigby's family. A true unsung hero, Pete was keeping rear operations running at full speed without missing a beat. Paula thought it was most important that, before we departed, we thanked him for his selfless commitment and dedication over the past two weeks. But Pete was nowhere to be found. He was not with his old comrades who had long since retired, nor was he with the pallbearers, or his support team. He was in the car park, on his duty mobile phone. Expressionless, deep in conversation, he turned his back to us the moment he caught my eye. I recognised his demeanour. The intensity in the concentration, meant only one thing. Colonel Patrick was on the phone, there had been another fatality.

Chapter Fourteen

The Epiphany
Mrs Paula Harding

Still unable to face the summer overtones emanating from the radio or television, fearful of hearing another news report from Iraq, the only sound came from the X-Box where Chris and Jake distracted themselves with mindless games. Normally, I would restrict their time on games by using a small Casio alarm clock, but now, I didn't care how long they sat on that sofa. It was the only means of diverting their attention from the grief we were all suffering. In the same vein, I thought I could do simple tasks to distract myself. But, inexplicably, clothes washing and housework took so much effort. During the easiest of tasks, I would cry silently the whole time. The relentless crying would cause disorientation and I couldn't remember where I was, or if I was at home or not. I could only recall constantly drying my eyes. No sooner had I composed myself, I would find myself sitting on the sofa staring at Paul's framed photograph, the one we used for his funeral service, and I would talk out loud to him. During one of these one-way 'conversations', I recounted the moment we entered the Cathedral, and the bugler dropped his mouthpiece, and Paul's hat fell to the floor. Perhaps I was reading too much into things by now, desperate to know if Paul was at peace somewhere, but the similarity between my entrance to our wedding, with my headdress being whisked off by a gust of wind as I entered the church and the music being stopped, really struck a chord with me. It was hard not to interpret this as some kind of secret celestial signal.

Astounding amounts of letters were still arriving every morning by the bundle. Our postman had now banded the letters into manageable sizes so he could squeeze them through the letterbox without delaying his round too much. The Monday after Paul's funeral, Chris had got up for a run for the first time. It never came into question that he would not be returning to Exeter University in the Autumn, having just completed his first year of a four-year Master's Degree in Civil Engineering. I knew he could not let this life-changing blow steer him off course, as he had been working so hard to get his career off to a good start. As captain of the Ninjitsu team, and sweeper in the mens' field hockey team, he needed to maintain his fitness. He had gathered up the post from the doormat and left it on the breakfast bar in the kitchen. Subsequently, Jake had come down and moved the letters to one side, to sit and have his cereal. I had eventually mustered myself from the bed, showered and made it downstairs. Still unable to eat, all I had managed to force down was a cup of milky sweet tea.

Standing at the breakfast bar, slowly sipping my drink, I began to sift through the envelopes, cautiously choosing a couple to open. The cards and letters were so moving, that reading them was emotionally exhausting. As painful as they were comforting, I would open one or two at a time, spreading them out throughout the day. As I sifted through, I came across a buff envelope, in black type. I read my name and full address. It looked like any other innocent correspondence. As I went to slide my finger into the corner of the seal, I felt pressure down the right side of my body. I froze. It was the strangest of feelings.

I was alone, and yet there was a physical presence of someone leaning over my shoulder, it was surreal. Trying to compute what this feeling was, a voice repeated in my head, 'don't open it'. Deep in grief, barely functioning and now trying to make sense of this bizarre experience, I cautiously opened the envelope. With my index finger and thumb, gingerly I eased the letter out a few inches. The words *'Your husband has been called a hero, but he is a murderer'* jumped off the page so I immediately pushed the letter back into the envelope. After everything I had been through, it wouldn't take much to tip me over the edge. And if that was the intent of the mindless idiot who sent it, he had failed dismally. I wasn't upset by it, I was furious!

Reaching for my mobile I rang Gaz to seek advice.

'Don't read anymore! I'm on my way' he said firmly. The noise of his motorbike seemed to fill our close in record quick time. Watching from the kitchen window, I saw him put his bike on the centre stand, pull off his crash hat and remove his jacket, as if ready for a fight all at the same time. Opening the door to him, I was shocked by his expression. A red mist had descended, and he hurried past me without formalities and straight into the kitchen. Picking the envelope up and pulling the letter out he read it quickly. 'It's written by an Arabic speaker. I can tell by the lack of vowels, and its structure. How much did you read?'

Not much I explained. Gaz took a long deep breath and fell silent. I could see he was composing himself.

'I'm OK Gaz, really. I feel sorry for someone who would spend their precious time writing hate letters to a grieving widow. They are to be pitied'.

Jake then came out of the snug realising Gaz was there, just as Chris returned from his run. Gaz reverted to his usual upbeat self and casually asked if either had touched the post? With all the skill of an accomplished Poker player hiding his hand, Gaz changed the subject and asked Chris how far he had run, and what game was Jake playing. Then as quickly as he arrived, he was gone.

Jock and Debbie continued to visit us most days. Their son Matthew and daughter Stephanie, were home from school and had become the main component of the support for my boys. The three boys would play golf while Steph buoyed them up with her antics and humour. A beautiful young lady inside and out, she would keep Jake busy by baking cakes and cycling around the village. Anything that kept the boys busy was heaven-sent. Just before Paul's deployment, Jake had sat at our dining table with Paul's military driver. Every company commander in charge of a fighting infantry unit has a nominated driver.

A lovely young man, he shared a coffee with Jake while Paul was getting ready to go out on an official engagement for the evening. The young soldier filled Jake with stories about how he kept ferrets and explained the joy they brought to his life. Jake had asked Paul if he could keep ferrets, but we just laughed and categorically said no! Now though things had changed, and when Gaz rang me asking permission to give my number out to Paul's old driver, who wanted to offer Jake a couple of ferrets, I agreed. So, my lovely vegetable patch was turned into an enormous ferret run, and two quickly became six as I would drive Jake around to various rescue centres to gather up the homeless. He named each of them after a character from Bernard Cornwell's 'Sharpe's Rifles' books, in honour of his Dad, and 'Sharpe' quickly became my favourite ferret. For the first time since the night that Pete came to call, I began to see Jake's eyes smile again.

THE EPIPHANY

One morning, shortly after I had received the strange letter, Gaz rang to say he would be picking us up later in the morning and taking us to Winchester Police Station. Everyone who had touched the envelope needed to be identified. Our fingerprints, along with Gaz's, needed to be taken so that the writer's prints could be isolated. So, for the first time in my life, I found myself in a Police station. What is more, we were led through the front door, past the custody Sergeant and into the detention area. As we filed past the open-bar cells with suspects urinating in the crude urinal, I shook my head and actually laughed. What would Paul be thinking if he were watching? Our escort ushered us into a small room, and as the boys were having their fingerprints taken, I noticed a strange look cross Gaz's face. I was beginning to understand Gaz. I could sense when there was unease, but this was a new expression that I couldn't read. He was seriously uncomfortable.

'What is it?' I whispered to him. With an awkward smile, he replied:

'I'm wondering if my past life in Liverpool is about to come back to haunt me'.

We both laughed out loud as the officer in charge of the proceedings gave us a look of confusion. A couple of weeks later I received another identical envelope, and as Gaz had instructed, I placed it into an evidence handling bag without touching it, and he duly came and collected it. By now, the C.I.D and a specialist Police unit in London were investigating other letters that families of the fallen were receiving. Not decrying the heart-wrenching pain these letters were causing to grieving parents, children and spouses, my way of coping was to make light of it. I was confident the authorities would not rest until they found the idiot who was sending them. Gaz would relay to me one day that, at the meetings with the CID in London, he was asked how I was coping. He took great pleasure in saying, 'Mrs Harding calls him her pen-pal, and in truth feels sorry for him'. Eventually, the letters were being intercepted by the Royal Mail and their source was located, only to find my pen-pal had fled to France, shortly before an arrest was scheduled.

As everyone who has lost a loved one knows, special days that mark a full circling of our sun are the hardest, especially the firsts. The first anniversary, and every anniversary thereafter. Birthdays and holidays are particularly difficult because the void left by the absence of that person seems to grow even more. It doesn't 'get easier over time'; that statement is wholeheartedly untrue. For us, Paul's birthday was the first of these dates we had to face. In anticipation of the emotional turbulence, Jock had taken the day off work, and come over with his children. Together we had all gone to a local wood for a dog walk. Whilst the kids messed around Jock and I reminisced about his and Paul's time in Germany, better known as 'Minden Days'. Their many trips with Jock on the back of Paul's bike. Weekends riding around Germany and the occasional trip back to Paul's parents in the UK for Christmas leave.

Just as we were meandering our way back to the cars, a whistle sounded, and I froze.

'It's Paul' I said out loud.

'What do you mean?' Jock asked.

'That's Paul's whistle for the dogs'. Just then Chris appeared through the trees and I heard him whistle three times. I burst into tears. Chris came running to me, followed by Monty and Bella at his heels. Grabbing and squeezing me to him he panted:

'What is it, Mum?' We stood still for several minutes as I explained how I had thought his whistle was his Dad. He pulled away, and although I was upset, I could see that he was secretly chuffed.

We returned home after picking up some bread and cheese for lunch and retired to the garden when the doorbell sounded. My guard was down and breaking with our established routine, I assured the boys and Jock that I was fine to answer the door. A stranger stood on the top flagstone of my doorsteps. Mid-thirties, neatly shaven and smartly dressed, he gave me a broad smile and introduced himself as a journalist from the Daily Express. Explaining how he understood it was Paul's birthday he asked if I had any comments about Paul's death and the subsequent deaths of British service personnel in Iraq and Afghanistan during the 7 weeks since his death. Stunned, shocked to the core, I closed the door. There are no words to describe the feeling of having a journalist doorstep a widow on the day of her husband's birthday to ask her how she feels about her husband's death. I turned around and Jock had sensed trouble. 'Who is it?' He asked.

'A journalist from the Express.' I explained. The same red mist I had seen descend on Gaz the morning I received my first letter from my pen-pal filled Jock's expression. He returned to the door and, to my surprise, politely explained we had no comment and requested the journalist to leave immediately. Jock had demonstrated amazing restraint. We all knew he was missing Paul desperately, and this incident could have ended badly. I doubt that reporter ever realised what a lucky man he was. Jock would happily be sent to jail defending the wellbeing of Paul's family, and had the journalist not made the right decision, the notion would surely have become a reality.

The day came to meet Gaz at Sir John Moore Barracks and receive Paul's possessions. Gaz had gathered all of Paul's personal belongings from his office in Bulford, and from his sleeping bunk in Iraq. The boys had gone to stay with Jock and Debbie so I could go alone and take my time. It was strange returning to the camp, seeing the soldiers in uniform, boots polished, flags flying and listening to the sound of drill square bashing. We went into one of the Quartermaster's stores where the boxes containing everything remaining of Paul's 31 years as a Rifleman sat. I'd lie if I didn't disclose a sense of trepidation at what lay inside, but as Gaz took the lids off the MFO boxes the smell of Paul emanated, along with that of shower gel, tiger-balm and boot polish. Everything was listed, and one by one I sifted through each item dividing them between things to keep, and things that held no emotional or tangible connection.

Mid-way through the second box, I came across his toiletries. Opening his wash bag, I felt a wave of nostalgia. The image of Paul in his skimpy running shorts, towel over shoulder and wash bag under his arm, flashed before me. I could visualise him walking with me to the shower blocks numerous times on our camping trips. Even his pencil case held memories. His writing pens and pencils and the little notes that the boys had written to him when they were very young, declarations of their love for him, and how much they were going to miss him. These notes dated back as far as Paul's deployments during the mid-'90s to Kosovo, Bosnia and Sierra Leone. It was heart-breaking to learn that he had kept them all.

To my amazement, I had kept it together, right up until we opened the bag containing Paul's wallet, rings and watch. The wallet had been a Christmas present one year from the boys. Years of being stuffed into the back pocket of his jeans had moulded the shape of the cards into the leather. Inside the wallet, I flicked through his everyday receipts. Amongst the petrol and milk receipts, I pulled out his driving licence and saw Paul looking straight at me. I began to feel that chill in my bones, despite it being a very hot day. I took a deep breath and put the licence back before placing Paul's wallet into my handbag. Then I took out his diver's watch. On the bezel, between two of the grooves was the smallest trace of blood; saying nothing to Gaz, it joined Paul's wallet in my bag. I removed Paul's gold signet ring that his parents had given him for his 21st birthday, and the wedding ring he had worn for over 20 years. There wasn't a scratch on either, they were highly polished, and looked like new. I looked at Gaz quizzically and he crouched down on his haunches and gently explained that they would have been 'cleaned up'. I knew immediately what he meant and said no more.

Calmly, I slipped them on my fingers for safekeeping. This was futile because of the size. They would just fall off. Even my thumb was nowhere big enough to keep either of them on, and then I remembered Paul's hands, so large and strong. I remembered when we were in Paris for Jake's 8th Birthday. We had gone to the Planet Hollywood restaurant for dinner. On the wall by the entrance were the hand imprints in cement, made by Sylvester Stallone and Arnold Schwarzenegger (the owners of the restaurant chain). Jake had begged Paul to put his hands in them and was thrilled when Paul's fitted Arnie's perfectly. So, Paul's rings joined his watch and wallet in my bag. In the months and years ahead, I would lie in bed trying to sleep clutching Paul's wedding ring on my right thumb.

By the end of August Paul's ashes were ready to be collected from the Crematorium. Gaz went to get them for me and held on to them until we were ready to do the scattering. The boys and I talked about where the best place would be to lay Paul's remains to rest. We had so many wonderful memories of places we had frequented during their childhood. Favourites like the Lakes, Fells, Moors and Cornish beaches were discussed. But we all felt we wanted him close enough to visit from time to time. Danebury Hill, 12 miles northwest of Winchester kept coming up in discussions. We each shared memories going back 15 years of sledging in the snow, kite flying, dog walking, basher building and mountain boarding with Paul. We decided that was the place. I also wanted our little ceremony to be done at sunset, so Gaz arranged for Paul's parents and his sister to meet us there along with the Padre from Bulford Camp. One beautiful, still, late summer's evening as we climbed the hill I worried about my father-in-law. He had suffered a heart attack when I was pregnant with Christopher. He was on various medications, and I wasn't sure how well he would cope with the incline.

Eventually, our little party successfully climbed the hill. We stopped at a tree I had chosen the day before whilst walking the dogs. The Padre said a few words, a blessing and finally, we said in unison the Lord's prayer, before each taking it in turns to hold the urn and sprinkle some of Paul's ashes at the foot of the tall and majestic beech tree. The sun began to set, and we slowly walked down to the car park in silence. The air stood still; birds paused their singing as if God had called the world to order. For what felt like an eternity, the world was eerily silent. Then like the gentle rumble of a thunderstorm rolling in from the sea, the unmistakable roar of a fast motorbike woke us from our slumber as it shot along the Stockbridge Road cutting through the fields of harvest. Rebellious, cheeky, full of energy and heading for a new adventure, it disappeared into the distance. We said our goodbyes at the car park and Gaz and I took the boys for supper in a pub in Stockbridge. There was a sense of relief around the table. Paul's father had made it without a hitch, and Paul was now laid to rest. Out of nowhere, Jake remarked *'that motorbike was perfectly timed'*, and we all grinned and agreed with him.

As days merged unremarkably into weeks, I had to get help from my GP. I still hadn't managed a night's sleep so she prescribed sleeping tablets, but I had to use them sparingly, and not on consecutive days. I could not describe how incredible it was to actually sleep. I would take one tablet and exactly half an hour later, I would be in a deep sleep that would last at least 8 hours. It was a much-needed respite from the constant earworm inside my head. The constant words 'Paul's dead' still tormented me. But the sleep came with a downside. Frightful dreams as realistic as life itself. I would dream that Paul had come home and joked that everyone thought he was dead, then I would wake with a start. It would take a few minutes to separate the dream from reality, and like a knife to the heart, it was like losing him all over again. Sleep was becoming a bittersweet interval in my journey through grief. I was stuck between three states of distress: disorientated through exhaustion, disorientated through induced sleep, disorientated through facing life without Paul.

Maybe I wasn't always thinking straight, or maybe I was thinking clearer than I give myself credit for. One night lying awake in bed, uninhibited and rested, I had talked myself into believing that the boys would be absolutely fine without me. Sitting with the strip of sleeping tablets in my hand, the route to being back with Paul was evident. I began to imagine taking them all. The joy of never waking up again, never going through the realisation that I was no longer a wife, but a widow. A vicious tug of war was going on in my head. The blues yelling, 'Come on! Just do it! The boys will survive, they'll have the house. You have got life insurance'. The red team screaming at me, 'Be realistic. The boys would be crushed, devastated'. At 2 am, the hour I had come to hate, I felt that I just couldn't deal with it anymore. There was no one I felt I could turn to, no one I wanted to burden with this. I looked up the number for the Samaritans, and rang them.

My call was answered immediately, and I sat in bed for over two hours talking openly with one of their call handlers. It was just what I needed. I poured out everything that had kept buried deep in my subconscious. I wasn't judged, patronised or rushed, just allowed to process and come to my own conclusion, to see realistically how my loss would impact my boys. I will always be grateful to the Samaritans, and their service. The skill they exercised to talk me 'back off the ledge' certainly saved my life.

Friends stepped up to the challenge of spending time with us, even when I was far from being good company. We spent a lovely few days with Nick Haddock and his family at their Welsh holiday cottage. In the peaceful idyllic settings of the Welsh mountains, we went on walks every day only accompanied by the sound of the babbling brooks and songbirds. The girls were great bakers and the boys helped by polishing off the cookies and cakes on offer. One day we packed a picnic and headed for the beach. It wasn't quite Cyprus, but when everyone went for a swim Nick stayed behind with me on the sand. Knowing how much I loved swimming I think he was surprised that I hadn't been one of the first in. Despite my call to the Samaritans and knowing in my heart of hearts I could never voluntarily leave the boys, I still had niggling doubts. Occasionally Blue Oyster Cult's' lyrics *'Baby take my hand, don't fear the reaper. We'll be able to fly, don't fear the reaper. Baby, I'm your man'* would

THE EPIPHANY

come back to me and I longed to be with Paul. When Nick asked why I wasn't going in, without thinking I replied,

'I can't trust myself'.

As I looked into his eyes, I instantly regretted what I had said. I saw his concern, trying to put him at ease, I assured him that I could never leave the boys.

Summer came to an end and Chris returned to Exeter. It was bloody hard letting him go, but I knew he had to return. There was some comfort knowing the quality of his friends, and Laura, who he would eventually marry, would be ever ready to provide support. Laura was his rock, making him eat, getting him to lectures when all he wanted to do was stay and grieve alone in his bed. He got back into his sport. The camaraderie in sport cannot be underestimated and I am sure this helped, despite several injuries including a smashed finger that he didn't tell me about until he had had the operation to fit a metal plate. He 'didn't want to worry me'. He continued with his driving lessons and to keep him focused, I had bought him a little run-around. He was determined to get his test out of the way and gain that independence of having his own transport. Gaz and I would pop down to see him in Exeter. Gaz enjoyed watching him play hockey. We would take him for a pizza, or we would meet with my sister and her husband. Chris had considered Durham and Aberdeen when choosing Universities, but I was so very grateful that he had decided upon Exeter to study for his Master's; it would have been very different if he hadn't been just 2 hours away.

At the same time, Jake returned to Peter Symonds College for the second year of his A-Levels. His tutors and teachers were simply amazing. They did everything conceivable to support him, to enable him to finish his education. Other friends continued to support us from near and far. My bridesmaid, Maria, was now Jake's Godmother; she came every Wednesday from her home, after work, often driving over one and a half hours. She would bring in a take-away, often a curry from Jake's favourite Bangladeshi restaurant. And my old friend, Jenny, would often come straight from work, despite being a busy GP, and cook for us. Jock, Debbie, Jill, Alison and Jimmy and many other friends constantly gave their time and energy, whether by phone or a loving message in a card, it meant so much knowing we were not forgotten.

In late September, Gaz popped in for a coffee and catch-up. I knew he was extremely busy with his job and other responsibilities, and his own family, and felt guilty at being a burden, but he always made me feel better for a visit. We had joined his family for a day at Centre Parcs, where Jayne, Gaz's wife, had booked me a full body massage in the spa. Gaz disappeared with the boys into the tropical water park, and I enjoyed the luxury of a few hours of solitude. The massage highlighted the number of knots of tension I was carrying, and as I relaxed completely tears just flowed silently down the sides of my face. I have no idea what the therapist must have thought. Kindly she said nothing and completed the massage. Leaving the spa, I had relaxed for the first time since Paul deployed and promptly purchased myself a membership to join a local hotel gym and spa.

During our catch-up, I thanked Gaz for everything he was still doing for us. He found it so hard not to cry when he replied, 'Look, Paula, I am only doing what I know Paul would do if it had been me. He would be stood in my kitchen, making sure my family were supported.' And reflecting on this after he left I had to agree. Paul truly cared for every man he served with, whatever rank they were. I remembered a time in Omagh: We had to collect our post from 'the post bunk' near the entrance to the camp. One morning, in the pouring rain, I had walked the half-hour it took to get there with a 3-year-old walking, and a 1-year-old in his buggy. I opened the door to the post bunk and the soldier sorting the mail looked up.

'Name?' He demanded,

'Harding, please.' I replied. He saw me struggling to get through the door with the buggy and reprimanded me.

'Don't bring that in here, it's dripping wet!' Taken aback by his attitude, I leaned over the buggy to pick up the post he had left for me. Looking at it I realised I hadn't given Paul's name or rank, and the post he had sorted for me was for Lance Corporal Harding.

'Excuse me,' I said. Clearly unimpressed by me still being there, he replied; 'yes what is it now?'

'This is the wrong Harding'. The man looked aghast.

'Is your husband Serjeant Major Harding?' I looked him in the eye and replied a simple 'Yes'. His demeanour changed immediately and apologising, he opened the door and helped me in with the buggy. I told him to just give me my post and left. On my route home, I passed Paul's office and he popped his head out of the window to say hello. I explained what had just happened, and he was furious:

'I'm not having families discriminated against because of rank!' Reaching for his beret he quickly appeared at the door and exited in the direction I had come from. Watching his back as he strode off, I didn't envy the man who had just served me. Paul would have been upset by the tone taken by the soldier issuing the mail, but above all, he would have been angered by the prejudice on display. Paul never believed in people being 'superior' because of rank. A Rifleman is a Rifleman, all are equal in love, war and yes, even the post bunk.

Joining the local hotel gym and spa proved so therapeutic for both Jake and me. Jake had a weekly session with an ex-soldier, now the gym's Personal Trainer. Jake threw himself into the fitness programme, whilst I mostly swam and enjoyed massages, but it was good to be doing something together, and physical. After several weeks of eating out on the way home, or picking up takeaways, Jake said 'I miss your cooking'. Those four words hit home. For weeks now we had been eating rubbish. Deliveries, microwave meals, junk food or at the hotel. That night, I sat down and wrote a meal plan and shopping list. This meant I would have to venture back out into the public gaze, and shop at Sainsbury's. I wore dark glasses, terrified that someone would recognise me, or worse still approach me, and start a conversation. There was no way I was ready for that. Thankfully I completed my first foray without crossing paths with anyone I knew. Like an athlete who had completed an ultra-marathon, when I returned with my shopping, I was exhausted. I collapsed on the sofa, drained of every ounce of energy. I knew I had to be 'Mum' again. Develop a new sense of normality, create a new normal for us.

Paul had been taking Jake to PADI diving lessons down in Havant. Paul always had a passion for the sport and when Jake intimated his interest, Paul was keen to support him. When Gaz found out that Jake had the equipment, and that I was trying to still take him to lessons, he got in touch with an old Regimental buddy, who was a Dive Master. Explaining who Jake was and that he was training for his Rescue Divers qualification, Gaz's friend immediately offered to help. Gaz and I drove Jake up to Blackpool to Paul's old battalion, 1RGJ (now 2 RIFLES). Jake stayed with the Dive Master's family and subsequently qualified as a basic sports diver. It was another example of the wider love and support Paul's friends and colleagues were demonstrating. Paul would have been so proud of Jake. He had faced the bitter cold in pursuit of sport, lived with total strangers and loved every minute of it. His confidence grew and grew and the start of his transformation from a boy into a young man was complete.

After the October half-term break, I found the courage to return to Peter Symonds for work. I really wanted to try to go back to work. I had enjoyed my role there, but it was intense and testing. I threw everything at it in a hope that I could regain some of what I had lost, but by the end of the first morning, I knew it was going to be too much. My students had such complex needs, and my emotional reserves were spent. I knew I wasn't up to meeting their needs. I was still struggling to meet my own, it just wouldn't be fair on the students or my team. Sadly, I had to resign. Searching for a crumb of comfort in my disappointment, it brought me to realise the strength of character required to keep going. And whilst on this occasion, I couldn't find it, my sons had. They had found their inner resilience to keep going, to get up each day and try harder, and my admiration for them grew even more.

Gaz continued to stay in close contact with Chris and would come up with activities to do with Jake. Despite the 'beastings' Jake would get from his Personal Trainer, he still had a lot of energy. Like most young men of his age, he was hungry for excitement and the dare-devil streak deep inside him needed to be satisfied. He began to talk about getting a motorbike, which put the fear of God into me. In recent years our Parish had lost two young men to motorbike collisions, and I couldn't bear the thought of anything happening to Jake. Near us, however, there was a motor cross track, a very large semi-professional circuit where competitions were held, but on other days anyone could book a space and ride for a small fee. So I explained to Jake that I would support him in this pursuit if it was off-road biking for the time being at least. It was a perfect distraction for him. Gaz would come over and take Jake and his bike on its trailer down to the track where Jake would let off steam. He was a natural but had no fear, which was always a concern. Getting the balance right is difficult even when everything is perfect, but he had to do something and at least this was contained, I knew where he was.

Our next-door neighbours were especially keen to help Jake stay positive. The Dad was a Director at SanDisk, and when he found out about Jake's interest in photography, and that he was a qualified

PADI diver, he invited Jake to accompany him in November to the Annual SanDisk Underwater Photography Competition, in the Red Sea. It was an incredible experience for Jake. They flew to Tel Aviv, and Neill drove them by jeep down to Eilat. The following week Jake got to dive with professional and semi-professional underwater photographers. He would call me from his hotel room, full of the tales of big fish and deep dives. I couldn't have been happier for him. The week culminated in a spectacular award ceremony, where on a huge screen, they displayed photographs that had impressed the judges during the week. The images were chosen anonymously. So, when I found out that one of Jake's photographs had been chosen for the display, I was incredibly proud, but even more appreciative of the support from my friends.

Every silver lining frames a cloud and for us, there was a tsunami of emotional turbulence slap bang in the middle of it. As Jake returned from Eilat, closely followed by Chris returning from Uni for his Christmas break, 4 RIFLES were recovering from the worst fighting and losses of the Iraq War. A service of thanksgiving for those who returned, and remembrance for those who had not, would be taking place in early December. My heart sank when Gaz told me it would be taking place at Winchester Cathedral, although it made perfect sense. In the year before, on Saturday 8th July 2006, 2RGJ exercised their Freedom of the City in Winchester where Paul, as Officer Commanding B Company had, with absolute pride, led his Riflemen of all ranks on parade through the historic home of The Royal Green Jackets. Crowds lined the streets in the sunshine for what was a poignant day for the Riflemen. Veterans and dignitaries from around the globe gathered as it was the last parade before the Regiment merged with the Light Infantry, the Devon & Dorset Regiment, and the RGBW to form The Rifles. As 4 RIFLES had been formed from 2RGJ, they had inherited that freedom, and as the City had paid their respects at the loss of one of their own, it was only right and fitting that the same people would want to welcome the battalion home.

But personally, for myself, my sons, my family and friends it was excruciatingly painful. We should have been ecstatic at the safe return of Paul, along with all the other families. Instead, it felt like they were opening up a large raw wound that was in the very first stages of blood coagulating, pouring boxes of sea salt into it, and giving it a good rub. On one hand, and it goes without saying, I was relieved that the battalion had returned, and the majority of our families were welcoming their warriors home for Christmas. On the other, I longed to be one of those families with every fibre of my body.

The week before the service I decided I was going into town to choose a new dress for it; I wanted to make Paul proud of me, to be strong in front of his men. For a short while, I wandered meaninglessly around the high street stores of Winchester, before stumbling upon a suitable outfit in a large department store. The young pretty assistant smiled at me as she was wrapping the dress, and then she asked; 'was it a wedding I was attending?' It felt like my purpose on Earth had just ended. The blood drained from my body, and a fog descended around me as I walked away from the till. 'Paul's dead' was screaming inside my head. I could feel my heart pounding harder and harder, my chest was fighting to prevent it from breaking out between my ribs. Flashing images of Paul in the sangar, lying in rest at the funeral home, ready to be cremated in his coffin, tipped me over the edge.

For the first time in my life, I started to panic. I hadn't walked more than ten yards from the till before I dropped to the floor, and scrambled under a circular rail of dresses and matching coats. I curled into a ball, confused, and disoriented. I could have been under the clothes rail for five minutes, or five hours, it is impossible to say. I was emotionally lost, struggling to regain my grip on reality when the mobile vibrated in my purse. Pressing the green button, I heard Gaz's voice.

'How you doing mate?' I heard his scouse accent ask.

My instinct was to affirm that I was fine, everything was OK. In my head I thought:

'*You are OK! Pull yourself together and get back to the car.*' But realistically, I recognised the danger I was in. '*I couldn't drive in this state, my head spinning viciously out of control.*'

My response was organic:

'I'm crashing Gaz! I am hiding under a clothes rail in the high street, too scared to go down to the car park'.

I heard a sharp intake of breath, and then Gaz replied:

'Don't move! Stay right there! I am at the museum, will be with you in 5.'

Curling up into the foetal position, I concentrated on breathing slowly, until I heard Gaz arrive, whispering:

'Mate, come on out. It's all OK. I've got the car outside.'

I crawled out from under the clothes rail, still clutching my new dress and I followed Gaz to his car.

The following week Gaz expertly guided us through the whole experience, arranging cars to collect us, Jock and Debbie accompanied the boys, my mother and myself.

At all these public events people try their best to say the right things. You are angry if they don't try, and angry when they do. Some people say the stupidest of things with good intentions, like *'I know what you're going through, I once lost a dog'*. Or *'I know what you're going through, my husband left me for another woman'*. Such remarks arrive unsolicited, and it's difficult to manage a response. As we stood around in a side room, where senior officers and dignitaries mingled with each other, and the families of the dead and injured, I was stunned when one of the other company commanders' wives, who I had only briefly met at the Mess Christmas party, in 2006, approached me and remarked how well I looked, and how much weight I had lost. Patrick Sanders swiftly stepped in and eloquently changed the subject, as he ushered me towards another group gathered holding cups of tea or coffee. I heard her husband berating her for such a faux pas. I was pleased to be rescued by Patrick, but strangely I felt sorry for her. She probably blurted it out not knowing what else to say, trying innocently to be supportive.

Paul and I had booked a holiday for his Christmas leave. We had liked the idea of somewhere hot and chilled. Golden sands, private beaches, chilled wine and a laid-back atmosphere. Barbados or the Dominican Republic were high on my list. But now we were facing Christmas without Paul. Worse still, the beginning of a new year, another first, and one that he would never be a part of. A few days after the Cathedral service, I decided to go into the independent travel shop in Winchester and gather brochures to get ideas for a holiday, somewhere as 'least-Christmassy' as possible. We needed to escape, to fly away from the cold of England, to find the warmth and relaxation on our own. Rest and recuperation, or R&R as the army would call it. Paul had visited Kenya twice on exercise. He had always said it was somewhere we would go together, and do a safari. Then, one night having one of my one-way conversations with him, I decided that was going to be our destination. So, I returned to the agent and booked a fortnight away for the boys and me. We would fly out on the 16th December, Terminal 4, Heathrow to Nairobi, then catch an internal flight to Mombasa. I had booked an all-inclusive stunning beach resort, with a 3-day safari in the Tsavo West National Park. Just for good measure, the boys would take a scuba diving trip on a traditional dhow. It sounded a perfect escape for us, and Gaz agreed having been to Kenya with Paul in 1998. Coincidentally he had friends there who would take Jake diving.

On the morning of the 16th, Nick took us to Heathrow, and we checked our luggage in just as a snowstorm hit London. Flight after flight on the departure board flagged up the dreaded CANCELLED sign. Remarkably our British Airways flight continued to show, and to our utter relief, it then flagged up GO TO DEPARTURE GATE. Hardly believing our luck, the boys and I walked to the gate and boarded without a hitch. Apparently only long-haul British Airways flights took off that night. The heat hit us immediately the aircraft doors were opened. It felt good to be totally anonymous. The war in Iraq was of no interest to the Kenyans, so we were unlikely to encounter the subject for the next two weeks. The transfer to Mombasa went smoothly and we were met at Moi International Airport by the hotel's driver and minivan. The 45-minute drive to the hotel was interesting, to say the least. The dual carriageway narrowed to a single track that wound its way through the town. Slow-moving trucks, overladen with goods roped down, were being overtaken by frustrated drivers at every opportunity, passing each other by the slimmest of margins.

Our driver was cautious but ignored the unmarked speed bumps, which made for a painful experience at times. The town was heaving with people, shops and market stalls, all of which were squeezed in together along the sidewalks. Children, goats and chickens roamed freely. Jake had brought the camera Paul had bought him for his A-Level photography course, and he was enjoying snapping away at anything that moved. Chris then pointed out the billboards positioned on every possible wall advertising the candidates for the up-coming Presidential elections to be held on 27th December, the day after Boxing Day. I acknowledged him, but to be honest I had little interest.

After four nights of relaxing by the pool and acclimatising a little, we were picked up early on the 21st and taken to a hotel at a watering hole in the National Park. The scenery was breath-taking, it was just as Paul had described after his trip. The bright red tracks, bushy topped trees, and tall golden-sun-bleached grass, it resembled a scene from the Lion King. Our Safari guide knew exactly where to find the big game. The thrill of sneaking up on a pride of lions was intoxicating. Each day was packed with magnificent sightings and better yet, the nights were peaceful and trouble-free. When I closed my eyes, my thoughts drifted gently into a slide show of Paul. The albums of his photos, the collection of wooden animals dotted around our home, and the random souvenirs of his times here. It was comforting to see my boys smiling and captivated by this new experience. Returning to our hotel on Christmas Eve, driving through Mombasa, things felt very different. There had been a change in the atmospherics. Call it a mother's intuition, or as Gaz would say *'spider-senses'*, there seemed to be much less activity. Paul had taught me much during our life together. In Northern Ireland, he taught me to identify the presence of the abnormal, and the absence of the normal. They were both an indication of trouble, and what I was seeing in Mombasa was the latter of the two. No children, very few women and crowds of men on street corners. In my naivety, I presumed this was how Christmas looks in Kenya, it is after all 90% Christian.

When we checked into our hotel, we decided to switch off our mobiles and try to ignore the fact that it was Christmas. We had 8 days left and wanted to immerse ourselves in each other's company. But trying to forget it was Christmas was impossible. Relaxing by the pool, the boys sipping ice-cold Tusker beer while I indulged in several mojitos, every hour, on the hour, a full 40-strong brass band of Kenyan Santas, white beards and all, paraded through the gardens playing Christmas carols. I don't know if it was the good food, the alcohol, the surreal setting we found ourselves in, or perhaps a combination of all the above and just being together without any interruptions, but I felt a slight reprieve from the constant ache in my chest. We had also made friends with another family staying at the hotel, a Mum, grandmother and two girls, roughly the age of my boys, and in *'it's a small world after all'* way, they came from Salisbury, and the girls went to the same school as Jenny's two sons.

The elections took place on the 27th and the following day we were collected by our tour operator and taken to the docks where we boarded a beautiful 120ft dhow. We sailed to a local reef where we anchored, and the boys had a day of diving. I got talking to a crewman, who spoke perfect English. He explained that there was deep unrest in the country due to the elections. He, as did many others, believed that the elections were rigged and the ascendency of former President Kibaki was the result of electoral manipulation. As interesting as this was, I didn't think any more of it, until over the next 48 hours the tension among hotel staff became palpable. I had come to recognise several of the serving staff in the restaurants. One young waitress explained people were becoming increasingly agitated and violent, so the hotel owners had allowed staff to bring their families into the safety of the hotel compound. The resort had increased its guard force and heightened their posture. The men guarding the entrance and beaches were armed with bows and arrows. As primitive as it may have looked, it was effective. Our wine waiter then explained that all Kenyans carried a tribal identity card. Now, during election tensions, gangs of men had begun roaming Mombasa, looking for rival tribesmen, and attacking them. The boys went back to the poolside after supper, but I went to the main lounge and joined other guests to watch the CNN news, and watch the horror that was unfolding around Kenya. This was now deadly serious. I returned to my room and powered up my mobile. As soon as I switched it on countless texts pinged in, as well as missed calls, and messages from my family and friends. Several were from Gaz. I thought 'shit! Where do I begin?'

We were due to fly out the following evening, and so spend the New Year in the air, hopefully asleep. It was a deliberate ploy to travel through the arrival of the New Year and ignore the pain of not having Paul with us. But Gaz had been doing some digging and had found that our flights were most likely going to be cancelled due to the riots and attacks happening in the city. Kibaki had been sworn in as President, and his opponent, Odinga, encouraged supporters to engage in mass protest. In addition to staging several non-violent protests, opposition supporters went on a violent rampage killing Kikuyus, the tribe to which Kibaki belonged to. In Mombasa, the Kenyan coastal residents took to the streets to protest and support their preferred candidate, Odinga. Tensions rose as the landless indigenous coastal communities felt this was a time to avenge the grabbing of their land by the Kikuyu. Looting was now out of control and the authorities were swamped as stores in Mombasa were ransacked.

THE EPIPHANY

Trying to stay calm and think straight I returned Gaz's call. He answered in less than one ring. He had been unable to get through to the hotel and was clearly keen to ascertain that we were safe. He asked me to go to Reception and extend our booking past the 31st. Gaz needed more time to engage with UK authorities in Kenya and ensure our departure was safe. I duly carried out his instructions but it was explained to me by the concierge that there would be 'no room at the inn', as they were fully booked. Calling Gaz back, he emphatically insisted, making me promise that I would not leave the hotel, even if it meant sleeping on the floor of the lounge. It was at this point I realised this was even more serious than I initially feared. I explained about our friends we had made from Wiltshire, another Mum, granny and the girls, and how they had the same flights booked as us. He responded, 'find them Paula, and tell them the same, I will sort something out'. The following day, the 31st, we were packed and bags deposited in Reception, and ensconced by the pool when a member of the concierge's team came walking around with a sign and calling out 'message for Mrs Harding'. I was to go to the Reception, only to find the Mum from Salisbury there too.

We were told that a bus was going to take us to one of the company's other hotels, less than half a mile away, and to gather the rest of our party together. I returned to the pool and saw I had a missed call from Gaz. Taking a breath to tell him the latest, I was taken aback when I discovered that it was Gaz who had instructed the concierge to get us to a safer location. We were to move to the other hotel and stay there until further instructions. So, the seven of us were transferred half a mile down the road in broad daylight. I recognised this situation from all my time spent in Northern Ireland. These were 'special measures', UK agencies implementing pre-planned evacuation operations dreamt up for just such an occasion. The short trip to our new resort was telling. The streets were empty, but there was no hiding the evidence of riots and civil disturbance.

We booked into our new rooms and were given complimentary tickets to the hotel's New Years' Eve party. Inwardly, I groaned. This wasn't the plan. I wanted to be in the air and out the way at midnight, to forget the whole event. However, my boys were 17 and 19, and despite the circumstances, and quite understandably, both were keen to go to the party. We joined our friends at the lavishly decorated garden dinner. The entertainment was most African, circus acts, singers and dancers that wouldn't look out of place at a show in Las Vegas. Despite the spectacular scenario, I was really struggling. Feigning fatigue, I excused myself with the assurance that Chris and Jake would stay with our friends and be back in their room by 1 am, as we were expecting further instructions from Gaz. I went back to my room and as the fireworks exploded and the partygoers cheered, I lay in bed and sobbed. Why had this happened to us? I was full of grief. I hated the arrival of the New Year without Paul. At 2 am my phone buzzed, a text from Gaz. 'Get everyone together in the hotel lobby for 4 am. You will be picked up from there and escorted to the airport'. I texted Chris and the other Mum, both replied, and I snatched the briefest of sleep until my alarm sounded at 3.30 am.

Arriving in the lobby we all looked exhausted, but the boys had enjoyed a good time. Still high on the euphoria of the party, they giggled as they recalled the size of the bows carried by the guards securing the beach and gardens during the party. I felt very uneasy by the need for armed guards, but said nothing. Seconds later the Reception doors slid open and in stepped a Kenyan soldier. His bow and arrow looked suspiciously like an AK47! Fear and trepidation subsided as he offered the broadest of smiles, and in the deepest of voices boomed; 'Mrs Harding?'

'Yes.' I replied.

'Are all seven of your party here?'

'Yes'. I replied again.

'Then we shall go!'

We didn't need a second invitation. Grabbing our bags we followed him aboard a small bus with its engine still running. We acknowledged two more soldiers seated on the far side of the eighteen-seater cab. They looked less friendly as they nervously fiddled with the gadgets fixed to their rifles. We were told to sit in silence as we pulled away through the darkness and out of the hotel grounds. The streets were totally different from the previous sunny afternoon. Dozens of men lined the side-walks. As we meandered through Mombasa, the many dozens had turned into many hundreds. Some carried clubs, others carried machetes. Rows of men lay face down along the sidewalks. Tightly packed and hands behind their backs, it was hard to fathom out what they were doing. At first, I thought they were sleeping, but in hindsight, the truth was much more sinister.

THE EPIPHANY

In silence we sat as the bus drove through the town's outskirts, passing the shacks and mud huts. The further we drove, the smaller the groups of men. Eventually, the streets were empty. We merged onto the dual carriageway, and the soldier driving put his foot down; we started to gain real speed. I was just checking that the boys had their seat belts on when I saw a huge truck coming into my peripheral vision on our outside. Turning to get a better look, I saw that on the flatbed lorry was human cargo. Penned in by a flimsy side rail, at a conservative guess, maybe 50-60 men, faces glinting in the moonlight. I could see this was a violent mob. They were equipped with every primitive weapon conceivable, from axes to machetes.

As the truck drew closer and parallel to us, a man was leaning out of the cab window, gesticulating to our driver. Flaying his arms wildly, it was clear he wanted us to pull over. I looked at Chris and Jake, and then to the soldier who had met us in the lobby, he just smiled back at me and gave a nod to the two other soldiers in the back with us. Simultaneously they slid open their windows. Barrels first, they raised their AK47s into the aim. Immediately the truck slowed, and we pulled away. Eventually, the truck's two small lights disappeared into the distance. Making it to Moi International Airport in less than 30 minutes, the relief that flooded over me as we passed the entrance gates was intense. The soldier in charge stood up and gave us another huge smile. He looked around and seemed totally relaxed, before helping us out with our luggage. AK47 in one hand, my suitcase in the other, he raised his head and addressed us all.

'I hope you have all had a good holiday in Kenya?' He said in his own style of English.

'Yes. Lovely, thank you. And thank you for the lift!' I replied without hesitation, feeling a little imperialistic, and inconvenienced by the whole affair.

The rest of our journey was mercifully uneventful. Nick picked us up from Heathrow, and Gaz had tracked us all the way through what I now realised had been a hard extraction. But he too was clearly pleased to see us back in Blighty. It wasn't until I caught up with the news over the next week that I learnt of the dreadful violence that ripped through Kenya that New Year. The violence started with the murder of over 50 unarmed Kikuyu women and children, some as young as a one-month-old. They had locked them in a church before burning them alive in Kiambaa village, just on the outskirts of Eldoret Town. Kofi Annan arrived in the country about a month after the election, and successfully brought the two sides to the negotiating table.

Kibaki and Odinga signed a power-sharing agreement, but the cost of the crisis had totalled 1,500 deaths and the displacement of 600,000 Kenyan people. We were fortunate to have escaped unscathed. Once the full facts of our predicament were understood, I dwelt on the fragility of life. I thought endlessly of the children burning to death in the church. Mothers, fathers, brothers and sisters all robbed of their precious lives. So sobering had the experience been that it delivered my life's one and only epiphany. Yesterday I contemplated suicide, but having nearly had my life stolen, I valued it more now than ever. There would be no more self-pity, I could never be so indulgent again.

In 1998 Paul and I had competed in the famous original extreme race, 'Tough Guy'. Allegedly the world's most demanding one-day survival ordeal, it was first staged in 1987. The Tough Guy Challenge was described as "the toughest race in the world", with up to one-third of the starters failing to finish in any given year. Taking place on the last Sunday in January, so it could capitalise on freezing winter conditions, the Tough Guy race is staged over a continuous obstacle course stretching more than nine miles. Starting with a cross-country run, it included one kilometre of fifty-metre slalom runs up and down a muddy hill, then into a sequence of brutal physical challenges. These included deep trenches filled with ice-cold water, log jumps, aerial ropeways and military-style assault courses. Electric fences, stinging nettle walkways, and burning hay fields. It claimed to be tougher than any other publicly accessible worldwide race, a claim that had regularly been affirmed. If you overcame the freezing water pools, fire pits, rope bridges and cargo nets, including a hundred-metre crawl through flooded tunnels, balancing planks across a fire pit, and a half-mile wade through chest-deep muddy water, the race organisers would invent other ways to break your resolve.

There are many high timber towers to climb, the tallest of which is thirty metres high, and known as 'The Brandenburg Gate'. Marshals, dressed as warriors, drive amphibious tanks and fire blank bullets from randomly scattered cannons, as well as exploding flares and smoke bombs over the heads of competitors. Paul assured me that he and his team of fellow Riflemen from 2RGJ would wait for me. Of course, I didn't believe a word of it, and as the starting gun sounded, I wasn't surprised to see the backs of 8 men dressed in green sweatshirts emblazoned with the Green Jacket cap badge disappear into the distance. I stoically plodded on making friends along the way until finally crossing the finishing line an hour after Paul and the others had showered and changed into dry clothes. They were all there to clap and cheer me through, it was an experience I loved to reminisce about, but I had hated every minute. Then in September that year, I had also joined Paul competing in the London Triathlon. Unlike Paul, I spent far too long drying and talking between stages, and didn't fall in love with the sport.

The boys had often sifted through Paul's photos and medals and I wasn't really surprised when Chris asked us to sign his entry form for the January 2005 Tough Guy race. He needed parental permission, not only to enter but to have an Exeat Pass from school. Of course, Paul was fully supportive, and Chris did remarkably well. So that only left Jake to complete the race and prior to Paul's Iraq departure, Jake had asked his Dad to complete the Tough Guy challenge with him in January 2008. Paul was chuffed to pieces and completed the application straight away. Shortly after his death, Paul's application was answered. His and Jake's race numbers arrived in the post, both enclosed with their joining instructions. Jake was gutted. He had been so looking forward to doing the event with Paul, and he couldn't do it alone as rules state the need to be accompanied by someone over 18. The race was to take place three weeks after our return from Kenya, and Jake was feeling so down about not doing it with Paul. But Chris called from Exeter and said;

'I've been in touch with the Tough Guy organisers and explained the situation. They have changed Dad's number to my name, so we are going to do it together Jake'.

It was a brilliant idea and when we told Gaz he suggested asking for sponsorship from the battalion. After the race, Jake was able to present a cheque for a substantial sum to the Regiment's own charity 'Care 4 Casualties.'

The tidal wave of events and presentations continued. At his home in Amsterdam, an up-and-coming filmmaker and artist, Steve McQueen, was posting his tax return when he noticed the stamp on the envelope had a portrait of Vincent van Gough. The idea of using a stamp came to him: 'A stamp has a beautiful scale, the proportions are right, the image,

TRIBUTE TO A HERO

it is recognisable, and then it goes out into the world, who knows where. Perfect. Wonderful'. McQueen said.

When McQueen approached the Ministry of Defence for support, his suggestion was declined fearing it too sensitive. His idea was to immortalise soldiers, sailors and airmen of the Iraq War. The concept was simple. McQueen wished to turn the picture used by the MoD to officially announce the death of one of its members and turn it into a stamp. Undeterred by the abstention of the MoD, his researcher contacted the families of service personnel who died during the campaign and requested the use of their original photograph. Including myself, a total of ninety-eight endorsed his idea. McQueen designed sheets of stamps, each one containing hundreds of individual stamps of one who had been lost. Printed in the margin of each stamp, is the name, regiment, age and date of death of the individual.

Despite several government departments fearing public reprisals, the concept won widespread support from families, and a war-weary public. The art installation went on display at the Imperial War Museum (IWM) and Gaz escorted us to a private viewing for the families. With so many bereaved families in one place, you would have expected an air of doom and gloom. But so tasteful and respectful was the exhibition that you couldn't help but be impressed by this homage to our brave servicemen and women.

Standing with Gaz, I surveyed the other families. Knowing their pain, and the courage it would have taken to visit the IWM for this opening, I felt humbled as we all paid homage to those we had lost. I received our invitation through the post. Previously, Steve's PA had called and explained his work in detail. Now looking at the stamp on the envelope, I imagined letters falling through the millions of letter boxes across the world. On doormats and hall floors everywhere would be the face of a stranger who had given their life for our freedom and values. What an amazing concept Steve McQueen had thought of. Christopher and Jake were fully behind the project, and seeing that they could each invite a guest they asked to take Jock's daughter Steph, and Jill's son Zac, who were both still at school at the Duke of York's in Dover. Permission was granted by the school, and we met Steph and Zac at St Pancras Station. Gaz thought it a good experience for Jake to drive us up there. He had called in a favour, and we were able to park up in Chelsea Barracks, meet the kids and head over to the IWM.

THE EPIPHANY

So, as I said, I found myself gazing around the room with dozens of people, drawn here by the loss of their treasured son, daughter, wife, husband, father, mother, strangers, all knowing the same agony of a breaking heart. I caught Gaz looking at me, and he mouthed *'you OK?'* I gave a quick nod, and pulling my coat around me, I could feel that familiar chill creeping into my bones. Gaz knew I was beginning to struggle.

'So guys, what do you think Steve McQueen will look like then?' Gaz said to distract us from the emotional pain. Chris, Jake, Zac and Steph turned to look at him.

'Do any of us know anything about him?'

We all shook our heads. So Gaz continued, bar of chocolate for the person who gets closest.

'I think he will be like the Marquess of Bath, larger than life, eccentric with gaudy clothing.' He then worked his way around each of us, and we came up with our own imaginings. Chris alluded to McQueen the actor, laughing that he may arrive on a motorbike. Steph described a middle-aged man, dressed in hippy clothes, just back from Glastonbury. Zac shrugged, grinned that same grin Larry had and said: 'He could be Chinese?' And then it was Jake's turn:

'I think he is a tall black man.' And at that point, an announcement was made that Steve had arrived. It was perfect timing. We turned and fixed our eyes on the artist for the first time. Our mouths fell open as a tall, good-looking, well-dressed black man entered the reception. Every eye of our little party turned and gave Jake a quizzical look.

'I promise I didn't know,' he retorted,

'But, I'll have a Galaxy bar please Gaz'.

If it wasn't a national entity wanting to pay tribute to Paul, it was a local one. The Army Cadet Force wanted to name a trophy after him, the Infantry Squash Club, the Regimental football team, it seemed never-ending. So many people wanted to commemorate Paul in some way or another, from a sports trophy to park benches; it was humbling. Gaz seemed less enthused. He explained that whilst it was flattering, anything we agreed to had to have longevity. Something invented and then forgotten a few years down the line would do more harm than good. Every agreement had to survive the boys and their children, and in time connect all of us with these memorials. It had not crossed my mind to question someone's desire to honour Paul's name and protect his reputation and memory. So, when my Parish Councillor wrote to me in conjunction with the Royal British Legion, explaining that they intended to add Paul's Rank and Name along with 'Iraq 2007' to the parish war memorial in Sutton Scotney, I had already made up my mind how this should be done.

The war memorial standing in the heart of the village is unique, made in stone in the form of a three-sided closed lantern and mounted on a white stone plinth. The column stands on a six-sided stone base that bears the inscription and names of the fallen. It only bears the names of 48 men, all of whom hail from the parish and died during World War I, including brothers from the families; Wren, Baverstock, Butler, Parfitt, Rawlings, Purver, Woodward and Suckling. Higher up on the memorial, a further eleven names have been added of those who made the ultimate sacrifice fighting in World War II.

On 7th March 2008, Paul had been Mentioned in Despatches for Gallantry and Bravery in the Face of the Enemy. It is the oldest recognition in the institution of gallantry awards, and Paul had won it for his actions whilst in command of the PJCC when it had been attacked by over 200 militia in May 2007, I wanted 'MiD' to be added after Paul's name, but the council refused for reasons I did not understand. I discussed this with Gaz and he felt the same, so I replied to the council and explained my disappointment, if they were not prepared to acknowledge his MiD, I could not consent to his name being recorded on the memorial.

I understood those who felt I was being pedantic, but the memorial acknowledges the bravery awards of others. I was resolute that the same respect should be afforded to Paul. This honour is given at the behest of Her Majesty the Queen. It reflects her gratitude to his commitment, and it meant everything to the boys and myself. As Gaz had warned me, if we were not careful, Paul's name would be diluted into obscurity. I wanted all future generations of the Harding family to see MiD engraved next to Paul's name, and to know that he died protecting the vulnerable, and freeing the oppressed. His brave actions must never be forgotten. Thankfully the council agreed, and six weeks later on a warm summer's day, I sat on the grass and watched with pride as the stonemason carved Paul's name.

Chapter Fifteen

It Feels Like Yesterday
Major Garry McCarthy

There was much investment required in my own household, an absent father since 2003. If it hadn't been Iraq, it was Kosovo. I had not spent more than 48 hours at home since 2002. Three operational deployments in three years had taken a toll on my family. Never had their support diminished, nor had they questioned my priorities, despite there being just cause. Still, the events of the previous sixteen days replayed through the MAXI cinema located in my deep subconscious. I dwelt on the pain being suffered by Christopher and Jake. I feared for Paula and how she would provide for the boys. And as strange as it sounds, my sympathies went out to the battalion in Iraq, from the Commanding Officer to the newest Rifleman. I knew their pain so very well, and while the situation in Iraq continued to deteriorate, much worse was to come. Like all soldiers, I wanted to be there with them, to share the burden, to fight the most evil of enemies.

Monday morning ushered in a feeling of dread. Work had been piling up and despite spending most of the weekend sitting at the kitchen table attempting a regain, I had achieved next to nothing. Fatigued, and spoiling for a fight, I decided to ride my Kawasaki Ninja to Bulford Camp. The bike afforded me just a hint of pleasure ahead of another difficult day at work. As a young soldier, I would see the old LE officers wandering around camp looking miserable as sin. Never smiling and always grumpy, I thought they were just born that way. It had taken nearly thirty years to understand why, but now, here I was, feeling exactly the same way. I felt like I was carrying the weight of the world on my shoulders. As a priority, my Visiting Officer reports needed to be produced. Consequently, I was facing a marathon session of writing. Each meeting with Paula was recorded and summarised for Brigade Headquarters, and JCCC. The reports would help the compassionate system understand the needs of the family and track problems in a hope that they could find solutions, before they ran out of control. But with seven very busy days to report on, the door of my office remained closed until just gone 1000 hrs.

My mobile phone vibrated uncontrollably as the Iraq international number flashed brightly on the LED screen. Colour Serjeant Taff Evans greeted me from Basra. He was providing the logistical support for B Company, but was due to be replaced in the next few days before coming to work with me. Taff was a positive character, always full of cheek and wit, but very capable and highly respected. A career soldier without being over-ambitious, he was liked by everyone he served with. We chatted briefly about his forthcoming appointment before the conversation switched to the recent fighting. His voice lost tempo, his delivery was intermittent. He was one of a group of SNCOs, all of whom were known to be hard as nails. Along with Colin Nuffer, Lee Roberts and Gaz Case, Taff was keeping everyone's fighting spirits high. It was a tough ask given the recent high levels of attrition.

The attack sirens sounded, and Taff hung up. It was confirmation that life in Iraq was truly unpleasant. Hearing the haunting sound of the siren bouncing off the walls in Saddam's Southern Provincial Palace transported me right back to Iraq in the blink of an eye. It was a base I had visited often. The Shat Al Arab ran the full length of the eastern flank which limited entry and exit points. Worse still, the only route to the Palace was through a densely populated city full of *'rat runs and through shoots'* as Jez Cooper, a fellow Rifleman, would say. There was no tactical advantage in its location, it was little more than a very well-built landlocked version of Alcatraz. On more than one occasion, I nearly lost my life at the Palace. Recalling those near misses had me fixed in a trance. Sitting at my desk, thoughts erratically jumping between, 'then and now' I could feel myself slipping into a black hole. The walls of my office seemed to close in, and the morning light faded. Like clinging to the edge of a virtual whirlpool, the feeling of being sucked under by an unstoppable power was gnawing at my mind. Had it not been for my phone once again vibrating uncontrollably on the hard surface of my desk, I would have disappeared into an abyss. I was even more relieved to discover a chirpy colleague on the other end, keen to talk football and take my mind off the day that lay ahead, albeit one stuck in the office until 2000 hrs.

The following day, I returned to see the Hardings, and check on their wellbeing. The house was now empty of visitors. Jimmy Mitch and his wonderful wife Alison had returned Hertfordshire. The unbelievably strong Jill and her children had travelled back up north, and Jock and Debbie had to get back to work. Now more than ever, this was where the support needed to kick in. From the 1000 or so supporters of last week, Paula was left with just me. It was something that I feared. Once the chairs and tables were empty, she would descend into a trance-like pitiful state similar to Ms Steel. But, Christopher and Jake had different ideas. If ever there was an example of two young boys becoming young gentlemen overnight, this was it. They had set out several achievements that needed to be attained in order to keep their lives moving forward in a positive nature.

Driving licence, dog walking, summer jobs, new hobbies and charities; their plans were grand, spectacular and ambitious. More importantly, they were spread out over a long period of time, purposely always giving them something to look forward to. If there was one thing clear to me now that the crowds had gone, I would need to give equal attention to the boys. Both Jimmy Mitch and Jock would endeavour to fill the parental void left by Paul, but for two busy family men, it would not be an easy task. Where possible, I would breach the gap and try to bring the fun and excitement to their lives, if for nothing more than to bring about a small distraction to their pain.

One week after the funeral, I accompanied Paula to the solicitor's office to finalise the issue of probate. The complex issue proved too much for the pair of us, and kindly SSAFA (the Soldiers, Sailors, Air Force Association) provided an expert to help us achieve the release of the estate. A day later, Paul's personal belongings had arrived back in the UK from Iraq and needed to be returned to Paula's care. Two large boxes and a number of large luggage bags contained all of Paul's belongings that had been either in his office at Bulford, or with him in the PJCC.

After thirty years in the Army, I had packed up the personal effects of fifty soldiers or more. The majority of these soldiers had been AWOL before ending up in jail, and subsequently dishonourably discharged, others were hospitalised never to return, and some sadly died whilst serving. I had counselled my fair share of parents, spouses, sisters and brothers alike. I had learned that no two events were the same. If a soldier died wearing his own clothes, the next of kin may wish to have the clothes returned. They are emotionally and spiritually connected to the deceased. The smells, the sweat stains, the history, the deep memories of certain items often become the abiding memory for relatives to hold on to. But do you wash them first, or leave them as they were found, possibly soaked in blood? Some next of kin wanted a 'warts-and-all' service, others wanted nothing back. 'I just want my son back', they would say. But keeping with the philosophy of protecting the happy memories of the home, the action of reintroducing Paula to Paul's personal belongings would be choreographed on neutral ground.

The Quartermaster of Army Training Regiment Winchester (Sir John Moore Barracks) kindly agreed to give me the use of his transit storeroom so that Paula could sift through Paul's belongings, and decide what she wished to keep. The Quartermaster would then dispose of everything else respectfully. Knowing how painful this was going to be for the whole family, we chose to do it on a day when Christopher and Jake were busy. This would allow Paula the space to grieve openly without fear of upsetting her children. As protocol demanded, every item had been logged and accounted for by an office, each item described in detail, documented and recorded in the inventory to prevent fraud or theft. Meticulously, these items would be numbered and placed in a specific box, the whole process referred to as two-five-three-ing. (The military number for the inventory form MoD F253).

In the empty storeroom, with two large cardboard MFO boxes and three extra-large black canvas bags, Paula and I sat on two hardback plastic chairs ready to begin. Wringing her hands, the strain and anxiety suppressed, Paula watched as the seal was broken on the first box. Instantly the natural and cosmetic smells from Paul's sports shirts leapt out and filled the room. I recognised that smell at once. It's the sweat and deodorant smell you get in a sports changing room. The mature lingering smell of physical exertion with just the faintest whiff of Ralgex. Sitting at the top of the box was an array of Regimental T-Shirts and running tops. Anticipating Paula to wobble or burst into tears, I paused and watched her closely. A smile warmed our mood, as she pulled a T-Shirt to her cheek, and took a large breath.

The smallest of tears fell and splashed on the dry flap at the end of the box. A sharp intake of breath and Paula reached into the box and grabbed the letters she had sent to Paul. Letting out a huge laugh she exclaimed, I hope no one has read these. She laughed loudly again as the letters were shuffled between her fingers. Oh good, she said, holding up a Father's Day card Christopher had sent. It had been a concern for Christopher, he was desperately keen to know if Paul had received the card telling him he was the greatest Dad of all time. Training shoes, civilian clothes, belts, electrical items were all slowly placed in one of two piles: Pile one, take home. Pile two, leave here.

At the top of the second box was a clear plastic envelope with the top section covered by a white panel used for writing information on it. From experience, I knew this contained Paul's items he had on his body when he was killed. Inside the envelope were his wedding ring, watch and wallet. Paula inspected the ring before clutching it tightly to her chest. With unbelievable strength, she said nothing as she reached back into the box to pull out the next item. The sight of the wedding ring had tipped me over the edge, and for a moment I stood up and feigned cramp. I needed to turn away, to grip myself. The pain of watching this wonderful lady sort through the belongings of a Regimental legend, an inspirational leader, mentor and true gentleman, was a pain too hard for me to conceal.

With the last of the items being lifted out of the box, it had been a miracle Paula had not broken down. She had sifted through the memories of her life; all contained in two cardboard boxes, and somehow kept her composure. At the bottom of the second box, the last few items were retrieved - a towel with Chelsea FC emblazoned on the front, and a pencil case. I felt so relieved that it wasn't something with greater emotional attributes, like a family photograph, a teddy bear or sweetheart keepsake. But Paula's mood dipped as she held the pencil case. It was old and a little tatty, the Chelsea logo still visible despite its age. Slowly drawing back the zip, she looked inside to see the coloured pens and pencils every officer carries to mark his maps and write his orders. Stored with all the attention to detail of a craftsman, they lay peacefully in a logical order, for the reasons only a soldier would understand. *'He's had this since he was a corporal. All these pens and pencils went everywhere with him. Ireland, Bosnia, Iraq the first time'.*

Maybe it was the accumulated pain of the past three weeks. Maybe it was the history contained within the pencil case, or a delayed reaction from seeing the wedding ring and watch, but it was the first time Paula cried openly in front of me. The pain emanated from everywhere as she clutched the pencil case and wedding ring with several T-Shirts folded neatly on her lap. Slowly, she regained her composure, typically apologising for any discomfort she may have caused me. There was no hiding place for either of us. We sat silently amongst the remnants of Paul's life. There was nothing to be said. There was nothing anyone could say. No accolade, no wise words crafted into a poignant poem, no crowd of 1000 men would help ease the pain felt by Paula as we walked out holding just a small bag of items that she wished to keep. Along with other items too sentimental to throw away, they would be boxed up and locked away in the loft forevermore.

The following day, as I was passing through Winchester, I had called in to check on Paula. Spirits were high as Jake had discovered a love for ferrets & polecats. Jock had arrived to help Jake build an elaborate cage and play park for the small pack of animals. Dayglow tubes ran around the garden with ferrets scampering through them, climbing poles crisscrossed the cage and occasionally, a fight would break out inside the cage. The once tidy garden had been turned into a menagerie, cats, dogs, birds and now ferrets and polecats. The joy this was bringing to the home was palpable. Paul loved dogs, Paula and the boys loved all animals, and at this moment in time, it was a pleasant distraction.

But Jake was growing up quickly. He was at that age where he would demand a large degree of freedom to explore beyond the parental boundaries and school restrictions. It was clear to everyone that the route to independence was through learning to drive. For a young person to have the ability to escape the critical eye of parents and teachers alike, is to discover a whole new world. As a child, I was too keen to bridge these boundaries, but I knew the need was all-powerful. For the next few months, it became the main effort. We had to gift Jake the ability to get away from it all, to find his own space, to give him a focus that teased him with excitement. So, along with his regular driving lessons, I took a detour on the way home or sneaked an extended lunch break to teach him to drive.

He was a model student. He loved driving which made it easy for me and we shared a passion for cars. Paul had taught him the fundamentals on the open expanses of military training camps, all I needed to do was teach him to watch out for the other lunatics on the roads. With every session, he grew in confidence. Paula had bought him a small Renault Clio and the date for his test was fixed. In typical military fashion, we rehearsed the routes, and we invested many hours practising the most likely scenarios to ensure success on the day. During our last session, Jake drove perfectly. His confidence was high, his morale soaring. It could not have gone any better and quietly we were all confident that the gift of a driving licence would help Jake manage his pain with greater maturity.

On the morning of his test, I watched my phone impatiently, desperate for a confirmation of his pass. Ten minutes before he was due to start, Paula's number flashed on my screen. She was borderline hysterical. I could hear the anger and tears raining down on the phone. In the background, Jake too was angry and upset. The test centre had cancelled his test because of a vehicle technicality. The Clio was listed as a vehicle not suited for examinations due to a faulty bonnet catch, and without a safety certificate, the driving official cancelled the test. There was no way the examiner would have known the extent of misery his decision would inflict on Jake. But this was a disaster for Paula and Jake. I could feel the pair of them spiralling out of control, being drowned by the nonsensical decision of the test centre.

Jimmy Mitch and Alison jumped into their car and drove from Kent to Winchester to rally around Jake. By the time I had made it to Winchester, there was calm descending, but the anger still simmered. Amongst the obvious collateral damage, there was an overwhelming sense of love and support for Jake and Paula. Not being allowed to take a driving test may have sounded trivial, but to a teenager desperate for independence, it was the end of the world. My only thought was to keep Jake occupied, and together we agreed we would increase the amount of time we went out driving.

Although it would not change a thing, and the DVLA would have taken what they thought were appropriate measures, I felt the need to write and express my disappointment at the lack of emotional intelligence they had displayed. They would never respond, but it made me feel so much better. We set about keeping Jake busy while a second date was confirmed. In truth, this may have been a blessing in disguise. Those closest to the Hardings demonstrated their enduring support, but Jake had developed another layer of resilience, something that he would draw on many times in the coming years. In times of disappointment, it is critical to find a pick-me-up and for us, it was a trip to the Top Gear show in London. Christopher came along for the ride, and the two brothers loved every moment of the wacky behaviour of Clarkson, May and the short bloke.

A week later, Jake passed his test and started work with a local business. Christopher had returned to Exeter University, and Paula was able to draw her breath. She knew the next shock on the horizon was simmering, the return home of the battalion. There would be parades, celebrations, news stories and every media outlet would be filled with wives and kids hugging their returning heroes. Inevitably, those Riflemen who had not had the opportunity to express their condolence would wish to visit Paula, including the Commanding Officer, Patrick Sanders. There could be no denying the love and support each visitor wished to convey, but the emotional drain this was taking could not be allowed to continue. There was no policy or procedure to stem the onslaught of people turning up on the doorstep, or calling Paula.

The system needed to change. Helping to support the families of those servicemen and women who die wearing Her Majesty's uniform had improved beyond recognition, but there was still so much to learn. I found myself discussing improvements with the Brigade Headquarters, and eventually helped them revolutionise the way we prepare ourselves to deal with families after serious injuries and fatalities of any nature. That moment was the forward edge of significant change everywhere. The British Army had begun its withdrawal from Iraq and the Commanding Officer, along with his principal staff, would be leaving 4 RIFLES. With each change there was a small piece of Paul's life taken with them, until less than six months after the battalion had returned, there was hardly anyone left to recount the events of that fateful night.

As Patrick Sanders departed, the new Commanding Officer called into my office to introduce himself. He had seen the latest round of promotions and appointments and knew I was to be promoted to the rank of major, and imminently about to be installed as his Quartermaster. He had intimate knowledge of the support we were providing to the families of all those killed or injured in Iraq. The first question he asked was, 'How are the Hardings?' His understanding of what they were going through needed no explanation. For the briefest of moments, I explained the challenges faced by Christopher and Jake.

'Remind me please Gaz, how old they are?', he asked.

'Nineteen and seventeen. How old were you when your father died?', I replied.

'Gaz, I was thirteen, but it feels like yesterday.'

It was the most concise and accurate description of loss I would ever hear. The notion that time is a great healer is utter rubbish. The pain for the boys would be as great next year as it was on the day they were told.

The boys had met the new CO 4 RIFLES a few weeks previously at the Regimental Headquarters, in the former Peninsula Barracks, Winchester. Both Christopher and Jake had taken part in the annual Tough Guy endurance race to raise money for the Regiment's 'Care 4 Casualties' charity. Having raised a substantial amount of much-needed cash, they handed over a cheque to retired Lieutenant Colonel John Poole-Warren, the first Regimental Secretary of The Rifles. Both young men stood steadfast, vehemently proud of their father, and everything he stood for. In the background, a host of serving Riflemen, proud of Christopher and Jake, watched on in admiration of their resilience.

The promotion to Quartermaster 4 RIFLES increased my workload, but it did allow me to continue to provide support for Christopher and Jake. We charted the hurdles that needed to be cleared as both boys shaped their futures. Christopher's path was all but decided having already invested so much time studying engineering. He had found his soul mate whilst studying at university. Laura was very pretty and incredibly talented. It was evident to anyone who spent time in their company that they were deeply devoted to each other, and the conditions for a happy life together were set. Jake was still too young to be bogged down with thoughts of love or careers. Although he had matured quicker than any young boy should ever need to, he was yet to experience the carefree life, independence, and the occasional flirtation with adventure most associated with our teens. For Jake, this arrived in the form of motocross. It was great fun taking him to and from the track with the bike trailer hooked up to my car.

Late autumn, as we pulled up outside the house to offload the bike and trailer, Paul's BMW K100RS sat under its cover. Jake had been keeping it running for his Dad, but it was no substitution for regular use. Every day the bike sat idle, it brought emotional pain to the family. It was too valuable to give away and too sentimental to sell, but we needed to address the issue. In the weeks ahead, I would fail to find the answer until a chance encounter with Captain Bernie Bambury at a Regimental function. Bernie was on the road to recovery after a horrendous accident whilst tobogganing down the Cresta Run in St Moritz, Switzerland. There was never any doubt in anyone's mind that Bernie was a born warrior, a true gentleman, and as brave as they come. But after surgeons had reattached his leg, he had been faced with one of the most difficult decisions you could face as a human being. Living with the leg attached meant suffering pain for eternity. The alternative, agree to a surgical amputation. Bernie had chosen the hardest route to recovery.

Despite his own challenges, he was only interested in the Hardings, and how they were coping. For twenty minutes we chatted about Christopher and Jake. Bernie was like a sponge, he listened intently to the developments and probable outcomes. Occasionally, he would regurgitate a story about Paul and the part he had played in the development of the young officers within the Regiment. He recalled Paul's crazy moustache, his incredible athleticism, and his love of motorbikes. Again, Bernie listened attentively whilst I explained that Paul's own motorbike had us facing a tough emotional conundrum. Bernie nodded and acknowledged the need to find someone who understood the importance of the bike's destiny. The bike represented much more than an inanimate object; it was a family member. A few seconds later he declared that he would like to offer the bike a loving home, and wrote a cheque for Paula.

It was just one of many extraordinary demonstrations of the respect and love shown to Paula and the boys in the months after Paul's death. The Infantry Squash Association named a trophy after Paul, and The Rifles introduced the Harding Cane, to be carried by the best Junior Commander of 4 RIFLES. By the end of the first year, invitations were beginning to mount up and Paula, Chris and Jake shared the attendances. Humbling and inspiring in equal measure, each time we attended an event, we would listen to senior officers heap praise upon Paul's heroics, and admiration for Paula's fortitude. It was a pattern that we would follow for the next four years; if Paula couldn't attend an event, she would invite Chris or Jake to attend as well as Paul's parents.

Between the family, they had supported the military with every request. Intuitively, Paula, Chris and Jake knew the importance of demonstrating their resilience. The Riflemen from Paul's company needed the emotional comfort of seeing his family remain strong and committed. They were unequivocally inspirational to those young men struggling to come to terms with the violent nature of their combat experiences. Seeing the families of the fallen and knowing they were coping with their loss, helped returning Riflemen face their demons and take solace in the company of bereaved mothers, fathers, wives and siblings.

Except for the Inquest, Paula and the boys had not declined an invitation. But for Paula, the Inquest held little importance. It would not bring Paul back. Nor would it shed any more light on what she already knew. So, on behalf of the family, I attended as the representative of the Harding family. It was made slightly less uncomfortable for me because I knew all the witnesses very well. I listened to Colin Nuffer describe how he had tried in vain to bring Paul back to life after the attack. Despite knowing Paul had died instantly, it didn't stop him from trying everything he knew to reverse the damage. Colin had been involved in more than his fair share of battles with the enemy. Like Lee Roberts, John Allan, Danny McCrieth and Gaz Case, he was one of a very special group of steely-eyed Warrant Officer's who never accepted defeat. Risking his life to try and save a company commander didn't need a second thought. Not that he knew it was Paul who had been hit, Colin had fought his way to the outpost knowing someone would have been in there moments before it was blown up, and if he was still alive, Colin was going to be the man who kept him alive.

The day before the inquest we had been warned to expect anti-war demonstrations and media attention. It was not uncommon to encounter protestors at such events, and on this occasion, I had prepared a statement on behalf of the family. It read:

Major Harding gave his life to the service of his country. He spent a lifetime freeing the oppressed, rescuing the enslaved, protecting the victims of ethnic cleansing and tyranny. He believed that every man and woman should be free to live in peace. To live without persecution, without fear, to embrace diversity and tolerance. You may be surprised to learn that he would encourage the freedom to protest, and support peaceful disagreement. For it is thanks to his sacrifice that we are all gifted the right to exercise these freedoms. We are free to do so because he and many of his fellow Riflemen have volunteered to protect the democratic rights of the people who reside in our great country. The nation is lesser for his loss, but more resilient because of it. You are welcome to disagree, to challenge authority, to do nothing or do everything. And whilst there will be those who disagree with the Army's involvement in liberating Iraq, rejoice in your freedom to express your disapproval, for it's this freedom Major Harding has died to protect. These are freedoms, less than fifty percent of the world can enjoy, so please know, they do not come cheaply.

This profound statement was written with the knowledge that the nation we had grown up in had lost sight of its core values. As a child, the gratitude shown to our servicemen was not reserved for one day a year, it was noted daily. Reminding people of the price paid for freedom was part of our staple diet. We were but a few precious days away from being overrun by the might of German armed forces. Had this happened there would be no diversity, no free speech, no Muslim, Jewish or Hindu communities, just oppressive blandness. Now values are lost in the wash of fake news and distorted truths, by whoever has the most followers on social media platforms, perversely the dawning of a new type of battleground.

Always conscious that both Chris and Jake had an eye for adventure, the week following the inquest, I decided to take both of them out for some fun. The winter had brought heavy rain and Salisbury Plain had flooded, bringing a swift halt to all movement across the training area. All except the driver training ground. This allowed me to take both the boys out driving to teach them the finer skills of handling vehicles in difficult conditions. It's a skill all drivers should develop and one I enjoyed teaching. To lose Christopher or Jake in a road traffic accident was unthinkable, prudence pushed me to ensure that both boys were well versed with extreme road conditions so they may be prepared for life on the open roads.

Borrowing a mean-looking black Mitsubishi 4x4 Barbarian, we drove the off-road route of the Tidworth driving circuit. Christopher was the first to try the obstacle course. Deep mud ruts, ploughed fields and shingle tracks gave him every experience he most likely would encounter. He learnt to steer into the error, drift, and control the spins. At the end of the route, he faced a knife-edge, a slow climb to the top, and an even slower climb over the edge. Once he had crested the knife-edge the deep ruts had dragged him to the very edge of a precipice. Perilously we teetered on the edge as I tried to coach him out of the predicament. But it was no use, the danger of rolling was increasing. Jake was leaning to one side to prevent us from toppling and Chris invited me to take his place in the driving seat. It was only by the grace of God that we got out of the predicament. But he was not dissuaded. Once at the bottom of the hill, Chris resumed control. His next obstacle, the water hole. At full speed, we hit the water. Revs high, wheels spinning out of control, we forged our way to the other side with the bow wave riding over the roof.

Jake's turn. A natural at getting the vehicle in and out of trouble, he pushed the vehicle harder. Slightly younger and less fearful, the grin on his face spoke volumes. He was better prepared for the knife-edge and as scary as it was, he guided the Barbarian over the edge as if he had been doing it all his life. At the base of the hill, he paused and shifted the drive from low ratio to high. Foot to the floor, he attacked the large water hole. The thick brown sludge instantly rolled up over the bonnet and onto the roof. He had somehow found a deeper section than Christopher had. The water threatened to breach the doors. The mud too was thicker and sucked at the wheels with greater ferocity. 'Keep going! Keep going!', I shouted at Jake. But the pull of the mud was too much. We came to a grinding halt in the centre of the water pool. It was about sixty-foot square and four foot deep.

I was in deep water, and not just physically. If I had to call for recovery, I would be reprimanded for unauthorised use of the driving track. Worse still, if the water breached the cab or engine compartment, I would be facing a huge bill. Jake and I swapped seats. I rocked the car forward and backwards hoping the wheels would gain traction. Reverse gear, first gear. Ten minutes later, we were still stuck. If I had to get out of the vehicle it would need to be through the sunroof. To open the door would be to fill the car with water. I pulled out my mobile phone to call for assistance, but there was no signal and now it was getting dark. I was truly in deep trouble. One last time, I thought. Forward-backwards,

TRIBUTE TO A HERO

forward-backwards. Then just when I was thinking of jumping out through the sunroof and calling for help, there was a hint of grip. Then a bit more and more. Suddenly lots more. With the engine screaming and the steering wheel gripped so hard my knuckles turned white, the car dragged itself to safety. At the edge of the water, I looked back to see the size of the wake we left. A huge sigh showed my extreme relief, to which Christopher commented: 'It was never in doubt'. The dry wit was so like his father.

The boys and I would continue to do random stuff together. Jimmy Mitch and Jock Fleming would also look for ways to keep the pair engaged and distracted. For Christopher, life was busy enough as he approached the end of University, but Jake was still searching for a vocation. The thought of him joining the military was too scary to entertain, but he wanted to contribute to the well-being and safety of society and perhaps there would be no avoiding some kind of service. Maybe the Police service we thought? As luck would have it, my friend was a traffic cop working the A303 which ran past Jake's door, so I arranged a ride-along. This would meet his needs. Fast cars and public service. It would be genius if it came off.

For me, a deployment to Afghanistan was days away. Having watched Christopher and Jake both make unbelievable progress in their lives since their father had died, leaving them for six months was a little worrying. I had always been able to drop things at work and help them fix issues since the loss of Paul, but now I would be locked into a combat theatre and not allowed out. It had dawned on me that Paula too would be feeling anxious as she saw the battalion once again head off to war. The week before I departed there was one more official visit that needed to take place. Her Majesty The Queen had commissioned a medal to be issued to the nearest relative of those servicemen and women who had died serving their country. Paula would be one of the early recipients. The medal known as the Elizabeth Cross would carry Paul's details struck into the heart of the cross on the rear. It would only be issued by a representative of the Royal Family. As luck would have it, I would return in time to see the Duchess of Cornwall present Paula with her Elizabeth Cross.

Chapter Sixteen

Bright as A Rainbow
Mrs Paula Harding

Christopher and Jake constantly amazed me with their resilience. Not for one moment do I pretend that they were perfect, but they kept themselves focused on moving forward, improving themselves and looking for a way to create their new 'normal' after losing their father. Paul was the most influential person in their development, so it was understandable that, occasionally, there was a lack of direction or focus. But when they caught hold of an idea, there was no holding them back. Their Tough Guy sponsorship raised an incredible £2,650 for The Rifles own charity 'Care 4 Casualties'. The homespun charity was crucial to delivering support to our Riflemen, many of whom had suffered life-changing injuries or developed difficulties with their mental health, mainly through their active service, but not exclusively. The charity filled the gap between government pay-outs, and the cost of living a life with a modicum of comfort; a welcome helping-hand for those who had been peacekeeping in some of the most war-torn countries on Planet Earth.

Christopher returned to Exeter and, with Laura's determination to keep him on track, he settled back into his studies. I could recognise in Laura the same kind of early commitment that I had for Paul, the makings of a loving relationship built on mutual respect. An even partnership where both protagonists work tirelessly for themselves, and each other. The days of the man doing all the hard manual work and the woman staying home cooking are long gone, and in Laura, there was a hungry desire to build a quality life for herself and Christopher. Maybe it's a mother's intuition or maybe it was obvious to everyone, but the chemistry between the pair of them was incredibly strong. I dread to think how things would have turned out for Christopher if Laura had not been in his life. The comfort of knowing Christopher had someone to confide in, someone to love him, gave me the space to think about more pressing issues, and our future.

It was the future that worried me the most. Where do we go from here? Could I afford to live the lifestyle we had become accustomed to? Would I have to sell the house? The list of fears loomed large and lurked around every corner. As much as I convinced myself to take one day at a time, trying to suppress my brain from running away with the worst-case scenario was not easy. Occasionally, there shone rays of hope. Jake began to regain his confidence and concentrated on his A-Level studies. Still not knowing what he wanted to do with his life, Jake focused on his course-work and exams. With incredible support from his tutors, he began to imagine a future. It mattered not one jot that he remained confused with his choices, or that he had no idea what his grades would be. It mattered only that he began to dream of a future. It was something I knew that I needed to think about.

Only the grieving will understand this, but contemplating a new life brought no pleasure, just more emotional pain. I could retain my train of thought for less than a minute before the dark demons returned. As rational as it was for me to think about my future, it consumed me with guilt to do so. I had just turned 41. Life with Paul was all I knew. We had been together since 1985. That was my entire adult life, shared with one man, raising our sons, travelling the world, living in destinations determined by Her Majesty's Government. How could I possibly move forward without him?

It is hard to pinpoint the date, or when it happened, but eventually I found the strength to pick up a newspaper and read about current affairs. Slowly calibrating my mind to select only positive stories, I actively sought papers and magazines that were more factual than sensational. Sitting in silence at the kitchen table, glancing through our local rag, 'The Hampshire Chronicle', I noticed an advert for a course at our rural college in Sparsholt. The course was a three-year Veterinary Nurse degree with a placement in our local practice. I looked at the website and for the first time began to imagine returning to a work environment. Somewhere I could make a difference, and actually have something that would offer me a reason to get out of bed. Still lacking confidence, I consulted my closest circle of friends and family. Then I discussed it with my boys before deciding to apply. To my astonishment, I was accepted onto the course and placed with an amazing local veterinary surgery. My new challenge was trying to control the anxiety that comes with starting a new profession at such a mature stage in life.

My fears were initially unfounded. I quickly became absorbed into the cycle of studying and working within the world of animal care and treatment. My human nursing skills were transferrable, but the hours studying animal anatomy and physiology, researching treatments, and procedures, as well as memorising drugs, their uses, doses and contraindications associated with them, were taking their toll. Although grief still filled my chest, the never-ending phrase 'Paul's dead' that played on a constant loop in my head, started to fade. At the same time, despite achieving incredible results with his A levels, Jake was entrenched deep in his grief. We all shared his pain, and to watch him suffer so much was heart-breaking. I have no doubts that he struggled to find a vocation in life as he strived to contain the pain of losing his father. His saving grace was his inherent restlessness. The need to be doing something interesting all the time prevented him from sitting still for more than five minutes. It was a fortunate disposition under the circumstances. If it wasn't the ferrets, it was the gym. If it wasn't the gym, it was the motorbike. It was only a matter of time before he fell into a job. To my delight, it came in the disguise of a dairy hand at an innovative family-run business, located in a neighbouring village. Jude, and her scrumptious range of 'Jude's' ice creams, supported Jake and encouraged him to develop as a young man. It was the catalyst to regaining his confidence.

Jude's supportive environment ignited his desire to investigate what he might do as a career. We discussed various avenues with friends and family and Jake became increasingly interested in Operation Raleigh International. The aftermath of the 2004 Tsumani and its environmental impact was still etched in our psyche. The events of that disastrous Boxing Day were so horrifc and, as a family, we felt mortified by our inability to help. Several years later, Jake's empathy for the eastern communities and the incomprehensible scale of their loss was greater than ever. His love of wildlife, compassion for those in need, and his sense of adventure drove him to apply for a project in Malaysia.

If successful, three weeks would be spent rebuilding parts of a village school. The priority was repairing the water supply system with a further three weeks spent on an environmental project. Top of the agenda, building a watchtower to protect Java rhinos. The final phase would be an environmental study on a coral reef, which meant lots of SCUBA diving. Our elation at his successful application was tempered by the challenge of raising the £3,000 to take part, plus the £1300 cost of his flights. He worked all the hours that Jude's offered him. But even if he worked every day from August until the start of Operation Raleigh in February, Jake would still need to raise £2,000. It was a challenge that felt too great to overcome, with only eight weeks to raise the £3,000 we needed help.

Gaz would often still check in on us. He would claim to have some kind of spider-sense, and it was tingling when he called. Maybe it was Paul giving him a nudge, or he truly did have a sixth sense when we needed his assistance. He had worked on Operation Raleigh International as a selector, so he was thrilled when I told him that Jake had been selected. I explained the need for Jake to raise nearly £4500 and how he was thinking of doing a sponsored cycle or something. I wondered if perhaps 4 RIFLES might be interested in sponsoring Jake.

'Leave it with me', Gaz said and hung up.

Less than 24 hours later Gaz called Jake and asked him to write a letter to Brigadier Jolyon Jackson, detailing his plans to join the Raleigh expedition in Malaysia. Jolyon had been the Commanding Officer of 2RGJ when Paul was the Regimental Serjeant Major, and our two families had formed a wonderful friendship. Jolyon took up the mantle and wrote an open letter to the Regiment, and its associations, explaining Jake's intentions. He crafted the words so beautifully that the response was overwhelming.

Reminiscent of the days immediately after Paul's death, the postman began to deliver bundles of letters. However, this time every envelope was addressed to Jake, and every envelope contained a letter from one of Paul's fellow Riflemen, along with a cheque. If ever proof was needed of the love that soldiers have for one of their own, and their family, those letters to Jake said it all. Just when you think there is no hope and that you are in this on your own, the cavalry comes charging through your door. Every letter contained unconditional support for Jake's adventure. Ironically, it was the anecdotes and memories recounted by the hundreds of supporters that proved to be the most valuable. Tales of what Paul meant to each correspondent and how Paul had influenced the lives of so many were (the tales) priceless to Jake. He will always treasure these letters. Written by every rank from General to Rifleman, from regular soldiers and officers, to Cadet Forces and Regimental Associations. The support from the Regimental family was so uplifting, it was comforting to know we hadn't been forgotten. Within three weeks Jake had received £3,655, to add to his own savings. With his confidence brimming, and adventure in his eyes, he booked his flights and set off on the trip of a lifetime.

Christopher was managing well in Exeter, and despite him missing Paul very badly, Laura's support was phenomenal. I could see their love for each other growing stronger with every visit they made. Despite the pressure of preparing for a year of separation, through the ERASMUS Programme (European Community Action Scheme for the Mobility of University Students) there was already an air of assurance in their body language. They were emotionally inseparable and it was evident that they were intending to forge a future together. But the student exchange programme, established in 1987, was a fundamental part of both Laura and Christopher's Degrees. It meant Chris would be studying at the University of Modena and Reggio Emilia, in Italy, and Laura would be studying her degree in German at the University of Wuerzburg, in Bavaria. Despite knowing the strength of their relationship was mature beyond their years, I felt a resonance between the early separations Paul and I had endured in our relationship, and what Laura and Chris were about to face. There was never a doubt that their relationship would grow stronger as a result of this separation, just as Paul and I had during his many tours of duty in Northern Ireland and the Balkans.

My sons were carving out their new lives with strength and courage, but I still found myself struggling with grief. Even though I was working and studying over 50 hours a week, every moment I wasn't busy, my mind would wonder where Paul was. Was he at peace? Was he in heaven? Had he just disappeared into nothingness? All those questions about mortality and the afterlife danced around my brain demanding answers. Being brought up as a Catholic, I returned to the religious teachings of my childhood, but they no longer made any sense. How could God be Father, Son, Holy spirit, but still allow the suffering that my family, friends and I were experiencing? Paul was freeing the oppressed, he was fighting the good fight. All I had been taught seemed little more than hollow promises and lies. At the height of my doubts, the most surreal event took me on a journey most unfamiliar, and until the loss of Paul, unthinkable.

Early one morning, I was woken from a deep sleep at a startling speed. So abrupt was my awakening, I froze still and silent in the bed while I gathered my senses. Laid motionless on my left-hand side, my back to the window, there was a familiarity with the situation that had me confused. Eyes wide open, cognisant, and fully aware of my surroundings, every one of my senses was razor-sharp. I could feel someone lying in the bed beside me. There was an arm under my neck, and another over my torso holding me tight. I could feel the weight of a leg pressed gently over mine. I took another sanity check to ensure I was wide awake. My heart was pounding so fast that it was in danger of bursting out of my rib cage. The thumping in my ears concentrated my attention. For a few seconds, I tried to reason with myself and understand how someone could be wrapped around me in such a way whilst I was lying on a solid mattress.

'Is that you Paul?' I whispered. Ever so gently, the weight and touch just faded away.

In my mind, I replayed that experience over and over again. It was the second event that I couldn't explain or understand. It was comparable with the time in the kitchen when I had felt a presence warning me not to open the letter from my 'pen-friend.' The voice repeating 'don't open it, don't open it' was inexplicable. Was I imagining these sensations? Was my desperate state of loss playing games with my mind? Both events felt as real as life itself. My curiosity had been pricked, and it was something I would need to examine. Was I experiencing something real?

My old Citroën Berlingo was on its last legs. Just before Paul had deployed, we had looked at several cars and concluded we would renew mine upon his return from Iraq. All of my cars had been workhorses. Big enough to take us camping and travelling around France, as well as economical and practical. Space for the hockey goal keeper's kits, rugby kits, bikes and other stuff. But now, with all those days lost, I was looking for something a bit more fun, and dare I say, sexy. For a while, the idea of a new car had vanished from my mind. That was until I started to find myself paying out increasingly more money for various work on my old car. A family meeting was called with Chris and Jake and we decided to start looking for a new vehicle. Jake, as a bit of fun, suggested a Mazda RX8. We watched the Top Gear episode where Clarkson test drives a stunning red and black version around the programme's track, and I liked what I saw.

Fast forward a few hours, and Jake called Gaz. The two of them began searching the internet to see if any were available in the local area. Within a week I found myself sitting in a deep scarlet leather seat feeling like a film star, my hands sliding around the black leather steering wheel, while Gaz and Jake discussed the pros and cons of the 'Wankel' engine. Both stated their reservations, and despite the fact I loved the beautiful lines of the body, the immense feeling of indulgence the vehicle exuded, I was still undecided. Jake and Gaz were cautious, fearful about the engine power and the racy nature of the car. I was daydreaming in the supple leather seats, admiring the cockpit design, and playing with the controls when inadvertently, I turned the radio on.

Blaring from the speakers, *'Me and Mrs Jones.'* Sung by Billy Paul, the familiar tune filled the car and in the blink of an eye, I was transported back to a restaurant in late August 1985, to the night Paul asked me to marry him. *'Me and Mrs Jones'* had played that evening, and we simultaneously told the other how much we loved the track. It became 'our tune'. My heart was racing. I never tried to turn on the radio. It was a total accident that I did. Without hesitation, and regardless of what Gaz or Jake had to say next, I announced; 'I will have this one.' It felt as if I had Paul's blessing to indulge myself a little. From then on, my scarlet RX8 was known as 'Mrs Jones'. I loved her.

The suspicion that Paul was trying to connect with me remained powerful. There is no rational explanation for this and maybe you would need to walk a mile in my shoes to understand my next decision. My desire to know that Paul was at peace, wherever he was, grew and grew. I had to know if he could see me suffering. Did he know my pain and how much I was missing him? Did he know just how much he was loved? Then one day a friend from Peter Symonds College texted me saying that a well-known south coast medium would be attending a meeting locally, and suggested it would be therapeutic to attend. I was desperate to know that Paul was alright. As irrational as this sounds, if there was any chance of getting an answer to my questions, this was it. I decided to go and asked Debbie to join me. Sceptically, we sat in the back row of a packed, old and cold village hall. I was sure that this experience would put the issue to bed. There would be nothing for me to hear at the meeting, and I could stick all my surreal experiences down to stress.

Wrapped in our winter coats and scarves, we sat together in silence observing every move made, listening to every word spoken. In desperation I was praying that Paul would come through in all his glory and answer my questions just like Sam did in the Whoopie Goldberg classic film 'Ghost.' But nothing happened. Not a glimpse or a hint. For two hours we sat watching the medium. Dan gave messages to other people, naming loved ones that had passed. It was emotional to watch as people would cry, but I was very sceptical. Then, right at the end of the session, Dan brought the meeting to a close, and was in the process of taking his leave when he stopped dead in his tracks. He looked down at his feet and said:

'An old dog has just walked in. He's a funny-looking thing. Short legs and a reddish-brown colour. I hear the name Heinz. He's now walking down the aisle to the back of the hall. Does this mean anything to anyone?'

Debbie's grip tightened around my hand. We both sat frozen, staring straight ahead. Then Dan announced:

'Well, he's moved off now. Thank you for your patience, goodnight.' Then with not so much as an explanation, he left the hall.

Stunned into silence, Debbie and I headed for the exit. I noticed a side table with business cards fanned across it. Silently I scooped a couple up and surreptitiously deposited them into my handbag.

A few days later I broached the subject with Debbie, and she assured me that I hadn't imagined anything. She was sitting right there with me when Dan declared a dog had made a connection, and that its name was 'Heinz.' I took out one of Dan's business cards and dialled the number. A very polite lady answered, and asked where I would like to see Dan. I explained that I didn't mind, and that I had my own transport. With all the calmness of booking a hair appointment, she gave me an address in Bournemouth, a date and time. I was braced for a barrage of questions. In my mind, I expected her to quiz me about who I wanted to connect to and when was the passing, so she could do her research. But all she asked for was my first name, nothing else, then ended the call. A few weeks later Debbie drove us down to Bournemouth. I was all over the place. Should I be doing this? It was totally in contradiction with my Catholic beliefs. What if it's a scam? I was aware of my own vulnerabilities. The self-doubt mounted up. Am I playing with fire? If there is a God, will I go to hell for this? But the desperate need to know if Paul was at peace was overwhelming, and my faith wasn't strong enough to resist.

I got out of the car and went up to the front door of a modern bungalow. Primed and ready to knock, I saw a sign asking visitors to take the path along the side of the building. His office was at the rear of the garden, so I proceeded down the path to a rather smart summerhouse. Doing as instructed, I pulled my coat tight around me; I had purposefully worn several layers as I knew that my bones would start to chill if I became emotional. Dan is a giant of a man, at least 6'5" and almost as broad, his mop of jet-black hair framed a dark swarthy complexion. He was quite distinguished with deep dark-brown eyes glowing with warmth. Grinning, he welcomed me into the summerhouse and signalled for me to take a seat. Nervously I took stock of my surroundings and noticed a tape recorder on the coffee table, similar to the one I had been given for Christmas in 1980. Succinctly he explained that he could not guarantee a connection with a person that had passed, that he would start recording the moment he began the reading so that I would have a copy of what was said. I took a deep breath and waited. After a few seconds, Dan leaned forward and pressed the record button. This is the transcript of the tape:

'When you were walking up the garden path towards the summerhouse two men walked with you. A much older man, your father, and a younger man, your husband. Your father needs you to stop feeling guilty about the nursing home, he understands that you needed to do that, your Mum could not look after him any longer, it was too much. He is laughing because you would get cross about his socks going missing in their laundry.'

I then go to speak, and Dan stops me. He continues:

'The younger man is here with your Dad, he died instantly, I feel it could have been expected, but it wasn't a suicide, he didn't believe it would happen to him. He is showing me a soldier's uniform and an explosion. He says he didn't know he was dead at first, then he saw himself in a crumpled heap, (it looks like the corner of a shed) he tried to give himself resuscitation, then a man came in and he watched as the man tried to resuscitate his body.'

There was a silence for what felt like an age before he started again.

TRIBUTE TO A HERO

'He stayed around you for a while, not wanting to leave you but then his grandmother came for him, told him he couldn't stay any longer, and helped him over.'

I couldn't speak. I was shocked and dumbfounded. I felt a large tear fill my eyeball then run down my right cheek. 'Breathe.' I whispered to myself. 'Show nothing, give nothing away.' I didn't want Dan to have any clues as to why I had come to see him.

Dan continues:

'It was over in an instant, no pain. he didn't expect it'.

'You go to bed every night and put his wedding band on your thumb, and you hold it there until you fall asleep, he has sat there with you as you cry'.

'He is laughing and saying you can wash his pillowcase now, it must be starting to smell'.

'He is thankful for another soldier, junior to him, he is doing all he can for you, tell him to smarten up'.

'The boys are making him so proud, but why are you not going camping anymore?'

'Don't drink wine and walk the dogs in the dark, he saw you fall over in the mud on the track'.

And then the tape goes silent. Dan opened his eyes, and says: 'I am so sorry'.

I can be heard saying: 'I don't understand this, how does it work? Is Paul happy? What is he doing?'

Dan replies with a chuckle:

'Paul is in heaven. I see him running over mountains, doing everything that makes him happy, he is watching over those he loves, he loves you.'

Paying Dan my £20 I asked: 'When can I come back and see you?' A euphoria was coursing through my veins. I had a connection with Paul, and Dan was the panacea to my pain.

'I don't want to see you for a long time, at least 6 months. You need to adjust and grieve. Coming here frequently will not help you in the long run, and your husband needs to be at peace.'

I was shattered. As I left with the tape in my bag, my euphoria tinged by the disappointment of not being able to return as quickly as I would have liked, it was difficult to quantify what had just happened. I climbed back into the car and as Debbie silently pulled away, my heart was broken all over again.

Visiting Dan caused emotional conflict. Arriving back at home, I felt a buzz I hadn't expected. How on Earth did this stranger know anything about my life? The fact that my husband had been killed, that I had boys, that I took Paul's ring and slipped it onto my thumb every night? The only information I had given was my name 'Paula' and my mobile number. Paul was security conscious and by default, as a family so was I. None of this made any sense, unless Dan really had connected with Paul and my Dad? I had gone looking for answers. Now I had to decide whether I believed these answers were true, or not. But I must admit, I was comforted by the thought of Paul being in heaven with his wonderful grandmother Beatrice, and funnily enough, I had known all along she would have been there waiting for him. I don't believe in alien abductions or extra-terrestrials, but there is no denying what is on the tape. The information was so specific, not even the boys knew some of it. And the most bizarre comment, that random reference to a junior soldier helping. Gaz was renowned as the scruffiest bloke in the Regiment! When Paul was Regimental Serjeant Major, he had privately told Gaz on several occasions to smarten up if he wanted to progress to become an RSM, something Gaz never did.

That winter, our friends invited Chris, Jake and me to join them on their annual ski trip. There would be 10 of us, ages ranging from fifteen to fifty, no couples, just friends and, after a brief chat with the boys, I knew we had to do it. We flew out to the French Alps, hired cars and headed to the slopes. The days made me feel alive again and the nights of playing games, cooking together and drinking brought a sense of normality to our lives that we had dearly missed. Every morning I woke and felt alive, looking forward to a day's skiing. I could feel a touch of my old self creeping back. Not that grief was ebbing away or that it was becoming easier, none of that was the case. It was just that my mind was being occupied by engaging with others, physical activity and socialising. The moment we arrived back home and walked through the front door, all my fears and pains came flooding over me.

Jake excelled in his Raleigh International Expedition. He made friends with a fellow Englishman, a young lad who had recently lost his Mum to cancer, and two Dutch students.

At the end of their 12-week expedition, the foursome had decided to travel further afield, visiting Korea, Laos, Cambodia and China. I had to swallow my parental apprehensions and show absolute support for this next experience. Children are beyond precious, and it would be impossible to imagine the levels of trauma and pain associated with the loss of a child. I had not contemplated that my life could get any worse until I imagined the potential for things going wrong when my treasured son was 5,000 miles away. But fears are heightened after you suffer a loss. The carefree risk-taking you had once believed in is gone forever. What I wanted to do was wrap Chris and Jake up in cotton wool and not let them out of the house for the next thirty years; it was hard not to show my true feelings of trepidation.

At least with Op Raleigh, there was a safety net, but the attractions of the Far East have a reputation for derailing the best-laid plans, and Jake would have to rely on his senses and sensibilities. Memories of our near-disastrous trip to Mombasa were fresh, but I drew comfort from the knowledge that Jake had received the best tuition possible from Paul. I took the attitude of John's father in Arthur Ransome's book, *'Swallows and Amazons'*, and his telegram from Malta: 'Better drowned than duffers. If not duffers, won't drown'. Jake was not a 'duffer' and it was time to let him prove everything he had gleaned from Paul's guidance.

Meanwhile, Chris and his fellow students were exploring Italy in between studies and projects. They were developing several concepts in Modena as well as learning the language, raising their standard of education, and improving their prospects for the future. During his breaks, he would pack a bergen with the bare essentials and jump on a train to explore everything within a hundred-mile radius. His love for travelling offered me the opportunity to fly out and meet up with him in Rome, and enjoy a little bit of sightseeing. We did the conventional tourist activities, guided tours of the Colosseum, the Vatican and so on, but we had the best fun riding the open-top, hop-on, hop-off buses, playing our own private game of 'count the priests, monks and nuns.' All Hardings are competitive, and Paul's loss had not diminished the appetite to win. It was blissful to waste our time on pointless childlike antics. Every ten seconds or so, we pointed and shouted, counted and laughed. People must have thought us demented. I wished beyond all measure that Paul had been there with us too. Paul was always involved in every one of our conversations, and my heart broke over and over for what he and Christopher were both missing out on.

Shortly after the Rome trip, I found myself reading and re-reading Paul's last email to me. He had said that I must not let his loss bring my life to a halt; I was not to allow his absence to affect my future, and the enjoyment of my life. How naïve this sentiment now felt? Paul loved me but clearly had no idea how I would be feeling now. That I was so bereft, how could he or anyone else comprehend? His intentions were good, he didn't want me to feel guilty if I met another man, fell in love or…. that dreaded term that every widowed person dreads, 'move on'. Like every soldier fighting wars, Paul would have analysed the potential of death; it's an occupational hazard, the Riflemen say. Paul would have made sure that everyone who deployed under his command had put their personal life in order and this included a letter or note to their loved ones just in case they never made it home. Paul led by example, his email to me was exactly what he had told everyone else to do.

I know his words were designed to bring comfort, to show support and understanding, but what should I do? I certainly didn't want to become a worry to my sons. Not for one second did I want them to make a decision on their future that accommodated me. They needed to be free of commitment, able to choose their own path without obligation. But I did feel the need to prove that I was OK; that I was strong, and capable of moving towards a new and happy life. But, how on Earth would I do this? I had met Paul on holiday, aged 19, and he had been my world for 22 years. But four weeks after I turned 41, I was widowed. I hadn't fallen out of love. There was no divorce or adultery. My love had been stolen from me like a rainbow, bright and vibrant one moment and gone in seconds, it had succumbed to the darkness forever. One moment we were planning holidays and birthdays on the phone, three hours later his body lay lifeless on the sand floor of a sangar 3,000 miles from home. Paul was in the prime of his life with everything to live for, his promotion to Lieutenant Colonel on the horizon, wedding bells silently whispering for Christopher, and adventure awaiting Jake. How could I possibly find a way forward from this?

Have you ever had that experience of buying a new car then, suddenly, you notice the same car everywhere you drive? When I fell pregnant with Christopher, I suddenly saw pregnant ladies all the time, when beforehand I had never noticed a pregnant person at all. Now I was no longer half of a couple, couples holding hands, couples doing their shopping, couples walking their dogs, just couples really, couples were everywhere. Weekends were the hardest. I avoided leaving the house on the weekend as there seemed to be more couples stalking me on a Saturday and Sunday. I am sure this wasn't the case, but it seemed to accentuate the fact I was alone. When you are fragile, you seem to be more aware of stuff that wasn't previously that important. It's not jealousy, nor is it self-pity, it is the impact of loss and grief. It's like being stuck in a car crusher, everything closes in around until you view every detail in HD. Eventually, it closes so tightly that you can see nothing at all. Ultimately, for my sanity and self-preservation, I would have to find some grown-up company.

Breaking into the dating scene in your mid-40's is not easy, especially when the last time you had a 'first date' was 25 years ago. Where does one begin? I started looking on the internet for inspiration and ideas. It had now become the norm to find suitable company on dating sites. The dating site, *'Our Time'* struck a chord. Specifically, for mature widowed and divorced parents, this dating site depicted a caring virtual world, where everyone was prioritising and protecting the children from their previous relationship. I didn't have young children to protect but I liked the idea of a family-orientated man who held the same values as me. So, I took the plunge and posted a photo and profile. I was totally stunned by the response my advert received. It was ridiculous, dozens of 'likes' appeared and messages asking how I was? The screen was flooded leaving me questioning what the ceiling for these enquiries would be. I engaged in a few messages, trying to gauge how this alien world would empower me to enjoy another man's company. It became a real struggle to imagine a scenario where I could be happy.

Then, a few weeks later, a charming man who lived on the west coast caught my attention. He had his own business, was divorced with two children. We spent several weeks texting before moving on to voice calls. Eventually, we agreed to meet at a restaurant for dinner. He was engaging and understanding. He seemed to have empathy for my journey. Listening to his life story, I too could empathise with his disappointments, and how his aspirations had come to an abrupt end. He described himself as an entrepreneur, developing his ideas into businesses, and I was intrigued. He often teased me about my job as a vet nurse, and slowly convinced me that I would be an asset to his business if I wanted a change of job.

After several months of persuasion, I resigned from my job at the vet practice and started working for his business. We were doing very well, winning large contracts, and managing several projects. Everything seemed perfect, and so when he proposed to me, I felt safe to say yes. There is no denying that my acceptance was whole-hearted. Although it wasn't born from the head-over-heels feeling I had for Paul, nor was it an act of desperation.

Sadly the sincerity of the relationship ran out very quickly. In my defence, the only men I had ever known were genuinely selfless, loving and good people, who always ensured their loved ones were happy and content. My Dad, my brothers-in-law, friends and cousins were balanced, measured in their problem solving and tolerant of all those around them. They respected boundaries and encouraged everyone to do likewise. Naively, I presumed this was the case for all men. It was inevitable that I would eventually measure my new husband against Paul and in doing so, it was evident that the relationship was doomed. I had been truly blessed to have Paul as my husband and father to my children. Our exceptionally perfect life as a couple had been forged in true love. The fact that Paul made no demands of me, encouraged a healthy lifestyle, put everyone else before himself and believed in the nobility of honesty and integrity, meant my tolerance for anything but the highest standards of commitment and behaviour was limited.

My new husband had everything to be grateful for. Healthy, lovable children, a business that was going places and an extended family with lots of colour and energy. But the consistent lapses in self-discipline became more than bothersome. I understood that he wasn't a military man, and that alcohol was more of a social past-time than it was a reward for a tough week at work. However, the contrast in lifestyles picked at the threads of our relationship. I needed values as much as I needed physical companionship. My life with Paul was built on mutual respect. Paul had treated me like I was the most important woman on the planet. In return, he was my knight in shining armour. Even when he had just cause to be irked at me, like the day I ran the car dry of fuel, or I knocked his motorbike over with my car, he did little more than huff at my disposition. But, in my new relationship, there was a threat of violence, and a danger of losing control.

For a while, every effort was made to address my concerns. I made appointments for us to see a counsellor at 'Relate' but, on both occasions, I ended up going alone. It was becoming hard to see how we could make this work. I was desperately keen to find a happy life, and for a short while, I contemplated remaining very unhappy rather than face living alone again. I was stuck between a rock and a hard place. I gave up a career to win the affections of a man I thought I knew. I had left my house, shared my most intimate fears, and poured my heart out to a man I thought I would grow old with. Now, I needed to make a decision that was impossible to contemplate. As the situation deteriorated, I doubted myself frequently. Maybe it was me causing his anger issues and outbursts? I found myself making excuses for his behaviour, thinking that perhaps I had said or done something wrong, and actually throwing a coffee cup, or TV controller at me, wasn't that bad.

With an increase in the levels of violence and unpredictable behaviour, I feared for my safety and left him with his drinking and anger. I moved back to the family home that Paul and I had bought. Thankfully, I had let it out and the tenants were able to move with relatively short notice. It took months for me to feel like my old self, but gradually my anxiety dissipated, and my life began to return to a gentle and happy place. My family and friends were once again incredibly supportive. I felt intense guilt for putting them through more heartache and worry. But what doesn't kill you truly does make you stronger. I had to accept the fact, I had made a huge mistake, but I could recover. Onwards and upwards, keep moving forward, life is for living and I had so much to be thankful for.

Christopher and Laura were now married and settled in their own beautiful house, just 40-minutes' drive from me. After Jake's travels he had successfully applied to Chichester University and graduated after 4 years with a degree in Adventure Education and had realised his dream of becoming a Firefighter. Whilst at Uni he had met the love of his life. Alexa was everything Jake had dreamt of in a girl. Beautiful inside and out, athletic, bright and loving. She had graduated with her Post Graduate Certificate in education (PGCE) and was flourishing in her teaching career. They were engaged and had bought a beautiful town house. I was back in my village, surrounded by wonderful friends and neighbours again. Shortly after my return, there was a knock at the front door. To my surprise, it was one of our Parish Councillors. He gave me a warm smile and explained that one of the new roads in our neighbouring village, the one where the war memorial is, was going to be named in Paul's honour. The level of pride I felt were extraordinary. I loved the people in our community, and clearly, they felt the same way about us. Naming a street after someone is humbling. Winchester is full of famous names of Kings, Queens or heroic battles, now added to that list was our family name. 'Harding Close' was opened on Paul's birthday. Surrounded by my family, friends and neighbours we cut the ribbon after a short ceremony and blessing, immediately followed by a party at home. Paul's mother, sister and great-niece had joined us to make it a truly great day for Paul, and all those who loved him.

Chapter Seventeen

Once More unto the Breach
Major Garry McCarthy

In 2009, almost three years had passed and the scars of Iraq were still there for all to see. A new command team, company commanders and operational staff, but there was no time to lick our wounds and wallow in self-pity. Two-thirds of the battalion were deploying to Helmand Province in support of 19 Brigade ready for Afghanistan Elections, and the inevitable violence. Six months later, A Company would bolster 3 RIFLES under the command of 11 Brigade.

Concurrently, the battalion would also redeploy a reinforced fighting company to the Falkland Islands. If that was not chaotic enough, at the same time as the deployments, the battalion would move out of Kiwi Barracks, take temporary lodgings up in Picton and Wing Barracks, Bulford, before moving into their final destination of Ward Barracks, Bulford. Even then, the challenge of changing roles within the Infantry had caused confusion and friction. Before deploying to Iraq the battalion changed roles from Armoured Infantry to Mechanised. Then it lost all its armour and morphed into a Light Role Battalion, but with an ability to be Mechanised if required. Later it assumed a hybrid Light Mechanised role, similar to US Strike Battalions.

As Quartermaster of the battalion, in charge of all the equipment, accommodation, basing, and deployment of assets, all accountable to the National Audit Office, life was running hot. I had operational equipment in ISO containers travelling between India and the UK, Afghanistan and the UK and the Falkland Islands. At one stage I owned five camps, three vehicle fleets, and three equipment schedules. Just when I began to drown under the sheer volume of work, I was given an additional appointment as Company Commander Headquarter Company. Had it not been for the likes of Rob Cutler, Lee Roberts, Gaz Case, Colin Nuffer and Taff

Evans, all of whom shared my workload, 4 RIFLES would have failed dismally as it tried to achieve a succession of minor miracles.

At the height of our deployment, I recalled the pressure Paul had endured during our ill-fated tour of Kenya, in late-1997. He had been a captain for just a few months. He had been appointed the Unit Enplanement Officer, responsible for the deployment of all personnel and equipment to Africa. He would spend his days pacifying RAF movers, and other administrators, who normally take delight in managing your operation at their own leisurely pace. I had just driven into Nanyuki Camp, to be greeted by an angry Paul. It was the first time I had ever seen him stressed. The movers were pawing over the weights, heights, and shapes of the vehicles, demanding Paul prove their roadworthiness. Although it was me on the end of a short sharp shrift, it was the movers causing the friction.

In the hours before Operation Panchai Palang (Panther's Claw, in English) Brigadier Tim Radford had visited me to check on the progress of our arrival. We were nearing completion, with vehicles secured, personal weapons checked and everything else accounted for; everything that is, except our 81mm mortars, all 12 of them. Brigadier Tim remains one of the calmest commanders I had ever worked for, but his parting words to me sent shivers down my spine.

'Well done Gaz on getting everything here so quickly, and on time for the start of Operation Panchi Palang. I am not sure what we would do without the contribution of 4 RIFLES, and their mortars.'

He had no idea that the mortars had not arrived, but I was just about to experience the very same lethargic approach to combat operations that Paul had endured during our trip to Kenya.

The RAF movers at Brize Norton recorded the mortars had arrived and were in Kandahar. The RAF movers in Kandahar said they were in Camp Bastion, and the RAF movers in Camp Bastion had them still stuck in Brize Norton. With 24 hours to go before 19 Brigade crossed the start line to what would be the fiercest battle of the campaign, I was crumbling under the pressure. In a final attempt to locate them, I called the Operations Centre at Brize Norton. Intentionally, I dispensed with formalities and cut right to the chase in the hope that the mover on the other end would understand the importance of the call. A young RAF Senior Aircraftsman answered:

'Hello, SAC Smith, how can I help you sir?'

'SAC Smith, I am the Quartermaster of 4 RIFLES. In 24 Hours, we are crossing the start line to begin the biggest operation in military history since Operation Market Garden, and I am missing my mortars. I need you to pull out the manifest for flight Number C13/09-2 and locate exactly where my weapons are right now'.

'Oh. Emm. I am just about to go off-shift. Can you call back in an hour or so?'

'No SAC Smith, I can't. Did you hear what I said? I am about to go into a battle with the Taliban and at present, my weapons are stuck somewhere in the RAF system. So, I will try and remain as composed as possible, but you need to pull out the manifest and locate my weapons now. That is to say you're not finishing your shift until I know where they are! Do you grasp the importance of what I am saying?'

'No, not really, but you can't keep me here beyond my shift. I am going home so I will go and get you a Senior Non-Commissioned Officer to do your checks.' Smith put the phone on the counter and I could hear him walking away. Simultaneously I could hear him yell down an empty corridor.

'Sarge! Sarge! There is some army dude on the phone. He's gobbing off about making me stay after my shift! Can you come and stick him straight?'

It had been twenty years since I had felt the urge to be physically violent with a colleague. As an immature corporal, I had made several poor decisions to mask my ineptitude with violence. Although it was never going to be the outcome, I recognised the feeling the very moment SAC Smith labelled me an *'Army dude!'*

'Sergeant Harrison, RAF Movements Cell, how can I help Sir.'

'Sergeant Harrison. I am the Quartermaster 4 RIFLES. Do you know what a Quartermaster does in a Battle Group?'

'Yes, Sir of course. There are QM's in the RAF. Why?', Sergeant Harrison replied full of sincerity.

'Please put SAC Smith back to the phone and listen to what I say to him.'

The young Sergeant put the phone on speaker, and called back SAC Smith.

'Go ahead Sir, he is present.'

'SAC Smith. When a Quartermaster phones anyone, it means there is a serious problem, one so big, it cannot be fixed by anyone between the rank of Private and General. It means take note and be at your best. If he then says, his weapons are missing and 3500 soldiers are hours away from starting a battle without them, you should be reaching for the panic button. Describing me as a dude and telling me you are going home because your shift is over, is likely to get me on the next flight to the UK so that I can drag you here to Afghanistan, and put you in front of the Taliban, with little more than a dustpan and brush.'

Sergeant Harrison picked up the handset and switched the speaker off. He dismissed the young Airman and apologised profusely. You could sense the embarrassment in his voice. But, even after he had located my weapons, my desire to drag SAC Smith to the front line consumed every idle moment for the next six weeks. As I put the phone down, Colin Nuffer who was the Regimental Quarter Master Serjeant, looked at me in the very same way I had looked at Paul in Kenya in '97.

Operation Panchai Palang was fierce. It's hard to recall a day that went by without either 4 RIFLES, 2 RIFLES, the Welsh Guards or the Cavalry suffering a casualty. It was particularly bad for our sister battalion (2 RIFLES). Although 4 RIFLES were attached to the Welsh Guards, it was 2 RIFLES that I leant on heavily for support. I shared accommodation with Chris Lamb who was their Quartermaster and a lifelong friend of Paul's. He had kindly picked up the slack in the ad-hoc deployment of what was now called the 'Election Support Force' and when the Welsh Guards couldn't help, Chris and his team would. It was the very reason General Nick Parker wanted the Royal Green Jackets to merge into the biggest Regiment of infantry. He knew that being a large organisation would not only ensure we survived future defence cuts, but in times of war, we could lean on each other heavily.

No sooner had we got underway, than the first fatality had been suffered. From this point forward, Chris and I would spend our days at the Rose Cottage (the makeshift mortuary) or the hospital. If Chris or I weren't signing the official identification of the dead at Rose Cottage, it was Nicki Mott, QM of the Welsh Guards. Between the three of us, our days were spent receiving casualties from the fierce fighting that had gripped Helmand Province, and whilst there was no doubting the bravery of the soldiers fighting the Taliban, never have I been more inspired than I was by the staff manning the hospital at Camp Bastion. The care, compassion and dedication displayed by the regular and reserve doctors and nurses, could not be captured in a library of conflict, let alone one book.

Despite thinking I had become hardened to the consequences of conflict, every time I walked into the hospital and saw the extent of the misery being suffered by combatants on both sides, my enthusiasm for life lessened. But astonishingly, the medical staff thrived on the challenge of keeping people alive and reducing the impact of their injuries. Where they found their energy was hard to fathom. They had every right to feel depressed or saddened by what they were dealing with, but the levels of professionalism, enthusiasm and commitment were nothing short of phenomenal. At times they dealt with soldiers who had been blown up several times during the same incident, so battered and torn were their bodies, it was difficult to know which way up to place them on the stretcher. But the Chief Surgeon had made me a promise during my recce of Afghanistan. He said:

'Gaz, if you get someone here alive, I promise, we will keep them alive.' It was a bold claim, but one he upheld for the duration of our tour.

Back in Bulford, Batty was bracing himself for greater misery. Along with the new Unit Welfare Officer, Steve Harris, they were once again the focal point for repatriations and casualty visiting operations. By the midway point of the tour, they had managed two deaths and nearly thirty casualties, eight of which were life-changing injuries. While this on its own amounted to a huge task for a team of only five people, they still found the capacity to assist 2 RIFLES who had suffered thirteen fatalities between June and September. Moreover, it had not been lost on me that Batty had been at the coal face of repatriations and casualty management since the start of 2007. As a Regiment, The Rifles had been fixed for a prolonged period in Iraq and Afghanistan. To date, more than 62 Riflemen had been Killed in Action, around 30 had suffered a loss of one limb or more. Approximately 300 other soldiers were seriously injured, and Batty had been intimately involved in nearly 50% of this number.

Steve Harris and Batty were amongst the first to greet me as I returned to Bulford earlier than the rest of the battalion. As Officer in Command of HQ Company, I would now head up the homecoming parade and facilitate other crucial events. At the top of Steve's list was the visit of the

Duchess of Cornwall to issue several Elizabeth Crosses to the widows, mothers, fathers and relatives of those Riflemen who had paid the ultimate sacrifice. Following protocol, Steve passed all the information to me and asked that I relay it to Paula. It was standard procedure to reinforce the 'single point of contact' concept as it prevented the bereaved family from becoming overwhelmed by the constant change in military personalities. Until 2007, there had not been a strategy for dealing with families. There had been lots of effort, plenty of policies and incredible levels of empathy, but no strategy for helping families grieving from the loss of their loved ones.

Inadvertently, by insisting people contact me before dealing with Paula, I had accidentally begun to shape the model for casualty notification and visiting. I had been back for less than two days before I received a call from Ian Pointer, a civil servant running the casualty handling operations for 43 Wessex Brigade. Ian wanted to improve the practices and procedures used for those officers and soldiers tasked with Notification and Visiting duties. I was hugely impressed by his commitment, empathy and understanding. Whilst most civil servants watched the wars in Iraq and Afghanistan pass them by, there was a finite number who sought to join the effort by improving operations. Ian was just such a person. After a brief introduction, he explained that he had learnt of my approach to these duties and invited me to help him shape a course to train others. It was a genius idea, and his efforts formed the basis of the incredibly well-oiled machine the MoD now possesses. On the first course he delivered, he had six attendees, but so impressed had people become with what he was doing, that on the last course that I helped him deliver there were over one hundred attendees.

On the day I visited Paula to explain the presentation of the Elizabeth Cross, she broke the news that she had found love with a businessman from the south coast. For a few seconds, we said nothing, the news needed to sink in. It was not the surprise maybe Paula felt it would be. In my mind, I had always hoped she could find love again. Even at her lowest ebb, she was full of love and energy for everyone in her life. If it wasn't being expended on Christopher or Jake, she was smothering Beth, Steph, Chloe, Zac or Mathew with it. When they were not about, it was the dogs, ferrets, cats or anything else that entered her life. Such a beautiful lady with so much love to give, it was inevitable that she would cross paths with someone who would capture her love.

Cinemas are full of stories where a husband or wife finds love after the loss of their partner. An idyllic location, a wealthy replacement, and wonderful children play out a predictable path to happiness for our entertainment. But no Hollywood film set can reflect the true complexity of such a situation. Paula's new husband would need to be special beyond comprehension if he wanted to keep Paula's love. And while it would never be my place to give anyone advice on affairs of the heart, I knew that it would be near on impossible for anyone to fill Paul's shoes. He would need to be intellectually sharp, physically fit, witty, selfless, loving and possess a moral compass that was fixed on true north. The chances of this were slim, if not impossible.

Challenges aside, there was just a hint of hope that Paula, Chris and Jake could find some semblance of normality as Paula married in grand style and moved to the south coast. Tying the knot during a traditional Catholic service, she was surrounded by her immediate family, as well as those lifelong friends she and Paul had acquired over the previous thirty years. After all the tears we had shed since the fateful day in 2007, now there were tears of joy. There was nothing but unconditional love and support for Paula the day she married. We all wanted Paula to find happiness. Not only did she deserve to find someone who could love her as much as Paul did, but her irrepressible zest for life needed a focus and a blended family seemed the most logical destination.

On the day the Duchess of Cornwall visited Bulford to issue the first of a long list of Elizabeth Crosses, Paula appeared content and settled. She was by now well versed with this kind of event and acutely aware of how much effort people like Steve, Batty and myself put into any visit, let alone when it involves a member of the Royal Family. Paula had learnt much about the Duchess since she was appointed Royal Colonel 4 RIFLES. She was adored by the Riflemen, all of whom had learnt about her desire to visit the injured and bereaved. The Duchess was compassionate and sincere when she talked to servicemen and their families. She never made outrageous demands or ridiculous requests, she simply focused on delivering support to those in need. Steve had witnessed her visiting injured Riflemen at Selly Oak Hospital, and could not praise her enough for her kindness.

During a solemn ceremony with a mixture of bereaved families from the Iraq and Afghanistan conflicts, Paula humbly received the silver crafted brooch with Paul's name struck deep into the flat surface of the reverse. The Elizabeth Cross, once known as the 'Silver Cross for Mothers' has been around since the First World War but hadn't been issued since the end of the Korean Conflict. Winston Churchill is often quoted for saying 'a medal glitters, but it also casts a shadow', although he was warning Great Britain of the perils of lowering the qualification threshold for the issuing of gallantry awards and campaign medals. However, it could not have been more appropriate for the Elizabeth Cross, for in the shadow of that medal there stood a serviceman or servicewoman who had given their lives to secure democracy in the free world.

As with all Royal events, the national newspapers carried the stories of Royal visits. Predictably other news outlets would be stirred into action and come calling, including local TV. As strange as it may appear, where a media outlet had used an appropriate channel to contact Paula, she never declined to comment. Not so for any journalist who sneaked up on her, trying to catch her unguarded, or those who rocked up to her house and called without warning. There were no good intentions coming from that kind of journalist. The pretence of telling the world of Paul's bravery was just a lie to get Paula to condemn politicians or the conflict. But if a media outlet had approached the MoD and provided a good reason for requesting contact, Paula would give the issue fair consideration. When a news team from Southampton asked if they could have an interview and chat about Paul's valour and how Paula was coping, she willingly agreed.

Paula chose to interview at the original home of The Rifle Brigade, Peninsula Barracks, Winchester. She paid a moving tribute to Paul and all he stood for. Composed and proud, Paula explained Paul was a professional, a career soldier who knew exactly what he was doing. She stated that Paul's only desire was to free the oppressed, to allow people the right to basic services such as education, health and welfare. Her answers were brilliant. I hoped the person who had sent her hate mail was watching. I wanted him to see Paula more resolute, more determined, and yet, whole-heartedly forgiving. She was unbelievably inspiring without even trying. She had no interest in the political decisions made by Blair and Bush. There was no accusation of MoD underfunding, or equipment shortages. Complaining was not going to bring Paul back and she wasted no time on these issues. Instead, she focused on Paul's contribution, his family and what lay ahead for them all.

By now, both Christopher and Jake were forging ahead with their own lives. There would be occasions for me to step-in and help out with some fatherly advice. I was always ready to share some of their burdens and would always drop what I was doing if the issue was urgent or very important. When Christopher started his first job with a company in Winchester, they were quick to criticize him for failing to keep pace with the workload. After sixty days, they had decided to release him, and Christopher asked if I could attend the meeting with his bosses as they explained their reasoning. There was no reason for me to be there other than to provide moral support. Willingly, I visited his workplace and listened to the reasons his boss had cited for the release. They were harsh reasons, all of which were completely attributable to the turbulence Christopher had to work through during his studies.

There were few words of support for me to offer. With a few of his belongings in a box, Christopher and I left his office having accepted his fate. We sat in Café Nero mid-way up the high street and debated the next step. I was fearing a full-scale meltdown by Christopher. He just could not catch a break. He battled all the way through University to get a degree, and the first encounter with someone from his chosen profession was now ending in disaster. He had every right to burst into tears, but instead, he analysed the problem, focused on the positives, and strategised a new approach. For Christopher, this was not a setback, it was an opportunity. Now he was free of the commitment he had made to the Winchester based company. He could look for a job closer to Laura, and their home in Newbury. He was contemplating marriage very soon and this would speed up the process.

It seemed like less than a few days later and Christopher was snapped up by another company, and one that was closer to home. Just as he had planned in the hours after he was released, he had crafted the disappointment into an opportunity and capitalised on it. In no time at all, he was planning and executing projects on Britain's National Railway Infrastructure. There was no time for self-pity, he had to move onwards and upwards. Like every good man I have ever known, he was supported by a remarkable woman. Unquestionably, the only person who could help Christopher through life's greatest challenges, a future wife. The first time I had met Laura, I knew they would marry and live a happy life. There were just so well suited that it could only end in married bliss, and eighteen months later the Harding family and friends gathered for their wedding.

With Jake as best man, and with a one-minute silence as a profound salute to Paul's absence, Christopher and Laura were married in Berkshire, followed by a reception in the stunning grounds of Brockhurst and Marlston House. The old building had a touch of Hogwarts about it. Large blocks of granite stone and huge wooden staircases, the setting was fit for a king. The moving tribute to Paul was evidence of the impact he had made on both boys. As a father, you wish only to give your children the best possible start in life. Unconditional love allows a child to follow any direction they so desire. Parental love is as much about letting go as it is about holding on. To see Christopher standing in front of his family, his friends and his in-laws, affirming his love and desire to build a future with Laura, confirmed that Christopher was living the life his father had wished for him.

Jake too was overcoming the challenges of adulthood. He was fighting hard to find his vocation in life, and despite the hard yards he expended at University, he was always destined to be a public servant. There was an inherent desire to be a force for good. If he wasn't going to save the world as an environmentalist, he would do the next best thing and save people. Despite several rejections, he eventually made it into the Fire & Rescue Service. Although it was inevitable he would succeed in one institution or another, it was his inherent resilience that kept him stepping forward after each knockdown. From the very first moment he wanted to volunteer as a Firefighter, you could tell he would be an exceptional addition to the emergency services. On the occasions he was denied, he would have been justified in offering himself to the Police or Paramedics. But he had come from a family that was not put off by disappointment or failure.

With Paul's physique and dry sense of humour, coupled with Paula's good looks and charm, Jake was always likely to end up in a relationship with a beautiful woman. Like all people who survive the darkest periods of life imaginable, Jake's light was Alexa. It was not the luck of the gods that saw him win the heart of a schoolteacher, it was the raw DNA he had inherited from his mother and father. Naturally funny, determined, and with all the hallmarks of a true young gentleman, Jake was never going to stumble into a relationship that didn't have a future. Not only had life taught him to choose wisely, but he had learnt how to prioritise that which is most important to him.

At some stage in life, we are faced with making distant relationships work. It is a modern trend and one that is fraught and potentially fatal to young love. It takes courage to dismiss the fallacy that absence makes the heart grow fonder! Such a misnomer is for those who have never sampled true love, or have confused priorities. For Jake, separation in the pursuit of work or education was for the Victorians. For him, life was about investing in those closest to him, those who he loved, and those who loved him. For a young man to digest and understand such a complex conundrum is nothing short of remarkable. Like Christopher, he had found the ability to build a loving relationship amidst the most turbulent period of his life, by working hard at it.

Having spent twenty-five years of my life volunteering (extra murally) as a Youth Development Officer, I have often been dumbstruck by privileged children wallowing in self-pity. If it's not been the rich kid, it's been the poor kid who played the victim and declared war on everyone and everything. When I encountered children who were determined, honest, focused and pure of mind, their qualities had been shaped by the adults in their early life. It's more than cognitive development and a good education, it is about charging the moral batteries so they can withstand the onslaught of temptations to drift off course. Being able to fulfil social responsibilities, and balancing emotional intelligence with the art of logical decision-making. It's about ensuring our children understand the consequences of not making decisions, let alone the consequence of making decisions. In every decision Christopher and Jake were making, the golden threads of Paul's character and that of his professional career shone through brightly.

In my final assignment of military service, the Army had chosen to send me to Saudi Arabia. For the first time since Paul had been killed, I would lose the ability to drop everything and help either Paula or the boys if they needed it. Jock and Debbie had moved to Germany leaving only Jimmy and Alison available in times of crisis. In a desperate attempt to justify my lengthy absence, I visited Paula and the boys as often as possible. Family gatherings or impromptu meetings, every excuse plausible was exercised, the most enjoyable of which was the arrival of Axel, the firstborn of Christopher and Laura. Full of jet-black hair and a dead ringer of his father, Axel's arrival brought a new focus into everyone's life. The lift in the family morale was tangible and with it, a renewed energy for life. And if we didn't think things could get better, Jake proposed to Alexa.

The sense of contentment was palpable as I packed the last of my MFO boxes ready for storage. I was mulling over the journey Paula, Christopher and Jake had been on. They had been through so much, and for Christopher and Jake, it had occurred at such a significant age. But now, nearly ten years on, life was looking up. Not that I needed reassurance that the pain was easing for Paula, but the last text of the evening warmed my soul to the core. Full of energy and enthusiasm, Paula wrote a lengthy message to say that she and Jill had decided to return to the military social circles and attend the most enjoyable event of the defence calendar, the Army versus Navy Rugby Challenge Cup. In terms of military gatherings, it's the largest assembly of 'military personnel' other than that of war. As many as fifty thousand servicemen and women descend on Twickenham to socialise, reminisce and watch some full-blooded rugby. I felt so privileged to be part of Paula's and Jill's lives. Two of the most extraordinarily courageous women you are ever likely to meet, and I had been part of their lives.

Monday morning, and more packing. This time it was my desk at Army HQ. My penultimate job in the Army and there was much for me to hand over to my replacement. We had barely started when Paula called.

'Gaz, I don't know how to tell you this, but someone has stolen my Elizabeth Cross. I wore it to the rugby match and at some stage, it went missing.'

The phone went silent as we both gave each other time to comprehend the words. Paula was emotionally drained by the theft. She was sure that she knew the moment it went and had a good idea of who the culprits were. But none of this eased her pain. I could not begin to imagine the depth of her pain at that precise moment. The Elizabeth Cross, bestowed by Her Majesty, gifted for the ultimate sacrifice, stolen on the first occasion Paula had returned to the military fold. But this was not a time for dwelling on what happened; for our sanity, we needed to do everything in our power to recover the Cross.

By Monday afternoon we were at Twickenham rugby ground, deep in discussion with the stadium manager. A young man, hair on fire as he tried to turn the stadium around for the next international game happening four days later, his capacity to help was limited. There was no CCTV and no surveillance officers available to chat to. The security contractor was unavailable leaving the only option a physical search of the grounds. Occasionally, the labour force dismantling security fences and temporary regimental bars, helped us scour the floor. But the stadium and all the roads around it were awash with street cleaners and road sweepers. If there had been a chance that the Cross had been accidentally pulled off Paula's blouse and landed on the floor, it was now long gone.

Fearful that Paula would beat herself up over the loss, I promised we would replace it immediately. She had been invited to the Edinburgh Tattoo by Patrick Sanders, now a Major General, and she would be desperately keen to wear it given the importance of the event. But time was tight and the need to navigate through a heap of red tape was looming large. Had it not been for John Poole-Warren and his trusted aid, Ian Foster at RHQ The Rifles, both of whom found the money and used their contacts to speed up a second issue from the Medals Office, Paula would have arrived at Edinburgh Castle feeling half-dressed and full of anxiety, dreading being asked why she wasn't wearing her Elizabeth Cross.

It was never lost on me that as my relationship had grown with Jake and Christopher, Paula's relationship had grown with my daughter Lauren. It had not come as a surprise at all when my daughter asked if Paula would visit her whilst I was working away in Saudi Arabia. Lauren played all school sports including hockey. In the knowledge Paula had spent many years coaching hockey at numerous schools, I suggested this would provide ample opportunity for her to visit. It was the beginning of a valuable relationship, not only for Lauren but for Jayne and I who worried constantly about how our children would cope with our absence. Of course, the school had its own pastoral support and welfare services, but Paula was the nearest thing we could hope for when it came to providing motherly love. So, for the next two years, Paula watched

Lauren play hockey and netball, then picked her up and dropped her off at Heathrow.

As my time in the Army neared an end, Jake announced the date for his wedding. It would take place in the final week of my service, offering me the last opportunity to don my ceremonial uniform. It would be poetic and fitting that I would be present, dressed in the Green Jacket uniform Paul had worn for thirty years. It was to be the most fitting tribute to the Harding family possible and evidence of the enduring gratitude the Service held for Paul. Everything Paul adored would be standing in the pews of the church. The most junior Rifleman of the Regiment (Jimmy and Alison's son Joseph, who had passed training and now served in the very battalion Paul and I started in) plus myself, now the most senior LE officer of the Regiment would be in attendance.

But as Jake had become accustomed, life continued to conspire against his happiness. Covid 19 had gone from a minor inconvenience to a global pandemic. The wedding was postponed six-months, and the attendance had reduced, but it was still going to be a brilliant occasion. It would mark the beginning of the end of the most difficult period in the Harding family history. Both Christopher and Jake would have their own families, living in their own homes, planning their futures. But as the pandemic gripped tighter, it became increasingly obvious that no weddings were going to take place anywhere in the UK. Moreover, even if weddings could take place, there was nearly a year of backlogs to compete against if you wanted a church or high-class reception venue.

For Jake and Alexa, it was irrelevant. They had found true love, not even a global pandemic would derail it. A second cancellation was truly little more than an inconvenience. They decided to marry in a registry office with a wedding party of only five. It was unquestionably a tough decision, but having survived all that life could throw at them thus far, we had come to expect this kind of courage and decisiveness from Jake. As he explained to all his disappointed friends and family, it was important that Alexa and he married, and that celebrations would take place when it was safe to gather.

There was no complaining or wallowing in self-pity. If life had taught Jake anything, it was not to wait and allow the grass to grow under his feet. He had become the decisive man his father was, capable of separating the needless from necessity, and acted accordingly. Whilst much of the

UK was awash with a never-ending list of people complaining about the government, Jake and Alexa had taken things into their own hands. Their decision was the final confirmation that both Christopher and Jake had overcome life's greatest challenge. They were consistently making positive and logical decisions. Moreover, they were both decisive young men with warrior-like resilience. Shining brightly through every decision they made, there was a light leading the way back to Paul's influence.

Chapter Eighteen

John 15-13
Lieutenant Colonel Garry McCarthy

John 15:13 of the King James bible says 'Greater love hath no man than this, that a man lay down his life for his friends'. In an army built on Christian values, it is the epitome of selflessness and the ultimate commitment in the pursuit of freedom. It matters not that the conflict in Iraq never had the full support of the country, it matters only that a democratically elected government, chosen by the people of the country, invited a volunteer army to dethrone a tyrant, and dutifully they did just that. This is how democracy and freedom work, but contrary to popular opinion, freedom doesn't come for free. It has a cost and Major Paul Harding plus a further 178 service personnel paid the price of bringing freedom to Iraq. In the UK, people wander into a hospital A&E and demand free medical treatment. We have come to expect free social care, housing and education. With impunity, we can publicly berate state officials, complain and bring prosecutions against law enforcement organisations, or the aristocracy. These freedoms exist only because of people like Paul Harding, his comrades in arms, and their families.

From the formation of The Rifles in 2007, until the fighting had come to an end in Afghanistan, the Regiment had suffered 69 deaths in combat. Never a day passes where I don't ask myself the question: 'was it worth it? I can only console myself with optimism and say: today, there are Iraqi and Afghan people who have variations of freedom thanks to the sacrifice of the British Armed Forces, and her allies. It is acknowledged that this freedom doesn't look like mine. Notwithstanding that Kabul is back in the hands of the Taliban, they are at least less evil than they were before our intervention. It is too painful to dwell on the question. Instead, I prefer to contemplate the alternative, which was to watch on the side-lines as tyrants and murderers slaughtered many more innocent people whenever they felt the urge, and this I would never have accepted, therefore I would do the same again in a heartbeat if the situation demanded.

Sitting in the magnificence of the Guildhall, London, post-pandemic, surrounded by six members of the Royal family, including HRH The Duchess of Cornwall and three hundred fellow Riflemen, all celebrating the success of The Rifles since its formation in 2007, I had a freakish chance encounter that keeps me believing. In the most surreal of scenarios, a waitress filled my glass with water and announced herself as our host for the evening. I instantly recognise her name as traditional Iraqi. Keen to impress our attendant, I thanked her in Arabic and inquired as to her home town in Iraq. Slightly shocked to hear the Iraqi dialect emanate from an ageing white bloke, her face lit up. With a huge smile on her face, she declared Basra. For the next ten-minutes she explained her journey to England, the university course she was studying and how it all began when the British forces liberated her family from detention in 2003. I recognised the detention centre she described, on the south side of the Shaat-Al Arab. I had indeed been one of those soldiers doing the liberating. Whilst it didn't seem appropriate to inform her of this, from our conversation she suspected as much. Maybe it was my eyes welling up, or the sheer joy stretched across my face that compromised my involvement, but she knew. In the dying embers of the most magnificent of military spectacles, the young lady, her duty finished, hunted me down. With a heartfelt tender hug, a gentle kiss on the cheek, she whispered 'bismallah min kull-shay shuckran' (In God's name, thank you for everything). Through me, she thanked all the Riflemen in that room and the families of the fallen.

For the humble soldier, it's not about the politics or consequences, it's about defeating evil, defeating injustice, preventing extreme behaviour from becoming acceptable, protecting our world from being destroyed by dictators, militants and terrorists. I and ninety thousand others would have done the same as Major Paul Harding had done on the night of the 19th. He had gone to protect his Riflemen against an advancing enemy, and in doing so, laid down his life for his friends. Even with the knowledge of the pain I have witnessed since, and the emotional torture suffered by everyone connected with his immediate and extended family, I don't think it would have changed a thing. I would rather die on my feet than live a life of regretful guilt, or in a world of extremism, dictatorship and injustice. It was heroic in every sense of the meaning.

Conversely, during the Covid pandemic, popular TV presenters, social media influencers and celebrities frequently described the domestic duties of the decent people of the UK as 'heroic'. Unquestionably there would have been millions of people demonstrating remarkable levels of commitment and dedication to duty, but ultimately, there would have been profit and reward. Not wishing to demean the valuable contribution of the hard-working business owners during a difficult time, to describe their efforts as heroic is to cheapen the cost of freedom. Courageous by definition, heroic activity implies enormous personal risk, the willingness to trade everything you hold dear in your life, for absolutely nothing in return, other than to inflict a lifetime of emotional pain on those you love the most.

Yet, I will never fully comprehend the levels of resilience, fortitude and commitment I witnessed in the years after Paul's death. His family and comrades were loyal, unflinching and more determined than ever to reinforce the values treasured by the great British public. The advent of the Elizabeth Cross was much warranted and graciously received by Paula. For the rest of her life, she will be paying for our freedom. Along with all the other mothers, fathers, children and siblings of those who gave their life in defence of our nation and the oppressed, she will never escape the pain. It is only right that Her Majesty Queen Elizabeth acknowledged this sacrifice.

And amongst the emotional collateral damage, its shameful that the contribution of Pete Bullard and Andy (Batty) Batcock passed unnoticed by our great nation. From personal experience, I know that the emotional turmoil endured during their duties would have spilled out of their professional lives and into their private lives. Their wives and children will have suffered greatly by the burden of their duties. And in this reflection, we have focused on just one event, I know there is an army of people who have done the same as Pete and Andy, all of whom have lost a chunk of their emotional resolve in exchange for little more than a hastily written comment on an annual appraisal.

I frequently recall visiting Pete during the early days of the Iraq tour, and recount the enormity of his capacity to manage complexity. He would be attending a funeral on Monday, personally briefing the likes of the Duchess of Cornwall or Lord Dannatt on the Tuesday, visiting amputees Wednesday, repatriation Thursday, reassuring and visiting families on the Friday, all whilst commanding his own company of Riflemen in Iraq and Bulford. Furthermore, the weekend would have been full of phone calls back to the Chain of Command in Iraq, normally to manage the consequences of enemy action. It is the very definition of 'Home Defence'. Conducting operations in support of a deployed force warrants state recognition. It is time for the Ministry of Defence to consider Brigadier Jim Tanner's request to reintroduce the Home Defence Medal. Unquestionably, during the Iraq & Afghanistan wars, those who had deployed on 'Rear Operations' would have been physically and mentally exhausted in a fashion similar to those who manned the 'Rear Operations' during World War 2. They will have been battered and bruised in a manner that very few will ever understand.

Regrettably, whilst I subscribe to Sir Winston Churchill's desire to guard against giving out state-approved medals frivolously, I suspect someone in authority has interpreted this as 'managing quotas'. It is understood that the fighting element will always win the attention of the hierarchy, but the state must do better in acknowledging the commitments of Pete, Batty and the many other servicemen and women who selflessly dedicate their lives in support of national policies and the protection of our freedom, a task they were never trained for, or expected to do during a military career.

Unquestionably the greatest loss is suffered by the family. A loss that no one could ever comprehend, unless it had been suffered. A pain so intense that it is physical, crushing, confusing and all-consuming. Yet, against all odds, Paula, Christopher and Jake found the determination to continue, when 99% of the world would have given up. The loss of such a great man will never be overcome, truly irreplaceable, yet the Harding family found a way to include Paul in their lives and thrive on every sinew of his character as they built a life without his physical presence. If this life is all we have, then live it on your feet, not your knees. Paul's DNA runs deep in both of his sons, it is the essential ingredient that keeps their moral compass pointing north. He had instilled a family resilience based on Christian values, military standards and the love of a devoted father. Inadvertently, these ingredients had primed his family to face life's cruellest experiences conceivable. To be true to themselves and each other, to love in the face of hate, to shine a light on the shadow of death, Paul had prepared Christopher and Jake for it all. Swift with their courage, bold in their commitment, if it is true that we are products of our environment, the Harding boys are heroes and they owe this to their remarkable father, Regimental legend and national hero, Major Paul Harding MiD.

Chapter Nineteen

Life's Greatest Lesson
Mrs Paul Harding

Fifteen years on from that catastrophic night of 19th June 2007, I am happy. Of course, there are difficult days, and no, it doesn't get easier. There are days when I wish Paul was here, to witness the milestones every family enjoys, to share in celebrating their tribe's achievements, like when Chris graduated with his Master's in Engineering, just three years after the devastating loss of his father, or Chris and Laura's wedding day, it was so special. But Paul's absence was so overtly raw. When we celebrated Jake's graduation, my heart ached for Paul, and I could not stop the tears pricking my eyes at his Pass Out Parade as he achieved his dream of being a Firefighter. Recently, amid the Covid pandemic I dearly wanted Paul to be alongside me as I witnessed Jake marry the love of his life, Alexa. I so desperately would have loved Alexa and Laura to have known him, to hear his laugh and see the likeness he shared with their husbands. Their professional achievements astound me, but it is the love these women have for my sons that fills me with joy. I am so grateful to both of them, and their families, who have filled the void and offered our sons parental advice, as well as being so caring and understanding.

When our first grandson was born I was filled with immense joy, yet such pain, and I felt again that desperate need to know if Paul knew of his birth, if from heaven his spirit could be close to us still. It was then that I found myself thinking back to Dan Clarke and the meeting we had had. Googling his name I found that he now had a website, and making a booking with him was easy. I called the number and a polite voice asked what treatment I wanted to book. Taken aback I thought I had misdialled and quickly explained that I was wanting to book an appointment for Dan. Apparently, this was not a problem because Dan had a room in the beauty clinic once a week and she just needed a name and contact number to put me in his diary, and then I would pay £25 on the day. I gave her the name 'Helen' and my mobile number, and was given an appointment 8 weeks later.

Arriving outside the beauty salon I parked up and sat staring at the front window of the shop, fluffy feathers and sparkling writing confirmed I was at the right address, but I started to get cold feet. Is this right, should I be meddling, what if I am courting danger by trying to contact Paul through a medium. But the yearning to know answers was too much of a draw. Climbing out of the car I took a deep breath and headed towards the door. Booking in was easy, no further information was required and so I sat on the soft pale pink sofa and flicked through the latest 'Hello' magazine. Less than 10 minutes later the door to one of the treatment rooms slowly opened and a young woman, and what looked like her mother, stepped out. Both had red eyes and were sincerely thanking the tall swarthy man holding the door open. Dan looked exactly the same. I took a deep breath and stood up. As the two ladies exited I then entered the room.

Sitting down opposite Dan I found he was looking directly into my eyes; connecting with his stare, we just sat in silence. Then he said:

'I have a small, smartly dressed elderly lady here, she looks like she is ready to go to a wedding. She says "Paula". And with her are two men, an elderly man, your grandad, John. And your husband'

I didn't say a word, I wanted to be absolutely sure that I wasn't giving away any clues. But Dan continued. He described how I was feeling that my husband was missing out on everything, and how I wondered if he sees the achievements of our sons. This struck me, he didn't say children or daughters, he said, sons. Dan then sat straighter in his seat and said:

'You have recently had a grandson born. Your husband is very honoured that he has been given his name.'

This took me aback as my grandson was not called Paul, and then I realised he had been given 'Paul' as one of his middle names. I just nodded, and then Dan said:

'His first name begins with…' and stated the correct initial, followed by his name.

Tears rolled down my cheeks, as Dan assured me again that Paul saw everything, he dipped in and out of our lives witnessing our milestones, and celebrations.

I left the meeting with Dan assured that Paul was with us, always.

Life continues to offer surprises.

I laugh and love.

I share mother-son moments that fill me with hope and inspiration.

It has become my strategy to hop from one wonderful moment to the next. All these wonderful occasions and achievements are bitter-sweet. In private, tears still flow for what could have been.

I have tried to follow Paul's direction and do as he told me.

It's a journey no one should ever have to imagine, let alone travel. But freedom has a price: thanks to a small number of courageous men and women, we would otherwise not be enjoying the privilege of choice, the luxury of free health-care, the right to complain and criticise the United Kingdom that we are.

Collectively, Christopher, Jake and I remain fiercely proud of what Paul stood for. Not the politics, not the argument, not the divides, but the desire to help others live life.

Reflecting on the achievements of our sons, their precious wives and our grandchildren, I feel blessed beyond measure.

Paul's legacy is as Pericles said:

'What you leave behind is not what is engraved in stone monuments, but what is woven into the lives of others.

The golden threads that Paul wove into all of the lives that he touched are beautiful and strong, multicoloured, God-given and full of promise and hope, bright as a rainbow.

Acknowledgements

Christopher, Jake and I would like to acknowledge the continued assistance of our extended military family. For more than a decade and a half, we have all leaned heavily on the support of Pauls closest friends, their wives and children. It has been this enduring friendship that has given us a reason to get out of bed and face the toughest of days. Additionally, in paying tribute to my courageous husband, we have revisited both joyful and painful memories, we thank everyone for their tolerance and unflinching commitment as we played tag with the ghosts of our past. As Gaz would say; *'we have emptied the laundry basket and kicked its dirty contents all around the room for others to paw over.'* Without their resolve, love and empathy, our tribute would have been lost to the *'all too difficult pile.'*

- Jimmy & Alison Mitchell
- Jill Clarey
- John, Bridget & Emma Pentreath
- Mike & Liz Jefferson
- Lauren Melia
- David Wakefield OBE
- Dave Adamson

Finally, both Garry and I would like to express our most sincere gratitude to Harriet Fielding, Tara Moran and Margaret Moran for their kind and compassionate guidance during the publication process. We hope they realise that they have given voice to the thousands of bereaved military families, who thus far had been unheard. We note that; courage is not just a physical activity, the pen is often mightier than the sword.